ABSOLUTE RADIO

The Inspiring True Story of the First Private Radio Station in Ghana's Western Region

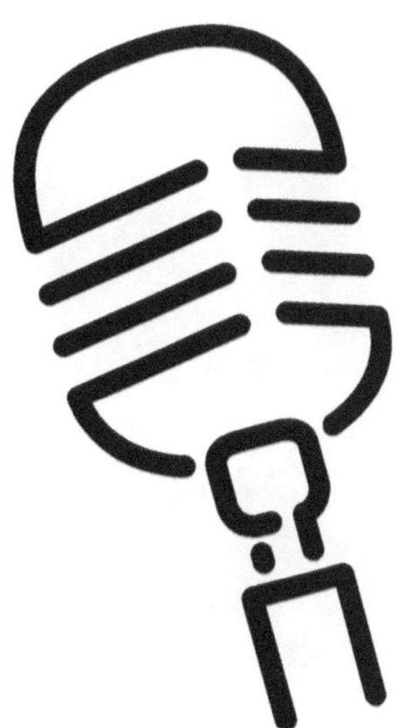

By Phillip Nyakpo

AfricanPod Media
(AfricanPod.com.au)
Perth, Australia
Phone: +61 493 219 774

www.nyakpo.com.au

ISBN:
978-0-6454252-1-5 - Paperback
978-0-6454252-0-8 - Audiobook
978-0-6454252-2-2 - e-Book

Dedication

To the good friends we lost along the way:
  Olivia Esi Gyan
  Mensah Nunoo (Uncle Opia)
  Kwesi Mould
  Samuel Ansah

Olivia Esi Gyan put up a gallant fight with cancer.

It would have been an honour to hear Uncle Opia tell the story in his own words.

Kwesi Mould remained "a bulldozer and caterpillar journalist" to the very end.

Samuel Ansah, an intelligent and easy mannered gentleman, became a Judge at the Circuit Courts of the Republic of Ghana, but passed away too soon.

To Susan Elliott and Matthew Scully in Sydney, Australia, thank you for showing me the path to broadcast journalism.

Contents

Nostalgia: Author's Introduction

The energy and passion to tell the stories in this book started in Australia in 1996 where I learned to become a journalist.

Susan Elliott at Channel 7 in Sydney invited me as a guest reporter for work experience. I love the immediacy of broadcast journalism, the energy and the thrill of storytelling.

I returned to my home in Takoradi, and it was a whole decade before I visited Australia again, a place which I have called home for the last 15 years.

When I returned to Ghana from Australia in 1996, I yearned to practice broadcast journalism, but the only radio station in Takoradi then was the Ghana Broadcasting Corporation's *Twin City Radio*, a public broadcaster clothed in thick bureaucracy. It had no room for adventure or experimentation, so I started writing for the *Ghanaian Chronicle*, the biggest private newspaper in the country owned by a Takoradi native called Kofi Coomson.

Soon, I started writing for *Radio and TV magazine (RTV)*, published by Robert Mills in Accra with Augustine Nelson and Kofi Asmah as young editors.

Private broadcasting at the time was a novelty that became legal only in 1995 and RTV magazine published juicy stories about the few radio stations that existed.

Working for *RTV* from Takoradi, I followed up on rumours that our city was about to get its first private radio station. Enquiries quickly brought me face-to-face with Wilson Arthur, a young man who envisioned the enterprise to build a radio station in a city that had lost much of its economic strength.

Smitten by Wilson Arthur's vision and enthusiasm, I became one of the early employees of the premier commercial radio in Ghana's Western Region when the station, Skyy Power FM, started in October 1997.

For nearly ten years, I was editor, reporter, news anchor and the top host for news and current affairs until I left for a stint with the BBC in London, in 2005. I later emigrated to Perth, Australia in 2007.

Even though Sekondi-Takoradi is Ghana's third largest city, its economy, supported by commercial rail service and a historic port had receded to the point where businesses suffered greatly.

As a result, the success of a private radio station in the mid to late 1990s was deemed impossible. Skyy Power FM therefore started almost like a joke, with a rag-tag band of mostly young women and men who went on to make history and changed the fortunes of an African city.

Across four continents, I found and interviewed all the major characters for this book -- more than 70 of them.

They were generous, kind and enthusiastic in sharing their memories and perspectives. This riveting story and pulsating historical account was made possible by their contribution and my own first-hand knowledge and experience from the past 25 years.

This book is a story of heroes captured with a complete range of human emotions, both low and high. It celebrates entrepreneurship, youth empowerment, talent identification and acquisition. It also reveals how a unique broadcast media entity integrated with a community's culture and tradition.

The story is a vista of ordinary girls and boys in an African media who followed their passion and flourished to become extraordinary women and men of substance. The main characters gave their very best, and in return, received the full devotion of a community that embraced their passion to spread opportunity and dreams.

Phillip Nyakpo
Perth, Australia
September 2022

"The Folly of a Private Radio
Station in Takoradi"

"When I became a Member of Parliament in January 1997, I visited Kwasi Twum, the Chief Executive of Joy FM in Accra. He told me he and his people had already looked into establishing a radio station in Sekondi-Takoradi and concluded that it was not financially feasible. I remember the conversation very well."
— *former Member of Parliament for Sekondi and Ghana's High Commissioner to the United Kingdom, Papa Owusu—Ankomah on his first memories of Skyy Power FM*

Papa Owusu-Ankomah had just completed his three-year-long duty tour in London as Ghana's High Commissioner to the United Kingdom when I called to speak to him on the phone. He had returned to Accra, Ghana's capital, a few days before.

"Why is your photograph and profile still on the website of the Commission as the head of mission?" I shoot the question straight at him, curious that information on the Commission's website had not been updated.

"There is a good explanation," he replies, and I listen closely for the reason. "It's not been made public yet," he says, "but President Akufo-Addo has reassigned me for another three-year term as High Commissioner, so I will be returning to London very soon."

This call is the first time we have spoken in more than 15 years. I used to speak to him regularly as a reporter and news editor for

Skyy Power FM in Sekondi-Takoradi, when he served as a Member of Parliament for Sekondi.

I introduce myself in less than five seconds after he answered the call.

"Hey, Phillip, it's been years! I heard you went to Australia," exclaims Owusu-Ankomah. The sound of his voice reflected his advancing age, and I was infected by his genuine and childlike excitement. It put a bright smile on my own face, as I speak into the microphone in my home studio from where I made the call.

"The last time I spoke to you, you were Attorney General and Minister of Justice for former President John Kufuor," I say, trying to recall the past.

"That was many, many years ago," says the High Commissioner. "I ceased being Attorney General in January 2005."

I told him that I was researching to write the transformative story of Skyy Power FM and explore the enormous impact it had on business, entrepreneurship, culture, and human resource development in the city.

"A quarter of a century has passed since the start of the experiment. You were one of those who saw it from the beginning, so I wanted to interview you about it," I add.

"I can remember those years," he responds. "I wouldn't have thought it was 25 years ago. Of course, I was then very young…" he says, and grants me permission to record the interaction.

Ground Zero

Sekondi-Takoradi, a twin city, is Ghana's third largest city. The foundation of its economy was the Takoradi Habour, constructed in 1928. The railways played a similar role, but both industries deteriorated through the 1990s and into the 21st century.

Known for its unique multiculture, language, and entertainment, the twin city had become a shadow of its former self, existing only in past glory.

"Everybody knows the Takoradi Port was dead," says Paul Ansah, who was deployed to Takoradi in the year 2000 to resuscitate the port.

Paul Ansah would later become the Director General of Ghana Ports and Harbours Authority after his success in Takoradi.

Skyy Power FM went on air in 1997 in the midst of the depressed outlook in the city, becoming the first private radio station in Ghana's Western Region, as well as the adjoining Central Region.

Private broadcasting in Ghana was a novel idea that occurred just around the time the country returned to constitutional rule after two decades of military dictatorship.

Political freedom was slowly expanding with the help of private newspapers which asserted their right to publish news, especially the sort that unsettled nervous political leaders.

The country's first commercial station, Joy FM, was established in the capital in mid-1995. It was easy to predict that, with time, private radio stations were likely going to be opened in other parts of the country, including the twin city.

Because of the dwindling fortunes of Sekondi-Takoradi, it seemed 1997 was not the year the city would get its first independent radio station. The necessary vibrant economy did not exist to support such an expensive venture.

Despite economic volatility, Papa Owusu-Ankomah was looking for a way to help start an independent radio station.

Dreams of a Private Radio Station

Owusu-Ankomah was born into a family of entrepreneurs. Even though he became a lifelong barrister and a politician, he grew up knowing what was necessary to run a successful business.

During the December 1996 general election, he felt an independent radio station would enhance the twin city's image. He won that election to start a 20-year career as Member of Parliament for Sekondi.

When he was sworn into office at Ghana's Parliament in Accra in January 1997, he still had in his mind an imaginary dynamic private radio station for a city he loved.

"I wanted to see an independent station that could educate, inform, and entertain," says Owusu-Ankomah.

"It is Not Financially Viable."

Shortly after he assumed office in Ghana's Parliament in Accra, Owusu-Ankomah thought of an idea that could bring independent radio to Sekondi-Takoradi. The plan involved an old schoolmate from his days at Mfantsipim School in Cape Coast. The schoolmate, Kwasi Twum, is the man who built Joy FM in Accra, under the Multimedia Group umbrella.

Before the end of January 1997, Owusu-Ankomah approached Kwasi Twum with a verbal proposition he believed would make a difference in Sekondi-Takoradi.

"I visited Kwasi Twum and suggested to him that it would be worthwhile for Joy FM to set up another station in Takoradi," says Owusu-Ankomah.

His verbal proposal imploded as soon as the Joy FM Chief Executive heard it.

"Kwasi Twum told me he and his people had already looked into it, and after some studies, they concluded that it was not financially feasible. I remember the conversation very well," says the former Member of Parliament.

Owusu-Ankomah said goodbye to his old schoolmate, and Kwasi Twum wished Owusu-Ankomah well on his new adventure as a Member of Parliament for Sekondi.

Where There is a Will, There is Always a Way

While Owusu-Ankomah was learning the bitter truth about why a commercial radio station in Sekondi-Takoradi would not work, a young man, Wilson Arthur, was finding a way to make it work.

After many months of hard work inspired by a passionate dream, Wilson was handed a broadcast license by the National Communications Authority in March 1997. Owusu-Ankomah would not know this until months later.

In the meantime, Wilson arrived in Sekondi-Takoradi in a jalopy old VW Golf car to start a small revolution.

"That car broke down many times on our way from Accra to Takoradi," says Kingsley Boohene, Wilson Arthur's childhood friend who travelled with him for the first reconnaissance mission to Takoradi. They arrived to learn how to build a private radio station that was also going to be the first of its kind for the twin city.

Wilson had a lot of things on his mind as he stepped out of the ageing car to work out how to start. The list he made, in neat handwriting, was long:

- *Find office and studio space*
- *Furnish offices*
- *Buy machines including a transmitter*
- *Build a strong mast*
- *Buy high quality microphones*
- *Recruit dozens of employees*
- *Don't run out of money before the station goes live on air*

Almost every item on his long list presented a daunting challenge. The one thing that came easy was his monomaniacal focus to get the job done. Wilson knew he had to battle many challenges to move from dreaming of the project to the point of flawless execution.

Given the low economic activity around the city, the most important question on his mind was: *would his passionate dream become a financial success or a shortcut to financial ruin?*

Meeting the Risk Takers

Papa Owusu-Ankomah eventually heard the rumours of the establishment of the new station. "When I heard that Skyy Power was coming, I was excited, but I was also a little bit apprehensive," he says. "Kwasi Twum had already told me it was not financially feasible, so I was apprehensive."

By the time he met Wilson Arthur, word about the establishment of Skyy Power FM was more than just a rumour. Wilson contracted a local graphics designer, Kwesi Bediako Quayson, whose glossy posters were everywhere in the city announcing the coming of the first independent radio station: *Skyy Power 93.5 FM.*

The posters showed the tagline, "Skyy is the limit," while also promising that the station would unleash "the power of news, the power of information, and the power of music."

The new venture was co-financed and owned by Wilson and his wife Adwoa Amofah, as well as Wilson's older brother, Kennedy Arthur.

Wilson Arthur and his brother Kennedy met Owusu-Ankomah together. "When I spoke to Wilson Arthur, he was very optimistic and told me that a private radio station in Takoradi was doable," recalls Owusu-Ankomah.

Through their conversation, Owusu-Ankomah learned that Wilson was born in Ateiku, a village only 100 kilometres from the twin city. Wilson was also an old student of St. John's School in Sekondi with teenage memories of Sekondi-Takoradi.

As he spoke to Wilson and his brother, Owusu-Ankomah kept remembering the conversation he had with Joy FM's Kwasi Twum about the inherent financial risk in building and operating a commercial radio in Takoradi. But he didn't say it.

"It struck me," says Owusu-Ankomah, "that Wilson wanted to do it because of his affiliation with Sekondi-Takoradi and Western Region. I have always emphasised that those of us from Western Region should be the first to take the step to introduce innovation into the region to speed up development."

So, despite his well-founded reservation, he wished for Wilson Arthur and Skyy Power FM to succeed, even as he feared that disappointment was possible. More than just a mere wish for the enterprise to succeed, Owusu-Ankomah says, "when Skyy started, I was committed to supporting it to succeed."

And It Really Succeeded

Looking back after a quarter of a century of Skyy Power FM's sensational success, Owusu-Ankomah says he has enormous respect for Wilson and the group of people who made the dream possible.

"Skyy Power FM captured the essence of Sekondi-Takoradi, when it came to music, culture, and lifestyle," says the High Commissioner.

Referencing the huge human resource developed through operations of the station, he says, "Skyy Power had a way of bringing out the best in those who worked there," adding, "including you." It was his way of showing that he knew me from the very first day I started working at Skyy as a journalist.

"I recall when you started," he says, referring to both Skyy and myself. "Very, very small boy Phillip, you worried people...," he laughs to suggest the memories of my youthful journalistic and annoying persistence in seeking information was playing on his mind.

He adds, "There were others beside you, and when they ended up in Accra after Skyy, they became national figures."

Apart from serving as Attorney General and Minister of Justice, Owusu-Ankomah also occupied other senior positions including Minister of Interior, Trade and Industry, as well as Education, Science and Sports.

Through the 20 years he served as a Member of Parliament, he was in opposition and in government. He experienced the excitement of freely talking to journalists like me while criticising those in power. Then, too, he experienced the tense relationship that occurs when journalists like me from Skyy pestered him for accountable representation when he served in government.

Decades later, he says, "I saw Skyy Power as a radio station that provided the opportunity to express varied views from that of the government. It was an alternative."

Living to Tell the Story

"Sekondi-Takoradi is a metropolis where everybody could belong, irrespective of which part of Ghana or the world you came from," says Owusu-Ankomah, and he believes Skyy Power FM made it even better.

Touching on the cultural revolution brought by Skyy, including helping discover and nurture musical talents in young people, he says, "Skyy introduced a greater sense of community engagement through the (masqueraders) fancy dress festival."

The festival has become a huge annual celebration that attracts people from all over the world.

Wilson Arthur and his friends came to Sekondi-Takoradi, an economically sinking city, with a venture to build the first private radio station, and then succeeded beyond what anyone would have predicted.

Skyy FM, with the addition of Skyy TV, became a brilliant ray of economic, social, and cultural sunshine that touched everything in Sekondi-Takoradi and the Western Region. The nearby Central Region, with Cape Coast as capital, fell into the station's orbit and benefited.

Owusu-Ankomah is just one of many hundreds of people who had a front-row seat to the story of Skyy Power FM. Like many of those people, he is alive to tell what he saw and what he experienced, in his own words.

This New Guy from London

These days, Dr. Jonathan Sowah lives in Ottawa, Canada. He is the Chief Executive and President of the multinational telecommunications company AstraQom International. In the mid 1990s, he was living in Ghana, working with Talal Fatal's Media Number 1 marketing company as the resident film director for commercials.

An essential part of his duties at Media Number 1 involved working directly with the marketing department, developing concepts for radio and TV commercials.

"I was told that we had this new guy from London who had just joined the team as one of the marketing guys," recalls Jonathan Sowah in an interview from his base in Canada.

Talal Fatal summoned Jonathan to a meeting so he could introduce "this new guy from London." The "new guy" was Wilson Arthur, who, in a few short years, would lead an experiment to build the first independent radio station in Sekondi-Takoradi.

"Talal was in his office; he called both of us there and I met this young handsome looking man, who seemed very calm, had a very nice smile on his face and it didn't take long for us to build a relationship. We got on very well," says Jonathan.

He continued, "He was a very hard-working guy. He had a way with people, which was very good. He had a way with clients. He was able to connect very well with various clients that he and I were working with. Over time, I found Wilson to be a very targeted businessman, very intelligent, very calculated in his moves."

The professional relationship between Wilson and Jonathan stood the test of time, and got even better with time. The two young men developed mutual respect for each other's ambition to succeed in business. Their conversations soon included how they could assist and support each other as their dreams slowly grew beyond their work for Media Number 1 in Accra.

The Biggest CD Collection in Ghana

One of the things Jonathan got to know about Wilson Arthur is that he brought thousands of music CDs with him from England where he lived and studied before returning to Ghana to pick up a job in marketing.

Apart from working as a marketing officer at Media Number 1, Wilson Arthur was also effectively running two businesses: a small one and a big one.

The small business he had was as a DJ to play music at different events around Accra, mostly on weekends.

This was in addition to running Music Paradise, a CD and Cassette recording shop, where music enthusiasts streamed in to record or buy music.

A lesser-known activity that could have been a third line of business was that Wilson rented CDs to Joy and Vibe FM to play. The two radio stations didn't have as much music as Wilson had in his collection.

Jonathan was yet to learn more.

"One of the interesting things I found about Wilson is that he was a man who was willing to use whatever he had, whatever lemon he had to make lemonade," says Jonathan, who was always observing Wilson's appetite for starting his own unique business ventures.

Stepping Out to Build a Radio Station

"One fine day, Wilson told me he wanted to go into broadcasting, radio specifically," recalls Jonathan. As Jonathan says this, the memory of his surprise at hearing the words is still evident in his voice. But what surprised Jonathan most was that Wilson also said he was taking his idea of private radio to Sekondi-Takoradi, Ghana's twin city.

As a marketing professional who had intimate knowledge of the Ghanaian market, he thought Wilson Arthur, more than anyone else, should know that advertising money that flows to Takoradi is relatively insignificant. As a result, Wilson's choice of Sekondi-Takoradi for a private radio seemed counterproductive. Nevertheless, he concluded that Wilson's crazy idea fit the person he had come to know.

"It was interesting that at the time when everybody was focusing attention on the main markets, Ashanti Region (Kumasi) and Accra, Wilson proved himself as not just a trailblazer, but also as a man with real real balls." Jonathan finishes the sentence, but quickly pleads, "you might want to edit that out."

"From what I remember," continues Jonathan, "people didn't want to risk it; they wanted to go where the money was, where advertisers felt the money was. But Wilson saw beyond this. He saw beyond what seemed to be the current reality. He only looked for his lemons to make the best out of it."

More than half a century after the fact, Jonathan's analysis was that Wilson observed and learned from Rupert Murdoch, the Australian-born American media mogul, whose company was an influential part of the vibrant media in the United Kingdom.

At the time Wilson Arthur lived in England, Murdoch's Sky TV was the UK's most popular digital TV service. Jonathan, who also lived and worked in England, says he can trace the UK Media's influence on Wilson's creativity in choosing the name *Skyy* (with a double y).

"When you take the impact of Sky broadcasting on the UK market, it is not surprising that Wilson chose to use such an icon to inspire him into the areas of radio and TV broadcasting. In my opinion, the name did not just reflect the best of a new brand, but also the best of a vision, the best of his inspiration in trying to do what the Murdochs did."

Visiting Takoradi to see Wilson's Vision

In early 2002, Jonathan Sowah visited Skyy Power FM's newly commissioned studio in Takoradi. He must have felt like coming to see the fulfillment of an old friend's dream. It was a good time to visit Skyy because, in a few short years, the radio station had turned up enough cash flow to the point that Wilson was adding a bold new operation: a television station later called Skyy TV.

Wilson Arthur and his management team poured all the profit from the radio station back into the business in order to make this new dream possible. It was another first for Ghana's Western and Central Regions.

Before Jonathan arrived in Takoradi, Wilson described him as a man whose presence and expert consultancy will assist our business at the radio station, as well as the new television service.

When Jonathan the consultant arrived, Wilson called me to his office to introduce me as the news editor. I walked to Wilson's office, and before I could be introduced, Jonathan Sowah and I got up into a big embrace, much to the surprise of Wilson Arthur.

Life Goes Around and Comes Around

I knew Jonathan Sowah when I was much younger, living with my uncle D. S. Kpodo-Tay at Teshie Nungua Estate in Accra. The house was always busy with many important visitors. One of them was Jonathan Sowah.

Even though just a few years older, he seemed to know so much more than me, but he was never pompous about it. He always kept people at ease with a permanently radiant smile that made you feel like you were the most important person in his life.

Geography separated Jonathan and me for more than a decade until the unexpected reunion at Skyy. Wilson Arthur's TV license was about to be granted and Jonathan Sowah was a consultant, advising Skyy on the best technology the company should use in deploying Skyy TV. The reconnection at Skyy brought Jonathan and me together again.

That is why I picked up a phone to call Jonathan in Canada to tell me about Wilson Arthur, the man he first encountered as "this new guy from London."

This guy, now decorated with grey hair, became a visionary that pioneered private and commercial broadcasting in Ghana's Western and Central Regions. More than that, he is, according to many, the one individual who has contributed to the development of private broadcasting in Ghana more than anyone else.

Nothing Induces Fear More than Dead Bodies

"I went to Korle Bu (Teaching Hospital), and I saw dead bodies, and it scared me out of reading medicine."
— Skyy Power Chief Executive, Wilson Arthur on why he changed his mind about pursuing a noble profession in medicine to the near ignoble profession in entertainment and broadcasting

Wilson Arthur had a dream. He wanted to become a medical doctor to help people in distress. He seemed to have the attributes: a satisfactory intelligence, love of learning, and a strong desire to do it. Prior to entering university, he enjoyed studying human biology.

Wilson tells me this in an interview I had with him on Skyy TV in late 2004. He built Skyy TV after the overwhelming success of his private radio enterprise.

"You see, Phillip," he tells me, "I wanted to become a medical doctor."

"You?" I interject, visibly shocked that the man sitting opposite me had once wanted to nurse people back to health.

I have only recently reviewed the video and cringed at my youthful skepticism. My obvious disbelief was expressed with a firm tone of ridicule. Wilson, to his credit, overlooked it and related his story.

According to him, before the dream of becoming a doctor took any recognisable shape, it disintegrated.

"I went to Korle Bu (Teaching Hospital)," he says, "I saw dead bodies, and it scared me out of reading medicine."

Just like the corpse he saw, his dream of becoming a doctor died.

The Interview

I had worked closely with Wilson on a daily basis for years. He employed me as a journalist when he set up Skyy Power FM. Given the speed with which Wilson developed his radio station and nurtured dozens of presenters into celebrities, the idea of owning and operating a TV station seemed like a natural progression for him.

Wilson is an indecipherable genius in making enterprising dreams come true. My colleagues and I saw this everyday, but the more we knew him, the less we understood how he made things happen to achieve lasting impact.

Wilson was all the more impressive because rather than being known as a boss, he was very much like an employee, mixing with the rest of us on the job every hour in a way that hardly distinguished him from the workforce.

"I am an average guy," says Wilson in the interview. It was a point he sought to emphasise. He also adds, "Maybe the difference is that I am focused, I know what I want and I try to go for what I want."

He reveals in the interview that the closed door to becoming a medical doctor made him find drive and purpose in the entertainment industry.

A Change of Direction

Wilson's spine-chilling experience of gazing at dead bodies in the hospital caused him to change his course. "I decided that I would go into a profession that will bring out the best in me," he says, adding, "I love entertainment."

Years later, he would add that "music is my first love."

His love of music and entertainment is one of the final motivators for seeking to build a profitable radio station in a part of Ghana that was written off as a possible location for a successful broadcasting business.

Roots from Ateiku

Wilson grew up as one of ten children in his family. His father, a retired army captain, died when he was only eight years old. His widowed mother managed the slim family budget with the combined skills of an entrepreneur and an economist. He enjoyed learning valuable entrepreneurial skills from his mother in Ateiku, a village not far from Takoradi. He observed intently as she bought and sold for profit anything she could lay her hands on.

"When we were young, we thought our mum was very rich because she could afford anything, to the extent of sending my older brother overseas to study," recalls Wilson.

"When someone comes to our home and the person gives us money, she would take the money and tell you she is going to help you make money out of this money. She invests the money in one of the things she is selling; so you see your money growing – and that was a big lesson I had when I was a child," says Wilson in the 2005 interview.

"I realised that if you put money into something, it grows and you can get money out of it and you can have whatever you want from the profit."

So, Wilson learned to become a creative entrepreneur at a young age from his illiterate mother, in a village not far from the Twin City.

Shooting for Sainthood in Sekondi

Young Wilson moved to Teshie in Accra before he turned twelve years old. While in school there, he formed a friendship with age mate Kingsley Boohene, which became a friendship that would last a lifetime. Decades later, Kingsley, known as KingB, would accompany Wilson to Takoradi when he arrived in mid-1997 on the first reconnaissance mission to build Skyy Power FM.

Long before this, however, twelve-year-old Wilson arrived in Sekondi as a student of St John's School. The child who would grow to change the Twin City through the broadcast media arrived with the highest mark in the common entrance examination.

Wilson didn't know anybody in Sekondi in those days, so he took refuge within the school environment, carefully sheltered by his school godfather in the Catholic boys-only school.

With encouragement from his school godfather, he became a member of the Scripture Union (SU), an inter-denominational evangelical Christian organisation that helps young people to grow with good morals. Often, young SU associates are described as being "Chrife," a term you will only hear in Ghana in light-hearted reference to some of the extremes to which some associates may take their commitment to SU principles.

Wilson became a "Chrife," quietly steering clear of popular dances, music, and fads; but it didn't last.

His deep-seated love for music, entertainment, and dancing quickly bubbled to the surface. He became a member of the Entertainment Committee at St. John's School. Upon the departure of his school godfather, Wilson was liberated to go as deep as possible in exploring his interests away from Scripture Union.

It was in the early days of backslide and break dancing, movements popularised by the King of Pop, Michael Jackson. With a few other friends, including KingB, Wilson, in his smallish frame, became a dancing phenomenon.

"I was a serious break dancer at St John's School," he says, almost trying to feign modesty, but the memories of his dance moves caused a cheeky smile across his face.

Wilson eventually ended up at the University of Ghana in Accra, taking with him his passion for music, entertainment, and dancing. At the University of Ghana, he became a member of the Entertainment Committee in 1989.

The Woman Wilson Arthur Married

The woman who eventually married Wilson, Adelaide Adwoa Amofah, fell in love with Wilson partly because of his gracious movement as a dancer. Adwoa Amofah, who was also a student at University of Ghana, went to a party at the Commonwealth Hall of the school where she observed Wilson dancing. His moves were effortless and graceful. Adwoa Amofah herself has impressive moves, the kind Michael Jackson describes as "divinity in motion" in his song, *Dangerous*.

Wilson and Adwoa Amofah danced that night, and they knew a union between them was something they both wanted. After completing studies at the University of Ghana, the two of them ended up in London where they formed a lasting partnership.

Three children later, they still share a dance with a constant memory of that first dance at the Commonwealth Hall of the University of Ghana.

A Profession in Music, Broadcasting, and Entertainment

Wilson made a major decision immediately after undertaking his National Service in the Volta Region in Ghana. Rather than looking forward to finding a good-paying job, he says, "I decided that I was going to be on my own." The brief periods he worked as an employee were mostly to acquire experience.

That includes the years spent in England.

As much as music and entertainment was constantly on Wilson's mind, owning a broadcasting entity never occurred to him. That was until Talal Fattal visited London from Accra in early 1995.

Talal, a businessman, met with Ghanaian students and provided updates on business opportunities back home. Talal himself is an electrifying character who is also a singer, songwriter, and producer. One thing in particular stood out for Wilson during the interaction with Talal.

"Talal Fattal disclosed that the National Communications Authority had started handing out licenses for private broadcasting," recalls Wilson.

After the event, Wilson and two other Ghanaian friends, Mike Cook and Robert Tamakloe, got together at Lewisham College in London to discuss how they could acquire a license and build their own private radio station.

"Mike Cook and Robert Tamakloe were both Takoradi guys, but I didn't know them until we all met in London as students," says Wilson. "We decided to take advantage of the opportunity Talal Fattal talked about."

At the end of the meeting of the three young men, they decided "Vibe FM" would be the name of their radio station when they would return to Ghana and build it together.

Wilson could not return to Ghana immediately with Mike Cook and Robert Tamakloe. They moved too fast and Wilson's obligations in London did not allow him to join them to bring Vibe FM to life.

By the time he returned to Ghana, Vibe FM was on air. Even though Wilson was left out of the partnership, he kept dreaming even bigger, and life started moving really fast for Wilson.

He eventually arrived at a point where he decided to build his own radio station. He spoke to his friends Mike Cook and Robert Tamakloe.

"They were very helpful," he said about his friends at Vibe FM. "In fact, they allowed me to use their proposal as a template to write the one I used in applying for the license," recalls Wilson.

Before obtaining the license, Wilson took a job as Marketing Manager for Media Number 1 in Accra. Media Number 1 was owned by Talal Fattal, the same man who met young Ghanaian students in London and told them about how the Ghanaian government had started handing out licenses for private broadcasting.

While working at Media Number 1, Wilson also set up Music Paradise where he rented out CDs to Vibe FM and Joy FM. Music Paradise was made possible by the thousands of CDs Wilson brought from London.

Wilson's childhood friend, KingB, confirmed the extraordinarily large volume of music Wilson brought to Ghana. "Wilson is a crazy music fanatic," he says. "He brought thousands and thousands of CDs from the UK, all genres."

Compact Disc duplication machines were rare in those days. Wilson knew this, so his business boomed, even as he continued renting CDs to radio stations in Accra, especially Vibe FM and Joy FM. No individual or entity had as much music as Wilson's Music Paradise in Adabraka, Accra.

The Drive and Enigma of Wilson Arthur

Sometime in July 1997, Wilson held a small radio receiver, turned it on and tuned to 93.5 FM. It was the first test transmission of Skyy Power FM. A tiny smile broke out on his face as his dream of owning and operating a radio station became something he heard for the first time. He imagined all the endless tracks his station would play to entertain and delight millions of people in the Western and Central Regions. With a lot more work to be done before commercial transmissions could start, Wilson's reflective thoughts on the impending success were only fleeting. He rarely took time to measure his own success.

"Do you ever stop to look at yourself and ask what sort of person you are in business?" This is one of the questions I ask him in the interview.

"I don't do that. There is always too much pressure on you to stop and even wonder what you are doing," he says, speaking of himself in the second person.

Wilson is always consumed by the power of his ideas and how to turn them into reality for profit. Those close to him notice it over and over again, and usually only after his ideas are about to bear fruit.

KingB, Wilson's childhood friend, saw it and says, "when Wilson makes up his mind to achieve something, he is very focused and would not give up until he gets it."

Thomas Dossah, a school mate from St. John's who later worked for Skyy, says, "Some of us never took him seriously in school, but he always seems to get ahead. After he returned from the UK and set up Skyy Power FM, you learned not to underestimate him."

Kwete Quaynor, an employee, says the first day he met Wilson in Accra at his music shop, Wilson told him he wanted to set up a radio station in Takoradi. "I didn't take him seriously because he didn't look like someone who could do it. Until he did it."

Jonathan Sowah, the resident film director who worked with him closely at Media Number 1, notes "I found Wilson to be a very targeted businessman, very intelligent, very calculated in his moves."

That is why, starting with Music Paradise, Wilson, in a few short years, built a business empire starting with Skyy Power FM, followed by Skyy TV, Ashh FM in Kumasi, a Music Recording Studio in Takoradi, and later owned Skyy FC, a football club in his hometown.

And those are just a few of his accomplishments as an entrepreneur and probably one of the best marketing and branding brains Ghana has ever experienced in the private sector.

"The Most Important Department is the Marketing Department"

It was Jonathan Sowah, Wilson Arthur's former workmate who suggested that Wilson is a "lemonade maker," a complimentary reference to how he can package and sell simple ideas and make them attractive. In my interview with Wilson, I ask him what he remembers of St. John's School after he started at the age of 12.

He off-handedly says, "St John's is a premium school."

St. John's, founded before Ghana's independence from the British, is indeed a notable school in the Western Region, but just by inserting the word *premium*, he gently led you to accept that it is a *premium* institution. His choice of words is part of his skills in marketing and branding. His skills in this area go beyond the choice of words. It found expression in ideas and solutions, often simple solutions that generate income to help many people and businesses.

As a journalist and editor, my biased position when I interviewed Wilson was that the newsroom was the most important department in any broadcasting organisation. Wilson had a different, well-grounded view, knowing the lifeblood of the private and commercial operation was tied to income and expenses.

He insists that "the most important department at Skyy is the Marketing Department." I quietly acquiesce and change the course of the interview immediately, for fear I would end up advertising either my bias or ignorance - or both.

Selling Attention

I remember an example of Wilson's marketing and branding skills from the early days of Skyy Power FM. Woodin, a fashion brand inspired by African culture and art, opened its showroom in Takoradi. Wilson's expertise was sought to help advertise the business. As if he had spent a lifetime preparing for this opportunity, he came up with a smart plan within minutes.

Ike Quartey, a former world boxing champion, was about to fight outside Ghana once more. The fight was going to be shown live on TV. Wilson's solution was simple: Skyy will provide live commentary on radio, to be sponsored by Woodin.

Adverts and jingles were quickly produced, announcing that Skyy would carry the live commentary, and each time Woodin was named as the sponsor. Woodin's location, its values, and commercial interest became part of the message, along with the appeal that it had come to Takoradi to help people see the best of Africa.

The combination of patriotic fever, the 100 percent support for Ike Quartey, and the love of boxing long established in Ghana became easy vehicles Wilson used to generate income for the still-new Skyy Power FM. Wilson repeated and reproduced powerful commercial messages like this thousands of times, while adding a powerful attraction of entertainment and promoting Sekondi-Takoradi and Western Region as the best thing Ghana had ever experienced.

He trained dozens in this process, leaving a trail of men and women who, while knowing he is imperfect, still feel a sense of gratitude to him for his passion and the power of his ideas.

Wilson, in addition to his marketing and branding skills, knew how to manage the egos of men and women who enjoyed celebrity status.

"You are dealing with talents. And talents like footballers, like musicians, the attitudes are very difficult to handle. You have people who are stars, who go out and they are pampered; they have big egos…you have to manage and get the best out of all these people. They are people who are very difficult to manage," reflects Wilson in my interview with him.

"How do you go around it?" I ask.

"I get to their level," he says.

"I eat with them, I flow with them, I jam with them, so they see me, more or less, like a colleague. They are able to tell me what they want to tell me, and after that, life goes on..." continues Wilson, projecting a demeanor that suggests he had accidentally disclosed a top secret.

Wilson's approach worked beyond colourful dreams, guaranteeing success for Skyy while raising the profile of the Twin City nationwide.

From Boys and Girls to Men and Women

The young man Wilson Arthur who came to Sekondi-Takoradi in mid-1997 brought with him a small army of other young men: Michael Griffiths, Root Eye, KingB, Sammy Arthur, Ato Parry, and Kwesi Fletcher.

They were all just boys, really. And they were joined by other young men and ladies: Maame Esi-Mark Hansen, Esi Gyan, Nana Fynnba Derby, Yuki Ampofo, Maame Efua DeGraft Aidoo, Kojo Frempong, Bob Gardiner, Elloeny Amande, Ato-Kwamena Dadzie, myself, and many more. A larger number, still mostly young men and women, joined later.

All of these young, outstanding boys and girls became men and women of substance by giving their best through private broadcasting in culturally and linguistically stylish Sekondi-Takoradi, the only place in Ghana where their story of inspiring a whole population could have been possible.

With few tools, skills, passion, and sometimes wisdom beyond their years, they made history.

Wilson Arthur, the son of an illiterate mother, supported by his wife Adwoa Amofah and his brother Kennedy Arthur, together with the immeasurable goodwill of the people of Sekondi-Takoradi and the Western Region, made history.

The full tapestry of their stories are worth telling and preserving in writing and in audio.

Childhood Friends

"My story, the story of Skyy and the story of Wilson Arthur... we go way back, back to when we were kids; I was 13 years old then."
— *Kingsley Boohene on his relationship with Skyy Power FM which started with Wilson Arthur when they were teenagers*

Of all the people who were employed at Skyy, no one is closer to Wilson Arthur and knows him better than Kingsley Boohene. Some of my colleagues may be seeing his family name for the first time in this book because we only ever called him *KingB*.

He became the first host of one of the daily weekday program called *Drive Jam*, leaving an indelible mark with his signature introduction of some of the best pop music ever played on any Ghanaian radio during late afternoons.

After the reverberation of one of Skyy Power FM's jingles, he would start the program saying, "This is *Drive Jam*, on Skyy Power 93.5 FM, live from 37 Windy Ridge. I am KingB, here to help you wind down. Check out this super rich classic called *Twisted*, by Keith Sweat." The rich stereophonic music would ring out on cue throughout Sekondi-Takoradi with the promise of a blissful late afternoon show carefully produced to ensure absolute listening pleasure during rush hour traffic.

I met KingB and Wilson Arthur as soon as they occupied the newly built property that they were determined to turn into a radio station in Takoradi. The two men looked like twins. Seemingly tired and fatigued, there was nothing about them that suggested they knew how to build a radio station.

The Proposal in Writing

KingB was one of the first people Wilson talked to about his idea to build the first private radio in Takoradi.

"When Wilson wrote the proposal to acquire the license to operate the radio station, I was the one who typed it out before submission," recalls KingB.

Ato Parry, who was working at Wilson Arthur's Music Paradise in Accra together with KingB also recalls, "At that time, Wilson Arthur didn't know how to use a typewriter, so he gave the proposal to KingB to type it out."

By the second year of Skyy Power FM operations, KingB had left for the United States, where for more than 20 years, Atlanta, Georgia, was his home. Wrapped with degrees in Computer Science and Biomedical Engineering, KingB manages the Medical and Radiation Oncology Systems and Apps at the Wellstar Health Systems in Atlanta.

That is where I reach him on the phone in March 2021 to interview him for this book and seek his cooperation. He is excited.

"That is such a great idea, Phillip," he says in reference to the planned book on Skyy Power FM. "You are the most qualified to write it," he adds, and leaves me flattered.

"How did you become part of Skyy Power FM?" I ask after he agreed to the interview.

Memories Not Quite Discarded

My rather bland question somehow startles KingB, and as he attempts to answer he stutters and fumbles repeatedly.

For the first few minutes, he struggles to recall some facts about Skyy Power FM's early days, and he can't even remember the physical address of the station's first location.

I gently interrupt the conversation to say, "it was located at 37 Windy Ridge," knowing he would appreciate that I was trying to be helpful.

But I am surprised he seems genuinely shocked that I remember the actual address of Skyy's first studio in Takoradi. "Hey, Phillip, you remember the address?" he says with some astonishment, accompanied by the unique laughter that I know so well.

For more than 20 years, KingB had not given thought to the early days of Skyy, a business he helped build. Soon though, it all starts coming back to him from a time when he was only 13 years old.

The Fog is Lifted

It was as if KingB needed a full warm up exercise to refresh a wealth of memories, and when he finds the key, I check to be sure the interview was still being recorded, because it is a story worth keeping.

"My story, and the story of Skyy and the story of Wilson Arthur… we go way back, to when we were kids, when we were about 13 years old," says KingB, after he clears his throat. "We met as teenagers in St John's School in Sekondi," he added.

Before he turned 12, Wilson the village boy from Ateiku in the Western Region, moved to Teshie-Nungua Estate in Accra. Even though the two boys first met in school, Teshie- Nungua Estate is the place that really cemented their friendship.

KingB's family owned a video theatre, where residents of Teshie-Nungua Estate and the surrounding neighborhoods were treated to nightly entertainment featuring the latest action movies and music videos. KingB took keen interest in the family business. He was allowed to assist in operating and maintaining all the gadgets for the movie theatre consisting of VHS video cassette players, fatback TV, entangled multi-colored wires running between multiple loudspeakers, and an amplifier constantly flickering with a scaled-down version of traffic lights.

Wilson and his family at Teshie-Nungua Estate visited KingB's movie theatre occasionally. There, Wilson observed the prominent role young KingB had in running the attractive nightly business.

The two boys whose friendship started from school got closer as a result of their common interest in music and dancing. They were especially attracted to the robot dancing and break-dancing craze, made popular by late pop music icon, Michael Jackson, and others.

"We love music!" affirms KingB.

When he says he and Wilson loved music, he stretches the word *love* to a breaking point.

With an extended intonation, he sounds more like, "we *loooooove* music."

Only the audio recording (to be released after this book is published) can fully convey KingB's excitement as he talked about their teenage escapades in discovering music deemed to be of global significance and thus defined a period of time.

"One very good memory I have between me and Wilson was when Midnight Star came out with the song, *No Parking On The Dance Floor*," says KingB.

No Parking On The Dance Floor, a quintessential "old school" music was released by *Midnight Star* in June 1983. As KingB recalls the memory, his voice changes with a heavy touch of emotion and elation confirming his deep love of music.

"Wilson and I would just hang around in his brother's house every day and listen attentively to decrypt the accent of the singers and write down the lyrics of all these songs manually. We would listen line by line to ensure we don't miss any details."

Lyrics of many dozens of popular songs were carefully written this way by the pre-teens, in an endless session of *play, pause, stop, rewind, play, start all over again.*

Wilson's older brother had the vinyl version of the Midnight Star album, including other hits of the time from London, which unlike the cassette player, made transcription easier for them.

Off to St. John's School, Sekondi

At St John's Secondary School, more than 200 kilometers from Accra, strict discipline curbed opportunities to explore the latest music and dance moves, but the passage of time resulted in more freedom for KingB and Wilson, along with like-minded schoolmates.

Their popularity soared. Along with a few other friends, their reputation was firmly established as two boys from Accra who knew the lyrics to so many songs and could dance like they were possessed.

Their friendship survived secondary school and the two boys returned to Accra. Shortly after their return, KingB left for school in the United States while Wilson attended the University of Ghana, and upon graduation, travelled to England for further studies. As they spent years apart on different continents, the two slowly grew from boys to young men - to the extent their new experiences could help them grow.

Reunion Back in Ghana

Later, they both returned to Ghana from their respective travels, and somehow, an invisible string pulled the old music lovers together again after years of separation. "It wasn't like there was any plan of meeting back in Accra," says KingB, "we hadn't even been in touch during our time away in the UK and the US," he adds.

One of the first things Wilson told KingB when they met again was about the thousands of music CDs he brought back to Ghana. Everyone who got to know about Wilson's goldmine of music was surprised about the huge collection, but not KingB.

"Wilson is a crazy music fanatic. I know him, so I was not surprised at all." The subtext of KingB's quick analysis is that as much as he shared the same love of music, Wilson's attraction to music is constantly at the extreme. Still, the sheer volume of the collection made him wonder why his friend had so many CDs. Wilson told him he had a business plan in addition to his passion for music.

"Wilson said he wanted to establish a recording studio. He found a small shop at Adabraka in Accra, and we started together," recalls KingB.

Signs of Owning a Radio Station

Private radio station ownership in Ghana became possible only about a year before Wilson Arthur returned to Ghana to set up Music Paradise. Joy FM was the first station to go on air, and by the time Wilson opened his music shop, other stations had opened, including Vibe FM.

Word spread about Wilson's extensive music collection at Music Paradise, and soon, the existing radio stations, including Joy FM,

Radio Gold, and Vibe FM, started renting music CDs from his shop. Vibe FM was a special case.

"Wilson was very close to the owners of Vibe FM. They were his friends, and they would often come to the Music Paradise shop to borrow CDs for their respective radio programs," says KingB. He is referring to Mike Cook and Robert Tamakloe, friends whom Wilson met in England and subsequently discussed building Vibe FM, except Wilson did not end up being part of the partnership. His friendship with Robert Tamakloe and Mike Cook continued, and Wilson would regularly visit Vibe FM studios located at Trust Towers in Accra, a few blocks away from the shop.

"Wilson was not always present at Music Paradise because he was also working as Marketing Manager at Media Number 1," says KingB. "Ato Parry, who was a DJ at the time, was often available to play music at different social functions around Accra."

According to KingB, during this time, Wilson also started looking for an opportunity to build his own radio station, and his friends at Vibe FM were helping him with ideas.

"Wilson wrote the proposal for the private radio license in his handwriting, and then I typed it out professionally with the office computer at Music Paradise," recalls KingB.

"One day," says KingB, "Wilson broke the news to me that Sekondi-Takoradi is the best place to consider building the new radio station later called Skyy Power FM."

Because the two friends attended St. John's School in Sekondi, they had a good idea about the city from when they were teenagers. A reconnaissance mission to Takoradi became an urgent need.

"It was a very exciting time," says KingB.

"Wilson and I took the trip to Takoradi for the first time to check out locations in the city. By this time, Wilson was an expert in marketing because that is what he studied at the university in England."

At the time, Wilson had what was possibly the oldest VW Golf car in Ghana. It moved alright and helped with daily business errands in Accra, but it was not always reliable.

"We drove that car all the way from Accra to Takoradi and a couple of times, it gave up on the road. We had to stop and work on the car before continuing the journey," recalls KingB, pausing to reflect on how he and Wilson survived the multiple trips they took in that jalopy car.

By the time Skyy Power FM started in October 1997, that old car was only fit for a graveyard, and Wilson Arthur, like most of the employees, didn't have his own car for a considerable period. He used taxis and occasionally walked on foot. Whether by design or accident, it helped Wilson establish an authentic image as a co-worker hustling to breathe life into a new enterprise, rather than a boss who lived a comfortable life at the expense of the workforce.

One of the first decisions Wilson and KingB made was to convince Uncle Opia to join Skyy Power FM. Uncle Opia was a wildly popular Fante language radio presenter who worked for the state broadcaster. He was well known for running a daily program on Twin City Radio, operated by the Ghana Broadcasting Corporation. He mixed the unique Sekondi-Takoradi humor with an uncanny ability to inspire the community to care about everything that makes a better society, from environmental hygiene to social justice. He earned the distinction as a man who represented the conscience of the people.

"With Uncle Opia on our side, Wilson was confident he could use his marketing and advertising skills to guarantee sufficient revenue to make Skyy Power FM a success," says KingB, as he recalls the early days before people got to know about Skyy Power FM.

There were multiple trips between Accra and Takoradi as plans went full steam ahead to build Skyy. Wilson and KingB were joined by Sammy Arthur and Ato Parry, both of whom were working with Wilson at Music Paradise.

Another early employee from those days was Michael Griffiths. Wilson knew him from St. Aquinas School in Accra. Two others were Kwesi Fletcher and singer-songwriter Root Eye.

"For many weeks, we would spend the whole day working at the studio with sound engineers, installers, setting up machines and radio equipment. We had lots of sleepless nights in those days," recalls KingB.

Apart from new equipment and gadgets for the radio station being hauled from Accra to 37 Windy Ridge in Takoradi, there was nothing else that made life easy in the new building. The owners of the property hurried up to finish the building because Wilson wanted to move in immediately, so it was yet to be furnished.

As a result, KingB and Wilson were practically sleeping rough, their quality of life just a little bit better than that of street vagabonds.

It was around this time, June 1997, that I first met Wilson Arthur and KingB. I was living in Takoradi, working for the *Ghanaian Chronicle* newspaper and also writing for Radio and TV Reviews (RTV) magazine published by Robert Mills in Accra.

I had a tip that Wilson Arthur had secured a radio license to build a new private station in Takoradi. I sought an interview with him and subsequently published it in *RTV*.

With a strong preference for the broadcast journalism that I learned at Sydney's Channel 7 in Australia, I knew I wanted to be part of a new radio station in Takoradi and play a leading role in producing the news and current affairs.

But I also wanted to confirm that Wilson Arthur and Skyy Power FM was going to be something worth committing to. Always operating on the assumption that nothing is what it purports to be until confirmed, I was personally unconvinced about the substance and future of Skyy - until test transmission started, followed by a recruitment drive to find talent, a process I followed with keen interest.

Furnishings at the 37 Windy Ridge studio were still sparse, and each time I visited, Wilson and KingB looked beaten up by the burden of building the station. Wilson always looked tired, and I found him either sitting or lying down on the newly laid carpet.

He was always consumed by a hundred different things that had to go right, and KingB was always the person he turned to.

Recruitment and Auditioning

Once test transmission started, KingB and Wilson found they now had the biggest megaphone in the city and community.

"We engaged in a recruitment drive, making announcements during the test transmission that we needed presenters for our new station," says KingB.

"That is how we secured all the amazing presenters like JM Caesar, Yuki Ampofo, Naa Adoley Thompson, Kofi Gyetsua Ankoma (KGA), Kojo Frempong (Shakes), Maame Efua DeGraft Aidoo, and Maame Esi Mark-Hansen. That is apart from the guys that came from Accra with us."

"Everyone we recruited and auditioned perfectly fit into Skyy. It worked so well that we became like family," says KingB.

"We did our best work in Takoradi and really enjoyed it. The people of Sekondi-Takoradi loved us, and they loved Skyy so much. We were superstars and didn't even know it."

Intoxicating Happy Memories

Throughout the interview, it was as if KingB is intoxicated by the joy of the memories of Skyy. The more he talks about it, the happier and fulfilled he sounds. He laughs so much as we recall so many funny events.

As a journalist, it was impossible to remain fully objective because I was part of the Skyy story from the start, as well as a fellow custodian of the memories he cherished.

KingB left Skyy to go back to the United States in the second year of operation, but he says his experience at Skyy was one of the happiest times of his life.

"We were so silly, and we had so much fun! Sometimes, it feels like we were all born into the same family and always knew each other."

For KingB, friendship with Wilson Arthur had the soundtrack of a thousand beautiful songs composed by lyricists who were also musicians.

The hours KingB spent with Wilson, singing and dancing, followed by the construction of a historic radio station became unbreakable ties between two boys who became men surrounded by workmates they called family.

The Seed that Skyy Planted

"Skyy became a place that educated us and informed us. Sekondi-Takoradi is probably the most pan-Africanist city in West Africa and Skyy, in a way, was like a pan-Africanist station because the guys who worked there came from diverse parts of Ghana, and they spoke like they belonged to the Western Region. They helped this city to stand on its feet."

— Paramount Chief of Essikado Traditional area in Ghana's Western Region, Nana Kobina Nketsia V, describing the achievements of Skyy Power FM, after a quarter of a century of operating in Sekondi—Takoradi.

Kojo Baffoe Maison is a larger-than-life character in Ghana. He is an intellectual who used to lecture at the University of Cape Coast, with a doctorate degree in history. He lives in Sekondi, Western Region.

Only a few people, mostly his students, know him as "Kojo Baffoe Maison."

That is because he now serves as a traditional leader, a chief, with the formal name and title, *Nana Kobina Nketsia V, Paramount Chief of Essikado Traditional Area*, part of the Sekondi-Takoradi Metropolis. The traditional leader possesses an uncommon combination of modern pragmatism and ancient wisdom, moderated by common sense.

Nana Nketsia saw the birth of Skyy Power FM and continually interacted with all the people who made it a resounding success over the last quarter of a century.

The day I call to interview him is also the day Ghanaians are engaged in a nationwide tree planting exercise.

"Today is a tree planting day in Ghana," he says, after we had been speaking for a while about the heroism of the past 25 years since Wilson Arthur and his gang planted Skyy Power FM.

"By the time the trees grow," he continues, "some of us will be dead. But these trees will offer shade to those who come after us." The insightful observation is directly related to the legacy of Skyy and what it achieved in the Western Region over a few decades.

"Unity, the First Point of Development"

Even though Skyy Power FM is a commercial venture in which Nana Nketsia had no share, he enthusiastically supported the station with everything he had. The exceptional support he offered stemmed from his strong belief that the essence of a leader, or a chief, is to inspire and enable the development of people and infrastructure, as well as the preservation of a healthy environment.

"Because of the traditional role I play, I was very circumspect about getting involved in the media or with the media, and yet I decided to throw my weight behind this radio station to make sure that it stands on its feet," he reflects. "I was even looking for people who could come and participate in discussions to ensure our citizens are not only well-informed, but better informed on issues of common concern."

The paramount chief of Essikado believes Skyy Power FM proved to be a strong unifier.

"When Skyy came in, it was a big boost to draw those of us from this region closer; at the same time, it created an identity of being one," he explains.

"Everything in this world depends on information. Skyy may have thought about the profit margin, but more importantly, it had a mission to inform and raise the profile of the Western Region. It was the people's voice in the Western Region," Nana Nketsia emphasises.

A Different Kind of Leader

On 15 October 1996, a year before Skyy was established, Nana Nketsia was enstooled. *Enstoolment* is a Ghanaian and West African English term that describes a meticulous and exhaustive proceeding with colourful rituals, punctuated by rhythmic drumming and dancing at which a nominated person is pronounced as a chief. The day Nana Nketsia was enstooled was the day his secular name, Kojo Baffoe Maison, became almost irrelevant.

He succeeded his revolutionary uncle, Nana Kobina Nketsia IV (*the fourth*) who had occupied the position since 1948, while also being a professor of Social Anthropology, Africanist, freedom fighter, and statesman. The older Nana Kobina Nketsia IV played a crucial role in events leading to Ghana's independence from Great Britain, leading a nonviolent civil disobedience campaign to resist the colonial masters. He paid a high price for his effort by being imprisoned in his own country, then called the Gold Coast.

The new Nana Kobina Nketsia V who proudly walks in the footsteps of his uncle believes the modern-day struggle is about helping members of his community, including Ghanaians and Africans, to stop looking out for hand-outs and rather help themselves to achieve their own successes.

Zero Tribal Instincts and Zero Partisanship

Nana Kobina Nketsia V made clear that the support and goodwill he showed Skyy Power FM was strictly for the general welfare of the people of the Western Region and was not partisan in any way.

"As a chief, you can't afford to move into any political party because you are the father of all," he says, adding, "That view must be constantly and consistently maintained. The stool [the authority and influence of a traditional leader] is not made for factionalism. As soon as you join a party, you've killed the stool; unless it is part of a national fight, just as my uncle did," he explains.

"Skyy Power represented the people's voice in the Western Region - it wasn't a partisan voice. The station represented our aspirations. Western Region is still suffering, but we also appreciate that it would have been worse without Skyy. Wilson Arthur and his band of workers did a yeoman's job for the region."

The broader context was that Skyy Power, as the first private and commercial radio station, had no competitor and benefited fully from the unlimited goodwill of the people, including the respected paramount chief of Essikado.

When the New Patriotic Party, one of the two main political parties in Ghana, won the general elections with Nana Akufo-Addo as President, Wilson Arthur accepted an appointment as a District Chief Executive (or Mayor). This was after his unsuccessful attempts to be elected to Ghana's parliament. The esteemed paramount chief thinks Wilson Arthur should have declined the political appointment and stayed far away from politics.

"Wilson Arthur is one of the most important people in the Western Region because of his contribution," says Nana Nketsia. He believes rather than enhancing his image, partisan politics could undermine all of Wilson's hard work and contribution. It is quite a thing to say about Wilson because Nana Nketsia was once recognised as Western Region's personality of the year, as well as the traditional ruler of the year.

As of the writing of this book, Wilson Arthur has decided to step out of politics and pursue his abiding interest in the media, as well as the development of football talents for the future.

Uncle Opia Introduces Wilson Arthur

For years, the man universally known as Uncle Opia was the most popular person in Sekondi-Takoradi, especially from 1994 when Ghana Broadcasting Corporation (GBC) opened its regional station in the city. Uncle Opia had a warm and affectionate manner of speaking to listeners in a way that won the hearts of the people.

That's why Wilson Arthur immediately poached him from GBC even before he identified a location from which Skyy would broadcast. Like many residents of Sekondi-Takoradi, Nana Nketsia knew Opia long before Wilson dreamt of building Skyy. He also interacted with Uncle Opia from a unique perspective when he served as Chairman of Ghana Broadcasting Corporation's Board of Directors.

"He was a typical Sekondi-Takoradi boy; he was part of the landscape," says Nana Nketsia in describing Opia, who died in 2006.

"Opia came and introduced Wilson Arthur to me. He was helping Wilson to find office space in the city for the new radio station. Wilson, at the time, was unknown to me; a bright-eyed young man and his brother, Kennedy," recalls Nana Nketsia.

After being introduced to the young Wilson Arthur, he knew he held a promise as a man with a community spirit and a vision to lead a movement to transform Sekondi-Takoradi and the Western Region.

In Sekondi-Takoradi, Everyone is a Friend

Another facet of Ghana's twin city is that there exists a strong social fabric where most people feel a sense of belonging. Nana Nketsia refers to this, saying "in Sekondi-Takoradi, everyone is a paddy; even the chief is a paddy."

To say someone is "my paddy" in Ghana means the person is a friend or a pal. Striking a friendship with someone in Ghana tends to be easy. In Takoradi especially, a pre-existing sense of camaraderie is the strongest currency and works like a glue that holds the population together. It transcends social status, and enables both old and young, rich and poor, famous people and ordinary folks to mix easily. "Takoradi is a small place" is a popular expression used to explain this aspect of the Twin City.

The city is also defined by its musical legacy, and some of its heroes include music icons such as C.K. Mann, A.B. Crentsil, and Paapa Yankson. It is not unusual to see C.K. Mann strolling on the street near his home at Anaji in slippers or Paapa Yankson walking on the streets of Amanful chatting to anyone about whether Hasaacas or Sekondi Eleven Wise Football Club is the best team in the Western Region.

Skyy Power FM became part of that fabric which made close relationships thrive easily. That is how the close relationship Paapa Yankson and C.K. Mann had with Nana Nketsia is just as special as the relationships that were played out on the street between them and ordinary people with no titles.

Both Paapa Yankson and C.K. Mann, who were fond of Skyy Power FM, have passed on, but the spirit and culture of friendship continues and is well and truly alive.

Kofi Kinaata, one of the most influential Ghanaian musicians, is from Takoradi, and he is walking in the footsteps of the giants that came before him. He spends a lot of time in Accra, but when he comes to Takoradi, he easily slides back into his natural role as a paddy to all.

When he scooped up a number of awards in 2020, he took it all with him to show the paramount chief at his palace. Photos of the visit made it seem like a very official event, but in reality, it was just two paddies, one young and the other old, who decided to celebrate another reason why the best is often said to come from Ghana's Western Region.

Something else Kofi Kinaata and Nana Nketsia have in common is their appreciation for Skyy Power FM. That is why a whole chapter of this book is about Kinaata, his relationship with, and his memories of, Skyy Power FM over a period of 25 years.

A Quarter of a Century in the Making

From its first day, Nana Nketsia has been close to Skyy Power FM and has used the medium to teach and inspire. That is how he became one of the few who saw the struggle of Wilson Arthur and his employees in the early days, long before success became a reality. He says, "Skyy virtually had nothing. Wilson was living from hand to mouth with his workers. Skyy was virtually scrambling and scrapping for existence." As Wilson Arthur himself often puts it, "money is the result you get from giving people what they need."

The people of Sekondi-Takoradi and the Western Region have an unusually strong emotional attachment to Skyy Power FM. The strength and enduring nature of the relationship is hard to explain, but Nana Nketsia puts it best: "Skyy became our radio station. Skyy became the place where we saw our truth emanating from."

That was before other private radio stations came to Sekondi-Takoradi, more than 30 stations at the time of publishing this book.

Twenty-five years after the experiment by Wilson Arthur and his gang, Nana Kobina Nketsia V still believes Skyy had a worthy idea: the idea of making Sekondi-Takoradi and Western Region a place where only the best comes from.

Returning to the analogy of a seed turning into a tree, he says, "Skyy planted a seed, and we need to go back to that seed, rethink it and water it for our future."

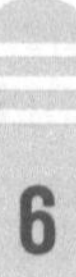

6

The Most Famous Address in Takoradi

"I told my friends and colleagues at work that a new radio station is coming, but some of them didn't believe me. When Skyy FM started transmission, they were all happy and excited. They said 37 Windy Ridge is your house, and it is all happening from your house!"

— Mrs. Kwansima Bedu—Amissah, landlady of the property from where Skyy Power FM started transmission in October 1997

The car driven by Mrs. Kwansima Bedu-Amissah in 1997 is described by its manufacturer as "the ultimate driving machine."

It was a BMW 3 Series.

In the late 1990s, Mrs. Bedu-Amissah was probably the only professional teacher in Sekondi-Takoradi who drove the ultimate driving machine.

During one early morning storm, Skyy FM's tall and heavy mast fell and nearly smashed this car.

When it was all over, the equipment, weighing tons, laid precariously, only inches from the shiny car.

The First Five Years

Mrs. Bedu-Amissah and her family owned the property at 37 Windy Ridge in Takoradi, the location from which Skyy started, spending the first five years there.

The mast that nearly smashed the fancy car was the first one Skyy raised to send broadcast signals to millions. As a small crowd gathered to see the mangled mix of iron, heavy cables, and expensive equipment, Mrs. Bedu-Amissah was grateful for two things: first, that no one was in the vicinity when the mast fell, and second, that it missed the car that she loved. "God intervened," she says, with understandable gratitude.

Finding a Location to Build a Radio Station

One of the immediate challenges Wilson Arthur and his brother, Kennedy Arthur, faced was to find a fitting physical location for the all-new private and commercial radio station they were seeking to build in Sekondi-Takoradi.

Most listeners wouldn't care very much about where a broadcast originated, as long as it met their needs. But the real estate principle of "location, location, location" was very much at play.

Constructing a new building for the enterprise was wholly impractical, so they decided to find a suitable property with multiple requirements. On arriving in Takoradi with a few friends on the reconnaissance mission for Skyy Power FM, Wilson and Kennedy realised they needed a local heavy weight as an ally.

That local hero was Albert Mensah Nunoo, better known throughout Sekondi-Takoradi as Uncle Opia.

Opia had already spent decades with Ghana Broadcasting Corporation (GBC) and was close to retirement. Wilson approached him with an attractive offer he could not refuse, and Uncle Opia became one of the first employees of the first private and commercial radio station in that part of Ghana.

A Visit to Essikado by Wilson Arthur and Uncle Opia

Uncle Opia's celebrity status in Sekondi-Takoradi meant he was also one of the most connected. In the era where mobile phones were uncommon, and yes, social media didn't exist, Uncle Opia's personal social network was the old-fashioned, but effective face-to-face knowledge of people, and he knew everyone who mattered in society. He introduced Wilson Arthur to all of them. One of the influential people Uncle Opia linked Wilson with was a lecturer at Cape Coast University: Dr. Baffoe Maison who lived in the Essikado suburb of the Twin City. The year before, he was crowned the paramount chief of Essikado, and assumed the royal name, Nana Kobina Nketsia V.

Underneath the royal robes though, Nana Nketsia is really a mix of a progressive minded traditionalist and a forward-leaning pragmatist, highly enthusiastic about doing everything possible to bring development to Sekondi-Takoradi.

Nana Nketsia could not assist with finding the most suitable accommodation for the new enterprise, but he was impressed with Wilson Arthur. Perhaps something more important than helping find accommodation was that the chief bought Wilson Arthur's dream of transforming the city with a private radio station. He threw his full moral weight behind the venture that eventually came to be known as Skyy Power FM.

The Property Search Intensifies

After many more unsuccessful attempts to find a property, Uncle Opia met Mrs. Bedu-Amissah, the posh Takoradi woman who drove the BMW 3 Series. Popularly known as *Teacher Kwansima*, she and her family lived in the fashionable suburb of Windy Ridge in Takoradi in a house they built on a hill.

On that same hill is a two-storey apartment, also owned by the Bedu-Amissah family. It was under construction and not yet ready for occupancy.

Wilson Arthur and Uncle Opia visualised what it would look and feel like when completed. They concluded it was the perfect property at a great location. It had all the important attributes:

Located on a high elevation

Large enough for multiple offices

Sufficient space for parking vehicles

Close to the Central Business District

Overall high quality to match a new trendy brand

"I had never met Uncle Opia until he came to visit me," recalls Mrs. Bedu-Amissah. "He introduced himself, and I was amazed. I recognised his voice because I heard it so many times on GBC."

Location: 37 Windy Ridge

By the time Uncle Opia made the request to rent the uncompleted house, Mrs. Bedu-Amissah was fully on board.

"I was so excited to hear that a private radio station would come to Takoradi and I was prepared to do whatever I could to help."

Uncle Opia had gone to start the negotiation with Mrs. Bedu-Amissah all by himself. Within a week, he returned with Wilson to finalise an agreement.

"My willingness to help the new radio station got even stronger when I met Wilson Arthur. He was so young, and because I am a teacher and a mother, I took him almost as a son."

Mrs. Bedu-Amissah was very serious about supporting the new and exciting venture. "I told Wilson that I want to help because the new radio station will create jobs for people. Also, I believed it would bring more variety in entertainment to Takoradi."

"Takoradi was starting to get boring, and even the harbour didn't have enough jobs for people as before, so I was really excited," says the future landlady. Soon, her actions took on a greater significance than her enthusiastic words.

"We were putting up the building slowly, but when Wilson Arthur decided to use it for the radio station, my family and I decided to finish it immediately so it could be used," recalls Mrs. Bedu-Amissah.

"When Wilson started to bring the equipment, I agreed to let him keep some of them in my home before the apartments were ready. We gave Skyy three apartments."

"My family and I decided not to charge a commercial rate on the property. We were reasonable and supportive because we knew the radio station was going to bring jobs and help Sekondi-Takoradi."

Each apartment had five rooms across the two-storey building.

The administrative offices were on the ground floor while the studio, production room, and newsroom were on the first floor. The adjoining apartment on the top floor served as a private residence for Wilson Arthur and his family.

A small detail Mrs. Bedu-Amissah reveals during her interview showed the genuineness of her excitement about Skyy and the benefits she believed the enterprise would bring.

"I recommended the first professional cleaner for Skyy, a man I knew who needed that job," she says. Twenty-five years on, it is clear that she took pride in her special relationship with Skyy Power FM.

"It is All Happening From Your House"

Mrs. Bedu-Amissah makes a confession when I tease her. "You couldn't keep the news of the coming of Skyy Power FM to yourself, could you?" I ask, imagining that she would have told her fellow teachers and perhaps students at school that a radio station was going to be operating from her property.

"It is true," she says, "I told my friends and colleagues at work that a new radio station is coming, but some of them didn't believe me."

"When Skyy FM started transmission, they were all happy and excited. They said 37 Windy Ridge is your house and it is happening from your house."

Millions heard the radio transmission from Mrs. Bedu-Amissah's property, but what they didn't know is that she and her family were very close to all the presenters.

"All the presenters at Skyy were like my children," says Mrs. Bedu-Amissah. "They all called me Mama and I enjoyed having them all here for meals."

"I was close to all of you, especially Kwesi Fletcher, Bob Gee, JM Caesar, you Phillip Nyakpo, Maame Esi Mark-Hansen, Aba Moses and Root Eye…" Mrs. Bedu-Amissah says, adding my name to the list.

"We all became like family."

Skyy Power FM's First Family

Of the multiple dozens of presenters interviewed for this book, almost everyone said "Skyy was like a family."

The foundation of Skyy Power FM's "family-ness" started with Wilson Arthur and his wife, Adwoa Amofah, who had a young family when operations started. With their three children, they lived in one of the three flats from which Skyy FM had its studio and offices.

The children, Maame, Kwabena and Kweku, were all under ten years of age. All three were born in England and experienced their critical formative years in Takoradi, Ghana, entirely surrounded by exciting radio presenters who adored them. It helped that most of the presenters themselves were young, either in their late teens or early 20s.

The family flavour also had roots in the easy love and affection from the landlady, Mrs. Bedu-Amissah, and her family. She and her husband had five children and lived next door to the studio.

Between Perth and Melbourne, Australia

Kweku Bedu-Amissah is one of Mrs. Bedu-Amissah's children. After a formal interview with Mrs. Bedu-Amissah for this book, we engage in a more relaxed chit-chat in which she says her son also lives in Australia, and she hopes that we would run into each other and relive the old days. Before long, I am on the phone to Kweku Bedu-Amissah. He was only ten years old when Skyy started. After 25 years, he is not that young anymore. I live in Perth, and he lives in Melbourne.

"I remember everything," he says about his memories of Skyy. "I was so excited that our property next door was going to be used for a radio station…" he tells me, his childlike enthusiasm still with him.

"Each day after school, I would run next door to the studio to see how everything was being set up. I was very young, but I tried to help as much as possible. I would run simple errands such as getting the technicians a drink of water or picking up tools from the floor as they work. I was especially excited when the walls of the studio were being prepared. My job was to place heavy glue on used egg crates which were pasted on the wall as part of soundproofing," recalls Kweku.

"Landlord Abodwese"

"Landlord Abodwese" (literally, Landlord with loathsome beard) is the title of a popular Ghanaian Highlife music by A. B. Crentsil. The song describes the tense relationship between humble tenants who sometimes feel intimidated by haughty landlords in an environment with a persistent shortfall in housing.

A. B. Crentsil, known for composing songs with both thoughtful and provocative lyrics, scored this perfectly for tenants who found their voice through the song. Many people had a thrill playing that music whenever possible, within the earshot of their landlord. The fact that *Landlord Abodwese* was pulsating and danceable made it all the more appealing.

Mrs. Bedu-Amissah was the landlady for Skyy at 37 Windy Ridge. One day, she heard the controversial song playing on Skyy. Her friends heard it, too. For a song that can be antagonistic, the outcome was a warm surprise.

"We heard your people on Skyy playing *Landord Abodwese*, but you are special, because they said you are a friendly landlady," one of her friends reported to her.

Mrs. Bedu-Amissah laughed, very pleased that Skyy Power FM is like a family to her.

9/11 Memories with Uncle Opia

One of Mrs. Bedu-Amissah's enduring memories at Skyy is the 9/11 attacks in the United States.

As a teacher, school re-opening days were especially important to Mrs. Bedu-Amissah. Tuesday, 11 September 2001 was one of those dates in Ghana. Mrs. Bedu-Amissah had travelled to the United States for holidays, but she made sure she returned two days before schools would reopen. She arrived on Sunday, 9 September.

Fully jet-lagged from the journey, she slept for most of the period leading to the infamous day, until Uncle Opia spoke to her, several hours after the attacks in New York.

"You must feel very fortunate to have returned from America before the attacks on the World Trade Centre (the twin towers). If you didn't, you could not have returned right now because all flights have been grounded," Uncle Opia sympathised.

Mrs Bedu-Amissah had no idea what he was talking about. Opia then explained the whole world-shaking event with details he learned from Skyy Newsroom.

She froze, unable to say much, only grateful to be home safely from America.

"This is one of the memories I keep of Uncle Opia, apart from the day he came to ask for our property to be used for the radio station," says Mrs. Bedu-Amissah.

Mrs. Bedu-Amissah's property remained the station's most famous address until February 2002 when Skyy moved into its own purpose-built complex on top of a hill at Fijai. The new famous address in Takoradi became 19/20 West Fijai. That property also became the biggest to house any private radio station in Ghana. Just as well, because Wilson Arthur built it to accommodate an all-new TV station that became the new dream.

7

The Funky Bean Counter

"I laughed off the job offer from Wilson," says Osei Bediako.
"I already work, so, no thanks," he told Wilson.
"What about after work?" Wilson asked
"Work after work?" thought Osei Bediako.

Osei Bediako's family history includes the fascinating fact that his father, industrialist Dr. J. A. Addison, procured and supplied thousands of tons of cement used in constructing the iconic Akosombo Hydro Electric project, which has powered the Ghanaian economy for decades.

It is a sterling example of the power of entrepreneurship that young Osei Bediako never forgot while growing up in Kumasi and later Sekondi-Takoradi.

By his late teens, he was sent to England for further education where he qualified as an Accountant. After more than eight years in England, and with the means to continue living there indefinitely, Osei Bediako had no plans of returning to work in Ghana.

But his aging father had other ideas.

"Young man, you are coming back home now to take care of the family business." It was an order he could not ignore.

Coming Back to Takoradi

So, in July 1997, Osei Bediako returned to Takoradi and settled at his new home in the hilly suburb of Windy Ridge. It took him less than ten minutes to drive to his office at Multiwall Paper Sacks, Ltd., which sits under the flight path for planes landing at the Takoradi Air Force Base.

He had no worries, and life was good.

Unknown to Osei Bediako, just a few houses down from him at Windy Ridge, an innovative new business was being born, one that would become part of his life for more than a quarter of a century. Through the business he would become known all over the twin city and even earn a new name: Jam Master Caesar, or simply, JM Caesar.

Osei Bediako became friends with Kobby when he returned from England. It was Kobby who told him about an emerging business, just walking distance from Osei Bediako's home.

Kobby himself was working with Mobitel, the first mobile phone company in Ghana and Takoradi which started operating about a year earlier. At that time, possession or ownership of a mobile phone was a clear indication that the owner was a person with significant disposable income.

Discovering Skyy Power FM

"I need to go and speak with Wilson Arthur. He is the owner of the new radio station, and they are doing the test transmission."

This was Kobby, telling Osei Bediako about Western and Central Region's first private radio station being built right in his neighbourhood.

"A radio station, I see," said Osei Bediako.

And that's all he said, and it was the first time Osei Bediako heard about Skyy Power FM.

"Yeah, come with me, let's go and see Wilson Arthur, the owner," said Kobby.

When they got into the car, the dial on the radio was already on 93.5 FM, and pulsating music was gushing out of the stereo loudspeakers. About halfway to the new station, the music was interrupted by a crystal-clear jingle.

"This is Skyy Power 93.5 FM test transmission, proudly sponsored by Mobitel."

Osei Bediako had just discovered Mobitel, the company his friend worked for, was sponsoring Skyy Power FM's test transmission. He took it all in, knowing he was about to discover a private and commercial radio station in his new neighbourhood.

Building the station was a financial challenge for Wilson and his two business partners, Adwoa Amofah and Kennedy Arthur. The relatively small market in Sekondi-Takoradi is why other investors chose not to set up in this twin city.

Hand-in-Hand with Mobitel

Under normal circumstances, a radio station will not earn any income until the start of full commercial transmission, a time when overheads soar with mounting bills and considerably high staff wages. Getting companies to commit funds during test transmission was not a regular business proposition.

But Wilson, a raw genius in marketing and advertising, knew how to make money from thin air with ideas generated in his head.

After almost a quarter of a century of operation, Nana Fynnba Derby, the lady who was the first to host the station's flagship morning show, looks back in reflection.

She says, "Wilson Arthur marketed effectively, with distinction. I think he studied marketing in the UK, so he knew what buttons to push in the community, and in the context of the culture, to create a niche for broadcasting for his station. He did a good job. I felt it as an employee."

After Wilson studied the Sekondi-Takoradi market, he made a convincing case to Mobitel that Skyy FM could make their expensive new cellular service more attractive to people than Mobitel could ever hope to do by advertising on giant billboards around the city.

Mobitel felt the debilitating fear of missing out as Wilson convinced them that Skyy is an emerging premium brand in broadcasting that will create ever increasing demand for services among old and young in Western and Central Regions of Ghana. He made Mobitel believe that their financial future was bright with Skyy.

Mobitel had already made millions in the national capital, Accra, as well as in Kumasi, the second biggest city in Ghana. The marriage between Mobitel and Skyy was consummated within a short period of Wilson's proposal that they sponsor the test transmission for the station. In return, Mobitel received the singular recognition as being associated with Skyy Power FM from day one.

Memories of United Kingdom

Osei Bediako and Kobby, the Mobitel employee, arrived at 37 Windy Ridge. It was deathly quiet that day in August 1997. No employees, no security, no cars, no chattering, nothing.

Apart from a modest antenna perched on a slim, multicoloured pylon, there was little to show that this was going to be the location of a groovy and transformative radio station.

The two friends found their way into the studio, located on the second floor of the two-storey building. Wilson Arthur was the only one in the studio, sitting behind the console playing music live on air.

A short introduction took place, but before any kind of conversation ensued, Wilson received a call on his mobile phone - a Mobitel phone of course.

And he excused himself.

Wilson spent about ten minutes on the phone. Before he returned, the music he was playing had stopped, giving way to a few moments of silence.

Wilson left Kobby and Osei Bediako on their own, surrounded by a stacked deck of CD players, an array of microphones, and a large mixer with knobs too many to count.

A big overhead earphone was resting on the mixer. The mixer itself, connected by fat cables, glowed with a million little traffic lights.

The setup is intimidating to the uninitiated.

But Osei Bediako found it alluring.

A-Class Studio Craft

In England, Osei Bediako used to play music at parties with a mixer and microphone connected to large loudspeakers through an amplifier. He knew how to change a CD and find a corresponding knob on a mixer to control the volume when the music starts to play.

Bediako anticipated the uncomfortable silence which was about to occur as the music faded away. He moved around and found a suitable track on one of the CDs to play.

He describes the maneuver rather simply in an interview. "I went behind the console, I changed the CD, and I played the next song."

When Wilson returned to the studio, he immediately knew someone had touched the machine, changed the CD, and started playing something rhythmic and funky.

"Who changed the CD?" asked Wilson in a mixture of relief and surprise, knowing an uncomfortable silence on air had been averted.

"I did," said Osei Bediako, feeling a bit guilty and self-conscious for doing something he was not expected to do.

"The previous song was ending, so I figured a new track ought to be played," he added, his justification, although logical, still sounded weak.

"Waaaooo," exclaimed Wilson, his eyes lit with excitement.

The Job Offer

Across Ghana, CD players were still novel in 1997, and Wilson had encountered many people who have not even seen one before.

"How did you know how to change it?" asked Wilson, genuinely wanting to know.

"I know how to do it,'" Osei Bediako offered, shyly.

Wilson, without asking for more details, said "we have been training people on how to use the console and they are finding it very difficult. You just walked in here and did it all by yourself?"

As if jobs at Skyy were like as easy to give as candies, he immediately made an offer to Osei Bediako. Bright eyed, he looked at him, asking earnestly, "would you like a job here?"

Elloeny Amande, who was later employed at Skyy and developed his capability as a radio presenter and sports journalist says, "you know, Wilson, he is very unconventional."

He truly is, and he combines it with an inexplicable instinct and ability to read people and instantly determine their capability and usefulness in radio.

Wilson's blindspot on this occasion, though, was that he didn't know that Osei Bediako did not need a job, and his family background also suggests he was not likely to need one in the foreseeable future.

He had a cushy job as an accountant, working for his father's business empire, while being guaranteed a comfortable life.

"I laughed off the job offer from Wilson," says Osei Bediako.

He did not know it, but he also had his own blindspot regarding Wilson. Wilson is a person who does not give up easily.

"I already work, so, no thanks," said Osei Bediako to Wilson.

"What about after work?" Wilson asked

"Work after work?" thought Bediako.

Considering and Accepting the Offer

The eyes of the two men were locked in the last minute or so as they talked. Somehow, they were beginning to measure each other's soul.

Wilson was building an army of radio presenters and he felt deeply that he had discovered a new presenter who somehow found his way to the studio.

Osei Bediako felt working with CD players, microphones, and a console was not much hard labour, and in fact, could be exciting and satisfying.

The memory of living and working in England flashed across his mind. Over there, it was not uncommon to hold down two jobs that required you to go to work again after you finished one job.

So Bediako said, "maybe, I will give it a try and see how it goes."

It was a deal done in about two minutes flat. A deal between two men who started seeing something in each other over an emerging private radio station.

Osei Bediako didn't realise that by saying yes, he was also agreeing to have his name changed from Osei Bediako to JM Caesar.

He was going to continue as an accountant all right--a bean counter, but a really funky bean counter! As of the time of writing this book, JM Caesar is the only employee who has continued with Skyy Power FM all through the station's 25-year history.

A Family's Man's Sacrifice

> *"Working with Skyy was like an apprenticeship for me. Wilson has been like a mentor. He is a very focused person, very talented and a visionary. When I look back, I am grateful that I was there at Skyy Power FM."*
> — *reflections of Michael Griffiths, one of the pioneers of Skyy Power FM*

Wilson Arthur's Music Paradise shop in Accra was like a magnet that drew people who loved music. Michael Griffiths, an all-round good-looking man with a fine heart, loves music and he sings as well. He chooses to sing mainly gospel music and avoids most secular music.

He became attracted to Music Paradise and loved hanging out there regularly with Wilson Arthur and the small crew that took turns running the shop.

Wilson spent a year at St. Aquinas School in Accra for his 6th form education after leaving St. John's School in Sekondi. At St. Aquinas school, he served as the entertainment prefect. Aquinas school is the link between Wilson Arthur and Michael Griffiths.

"Wilson was my senior in Aquinas. He was in sixth form, and I was in form three or form four, and so we got to know each other from then," says Michael.

Years after school, Michael and Wilson found each other again, by which time Wilson was working as Marketing Manager at Media Number 1, while also running Music Paradise.

It made sense to Michael that Wilson graduated from being entertainment prefect in school to running a music shop with the biggest collection of music nationwide. He was quick to check out Wilson's music shop.

Love of Music and Friendship

"I loved my gospel music and Wilson had the best of the vinyls and CDs, so I would go and make my selections there. I would pass through Music Paradise on my way to afternoon service at church. Wilson would arrive there after morning service at 11 am. I would listen to music or record some music before my service would start at 2 pm," recalls Michael.

"One day, Wilson shared with me his vision of starting a radio station in Takoradi. At the time, the media had just been liberated. Joy FM had started, and a few other stations were in Accra, and Wilson thought Accra was choked, so he wanted to go to Sekondi-Takoradi because he went to school there. He wanted to be the pioneer in private radio which he became."

"We talked about it over a few months, and one day, he told me he got the license and we should go to Takoradi to check out the environment. Eventually, Wilson, myself, KingB, and Ato Parry made the trip. Wilson had this old, old VW Polo, so all of us packed ourselves into this car to drive to Takoradi. Wilson and KingB were in front and me and Ato Parry were at the back. This car died a number of times on the way; it was very old," recalls Michael, while laughing at the memory.

Becoming a Pioneer with Skyy

Michael became part of the small group of people who had a hand in building Skyy Power FM from the beginning and subsequently became one of the first employees.

Michael was mostly uninterested in the secular aspect of the operations, so while helping with the entire set up, he designed *Skyy Christian Radio* for himself. It allowed him to play inspiring gospel music from all over the world. Wilson was pleased and approved of it. Akyen Aikins, an IT Consultant who helped various clients to connect to dial up Internet of those years, had a similar disposition to Michael, so he was brought on to help Michael with *Skyy Christian Radio*.

Michael's voice was prominent on air during Skyy Power FM's test transmission. The recorded voice was played every couple of hours or so: *This is a test transmission of Skyy Power FM from 37 Windy Ridge, Takoradi."*

When commercial services started, the same voice spoke with a slight British accent. His full name is "Michael Griffiths-Bentil," but since school he was often referred to without the "Bentil," so to simplify, he chose to keep it Michael Griffiths.

Being Michael Griffiths on Air

Michael's distinctive accent was the result of two things: time spent with highly educated members of his family and being educated in England.

Beyond that veneer, Michael says he is a typical boy from Accra who grew up around Bukom, the famed suburb where children learned to score points through hand-to-hand combat, especially boxing. Legendary world boxing champion Azumah Nelson was nurtured there.

"I know the place and streets very well, and I speak the language perfectly," he says.

As Michael romanticises about Bukom and his childhood, I imagine him devouring a local dish like *a large-sized kenkey with fried fish and fresh kpakpo shitor.*

The thought makes me lose focus for a few moments as I feel my mouth watering and nostrils fill with the imaginary, delicious flavour.

My imagination, though, is a far cry from the reality in my home studio as I watch the Rodecaster machine blinking to indicate my interview with Michael is still being recorded.

Beyond the adventure of being part of a pioneering enterprise, Michael made what he believed was a hard choice of moving from Accra to Takoradi to work full-time for Skyy Power FM.

Days of Encounter in Takoradi

The most vivid memory Michael keeps about his time at Skyy is the enormous sacrifice he made as a husband and new father.

"Moving to Takoradi all by myself was very difficult," says Michael.

"My sweetheart and I married in 1996, and by the time Skyy Power FM started, we had our first son, Wesley, who was only six months old. We settled into a comfortable life in Accra in our own home, and then suddenly, I found myself in Takoradi with Skyy Power FM."

"I didn't have accommodation immediately, and for weeks, I was sleeping rough on mattresses placed on the carpet in the studio. Later, I moved in with Kwesi Fletcher."

"*Skyy Christian Radio* starts at 4 am, and that means waking at 3 am. Kwesi Fletcher owned a taxi, and he would drop me in the studio, but it was inconvenient for him as he also starts work around 6am. Later, I had to walk through swampy fields of plantain at dawn to reach the studio," recalls Michael.

Something in his upbringing made him extra sensitive about leaving his wife and baby in Accra. The pain for him was so raw that even after nearly a quarter of a century, he speaks about it like it isn't something from the past.

A Kindred Spirit

Michael and I were very close when we worked together at Skyy. We confided in each other and offered support to each other.

"I was only three years old when my father died," he reminds me in the interview. "Because I didn't grow up with my father, I never wanted my child to grow up without seeing his father regularly. I loved being a father, and I am now a father not just to my own children, but to other children, as many children as possible to whom I can be a father."

As my interview with him continues, memories of Michael's sensitivity and gentleness hit me again, and I wonder if my decades-old relationship with him is making it too easy for him to get more personal than is necessary.

"You were an affable guy," he says in reference to me. "For some reason, I just gelled with you like, I mean a kindred spirit. Besides Kwesi Fletcher, I spent the most time with you. Even when I left Skyy, you were the one that I called."

To live up to his values, Michael returned to Accra and to his family a year into the operations of Skyy.

Still Full of Gratitude

"I don't speak of my experience in Takoradi as a form of complaint. I loved Takoradi and enjoyed my time there, but because I was not with my family, my heart was not there," says Michael.

Michael now runs *Family TV Ghana*, a multimedia company producing child-safe content for the family.

"Everything I am doing now with my own company is the result of everything I learned from Wilson Arthur and Skyy Power FM," he says, looking back with gratitude. "Working with Skyy was like an apprenticeship for me. Wilson has been like a mentor. He is a very focused person, very talented, and a visionary. When I look back, I am grateful that I was there at Skyy Power FM."

He continued: "I have had the chance to train so many people who are also managing media organisations in Ghana, and this comes from my experience at Skyy. We had so much fun at Skyy together," says Michael.

He recalls that Skyy Power FM was like a family in itself, but the real family he missed during his time there was his wife and his six-month-old baby.

In a different interview for this book, another former colleague at Skyy, Kojo Frempong, speaks fondly of Michael Griffiths, saying: "Michael has always been beautiful!"

Michael is a man who finds fulfilment by being the best family man he can be. Twenty-five years after Skyy, he realises that he had to go through a period of difficulty and sacrifice to gain the experience required to help him live his dream as a father for all time.

A Strong and Free Woman

"I was nurtured by parents and uncles and brothers who saw me as being more than just a woman. They instilled in me the fact that I am strong, free, and capable. I grew up around people who didn't put me down and that was my advantage in life."
— *Maame Esi Mark—Hansen, describing an upbringing that made her successful at Skyy Power FM*

It was the end of another busy week in April 1998 in Takoradi. Endless discussions and coaxing to cut back on work hadn't succeeded for weeks. By the time his wife returned from work, Reggie Mark-Hansen had decided it was no longer reasonable to allow her to go to work until further notice.

Anxious, desperate, and genuinely concerned for the welfare of his wife, Reggie issued an ultimatum.

The Ultimatum

"If I hear you on the radio on Monday, I will come and haul you out of the studio myself," said Reggie to his wife.

His wife, Maame Esi Mark-Hansen, was pregnant with their first child.

The pregnancy had run the full course of nine months, and the baby could pop out at any time. A tireless workaholic, Maame Esi did not contemplate taking maternity leave even close to the last trimester of her pregnancy.

Like a relentless mechanical bulldozer, she kept dragging herself to work, doing everything exactly as she did from the first day of her pregnancy. The only thing she could not control in her life was the increasingly growing baby evident in her expanding and glowing baby belly.

The steep stairs leading to the Skyy Power FM studio at 37 Windy Ridge were no match for Maame Esi. She worked seven days a week on-air and off-air as Marketing Manager and presenter of *Skyy Market* and current affairs programs. She spoke truth to power during contentious interviews with politicians.

Off air, she engaged in intense haggles with advertisers for better deals for Skyy. When her husband Reggie, out of concern, finally issued the ultimatum, Maame Esi complied.

"I was raised to be a strong and free woman, but I equally have appropriate respect for the men in my life," she says, adding, it was also a matter of honour that she listened to Reggie. So, when Monday came, Maame Esi finally took a day off work.

Reggie Mark-Hansen felt relief. He wondered if he could have perhaps issued the thoughtful ultimatum earlier, even as he dreamed of becoming a father.

The Skyy Family of Maame Esi Mark-Hansen

In the big family called Skyy Power FM, Maame Esi was like a big sister to all, especially to the other younger ladies. They shared a deep love and affection that they could never speak of without comparing it to the unique relationship in a blood-related family.

"I was quite young myself," says Maame Esi, "about 26 years old when I joined Skyy, but the other ladies were much younger, so I was like their big sister."

The younger ladies include Yuki Ampofo, Maame Efua DeGraft Aidoo, and Naa Adoley Thompson.

The ladies had never experienced a day in the studio without Maame Esi. So, on the first day she was missing from work, two of them, Maame Efua DeGraft Aidoo and Yuki Ampofo, went to visit their heavily pregnant senior colleague.

They met Maame Esi's sister who, like a lioness, was providing protection services, making sure her heavily pregnant sister was as safe and comfortable as possible.

Yuki and Maame Efua had no idea that their visit was inconvenient, and worse than that, it was not a quick visit. They made themselves exceedingly comfortable. An hour passed, and they were still hanging around. In the meantime, the pregnant Maame Esi was starting to endure unspeakable pain.

"I was in the early stages of labour pains but decided not to tell my friends. The discomfort was horrible and made worse by the fact that Maame Efua and Yuki would not just get up and leave." The Ghanaian culture almost always makes room for visitors, even when they overstay their welcome.

Maame Efua and Yuki overstayed, and they would not indicate when they intended to leave. When Maame Esi could not contain the ever-increasing labour pains anymore, she decided to kick out Yuki and Maame Efua as nicely as possible. "I used my big sister's privilege and practically ordered them to leave."

They did, after long hugs and gentle baby belly cradling.

Coming to Takoradi

Maame Esi Mark-Hansen and her husband, Reggie, were living and working in Accra around the same time Wilson Arthur was on a reconnaissance mission to build Skyy FM in Sekondi-Takoradi. They married a year before Wilson ventured into Takoradi.

In early 1997, Reggie was transferred to Takoradi by his employer, British American Tobacco. Maame Esi was working for an airline company in Accra at the time. At first, she had no immediate plans to join her husband, as she needed some time to transition from her own work.

But Maame Esi's mother advised her that letting her husband live in Takoradi alone, even for a short time, was not helpful for their marriage.

She understood.

"I thought about it a little and made a move. I didn't even tell my husband. I just resigned and immediately joined him in Takoradi," she recalls.

As they settled in Takoradi, Maame Esi turned their new house into a home, but soon, she felt uncomfortable. "I had become a housewife, bored out of my mind," she says.

The thoroughly restless Maame Esi craved the need to get back into the workforce at the same time Skyy FM was undertaking test transmission in Takoradi.

Going up to Skyy Power FM

"One day, I turned on the radio and heard that a certain Skyy Power FM was looking for people with experience to work with them. Interestingly, I had also just found out that very week that I was pregnant."

The discovery that she was going to have her first baby did not dissuade her. She dressed and went up the hill to 37 Windy Ridge where the station was located.

Her memory of that day is still sharp and vivid.

She explains, "I got there, and there were two gentlemen; one neatly dressed and the other looking casual and slouched on the carpet. I focused, of course, on the one neatly dressed."

At this point of our interaction, Maame Esi regales me with a story about who the two gentlemen were, knowing it would quickly get both of us into a fit of laughter because of having worked together and knowing the full dynamics of Skyy and the hilarious family environment it was.

"KingB was the one who was neatly dressed," she says, starting to paint a contrasting picture.

KingB was always so sharply dressed that some of us at Skyy often joked that he would easily consider going to bed in a full three-piece suit.

"I remember this thing like it was yesterday," Maame Esi continues her story, deliberately pausing to create suspense before revealing the identity of the other gentleman she met when she went to present an application to be employed at Skyy.

She continues, and finally drops her punchline, saying "...and the one wearing the bogolan [casual] shirt and just lying on the carpet was Wilson Arthur."

Maame Esi set me up to crack up with laughter. When she drops her punchline, I fall for it like a rock rolling downhill in my unrestrained laughter.

It was just the reality with Wilson Arthur in those days. He almost never looked like the boss or the Chief Executive and owner of the station.

What Maame Esi didn't know on the first day she met Wilson was that the full weight of creating the first private radio station was heavy on his shoulders and being the best dressed gentleman was secondary.

The episode has since become a running joke: Wilson Arthur would remind Maame Esi that when she first came to Skyy, she ignored him completely; and then Maame Esi would reply, saying, Wilson should have dressed like a boss to attract the attention usually given to a boss.

A Pioneer of the Experiment

Maame Esi became one of the first employees of Skyy. A few months after launching in October 1997, her baby belly became prominent. That is the only time anyone at Skyy noticed she was pregnant.

The culture at Skyy allowed for very many jovial references to Maame Esi's pregnancy. By the time her delivery approached, Wilson and the other Skyy family members worked out that she was pregnant before the station started commercial services. They would often marvel the awesome responsibility of carrying a baby did not dampen her spirit or slow her down in any way.

Maame Esi is built like a fully functioning working machine, with a constant readiness to simply get things done, no matter the challenge. She has a keen sense of what is right and what must not be tolerated, balanced with a boisterous sense of mirth and friendship.

It served her well in a broadcast industry driven by the need to meet constant daily deadlines while generating income through persuasion backed by concrete and verifiable results.

Life Before Skyy Power FM

Maame Esi has a strong creative spirit which she shares with her brother, Nat Brew, a professional and well-known Ghanaian musician popularly known as Amandzeba.

The strongest influence in Maame Esi's life, however, comes from Kwesi Brew, an uncle who looked after her from a young age. A tribute by the *Guardian* newspaper published after his death in 2007 describes Kwesi Brew as one of the first Ghanaians who served in diplomatic service after independence in 1957.

He went on to work in the United Kingdom, France, Germany, India, and the USSR, before serving as ambassador in Mexico, Lebanon, and Senegal. Later, he became the resident director of the Takoradi Flour Mills.

"I was nurtured by parents and uncles and brothers who saw me as being more than just a woman. They instilled in me the fact that I am strong, free, and capable. I grew up around people who didn't put me down and that was my advantage in life," says Maame Esi, recalling her upbringing.

In broad strokes, she paints a picture of her accomplished uncle and the influence he had on her.

"My uncle Kwesi Brew was an acclaimed poet and diplomat. Intellectually, he was way ahead of his peers, a quintessential gentleman who was unafraid to tell you if you are being an idiot. He would tell you to your face and make sure you don't repeat it; and the next moment, he is the same person coddling you and laughing with you and joking with you."

In describing her uncle, Maame Esi ultimately gives the clearest summation of her own character, as well as her rich family heritage.

Discovering Another Family at Skyy Power FM

Maame Esi places a high value on family, but she never once imagined that a corporate environment at Skyy Power FM would reflect family values. Her whole memory at Skyy is filled with the warmth and fun that is synonymous with a happy family. Maame Esi's younger colleagues at work looked up to her, and she felt proud and privileged to be an example in hard work and creativity, on-air and off-air.

"We had so much fun every day, and it seemed everybody liked to stay around the station all day, whether they had a program or not. Some of us worked seven days a week and we didn't even feel it. We were passionate about work while always having fun," recalls Maame Esi.

She also sees the experimental enterprise as genuinely historic.

"This thing," she says in reference to Skyy, "was organic. It was a pivotal moment in the history of broadcasting in Ghana because it was part of the early years in private radio, which was mostly limited to the national capital, Accra. It brought out the likes of Komla Dumor and Doreen Andoh, and in other places, ordinary people in their small communities popped out to showcase their talents for the benefit of all," she said, noting that Wilson Arthur's Skyy Power FM in Takoradi holds a special place in that rich history.

"Wilson's wife Adwoa Amofah and Kennedy Arthur also deserve commendation for their vision to establish Skyy in Takoradi against all odds at a time when Takoradi was not a profitable market for radio."

Then and Now

As my two-hour long interview with Maame Esi continues, the depth she reaches for her memories is matched only by the joy of sharing it on record. Suddenly, in the middle of one sentence, she says she has a surprise to share, and asks that we switch to a video call.

Standing with her was a handsome 25-year-old boy called Nana Poku. Nana Poku is the son that Mame Esi delivered less than one year into Skyy FM's operation in Takoradi.

I was honoured to be reintroduced to him as "Uncle Phillip in Australia."

He was just a few months old when Maame Esi started bringing him to work. He was a much-loved baby among all the Skyy Power FM presenters back then.

The last time I saw him, he was a toddler with an irresistible smile. This is the boy whose mother never took a day off work as he grew in leaps and bounds--in her womb.

This is the boy who, at the beginning of his mother's labour, was visited by Yuki Ampofo and Maame Efua DeGraft Aidoo from Skyy, and they overstayed their visit until Maame Esi politely insisted they leave.

As Maame Esi recalls, she gave birth to her son only an hour after her two friends from Skyy agreed to leave.

For Maame Esi, nothing tells the passage of time better than her son, and every day, she is reminded that family is the most important thing in life. Her extended family includes all the women and men of Skyy Power FM she worked with decades ago.

A Legacy Worth Celebrating

"Can we even properly value the impact of Skyy?" Maame Esi asks rhetorically as she attempts to describe the legacy of the enterprise after a quarter of a century.

"It was a phenomenon," she says.

"Look at the number of radio stations that flocked to that part of Ghana. Look at the number of people who went through Skyy who are now in other sectors of broadcasting. Look at Ewurama Smith, Cyrus deGraft-Johnson, Root Eye, Kwame Dzokoto, etc. Skyy has produced some heavyweights. Even for those of us who moved out of broadcasting, the exposure we had at Skyy gave us the ability to think outside the box for success."

Maame Esi once more recognises the courage and vision of Wilson Arthur and his team.

"I doff my hat to Wilson, his wife Adwoa, and his brother Ken for taking that leap of faith because I am sure a lot of people thought they were crazy to move out of Accra and go to the Western Region to establish Skyy Power FM."

Years after she left Skyy, Maame Esi and her family have travelled around the world with work. She lived four years in South Africa and another four years in America, but she still thinks the experience she had at Skyy, being part of an experiment that opened up private broadcasting, carries a lot more excitement and fulfilment.

William Shakespeare in the House!

"The leadership that Wilson Arthur provided us in terms of how to do radio was excellent. I would not trade my beginnings in radio for any other teacher, not even the BBC. Wilson would often say, 'just get it done and have no inhibitions.' To him, it was as if everything was possible."

— Kojo Frempong, also called Shakes, on the quality of the training he received at Skyy Power FM before he moved on to win awards in broadcasting

When I call Kojo Frempong and tell him I need his cooperation to write this book, he falls silent and immediately slides into a meditative mood. We had not seen each other for more than 15 years, and I still had only an old picture of him in my mind as a work colleague at Skyy Power FM. He was a lanky lad, loud, very loud, but also reflective.

He has piercing eyes that hide a genuinely friendly character. A 99% pure product of Sekondi-Takoradi, Kojo Frempong is intelligent and could be the head of an organisation that produces volumes of academic work to explain the unique culture of Ghana's only twin city. He loves Sekondi-Takoradi more than any other place on earth.

Kojo has a deep sense of appreciation for life and loves learning, but he is also a boy full of inexhaustible fun and mischief. Given the chance, he can talk and make scintillating conversation all day without asking for a glass of water. As if preparing for such a session, he puts me at ease as I start interviewing him.

"Let me say what a privilege it is, having worked with someone like you," he says, referring to me, adding, "incredible mind, straight to the point, unrepentantly professional. We don't always count our blessings, it is a privilege for me to be speaking to the editor, Phillip Nyakpo." I laugh calmly and gently to acknowledge this.

I have great respect for Kojo Frempong and his exploits since our days together at Skyy in Takoradi. He proved his value by going on to win awards in broadcasting and ended up at Harvard University in the United States before returning to Ghana.

"The Whole Trajectory of My Life Started With Skyy"

"You know, when I look back, everything I am and everything I have done in my life all started with Skyy Power FM. That period of our life was not wasted, and I am glad for the chance to look back," says Kojo Frempong.

Kojo's story with Skyy Power FM started at Daboase, a farming enclave, serving as the capital of the Wassa East District in Ghana's Western Region. It is about an hour's drive north of Sekondi-Takoradi, bigger than a village but smaller than a city.

When he was about 18 years old, he was sent there under a compulsory year-long Ghana government development program called *National Service*. The scheme deploys human resources from educational institutions to support public and private sector development across the country. On that assignment, Kojo served with a few other young graduates.

Out in that location, Kojo and his friends found out that they were the hottest and most sophisticated young men in town and constantly enjoyed princely attention.

The privilege made up for all the buzz they missed from living in big cities like Accra, Cape Coast, and Sekondi-Takoradi.

Soon after the boys started their service, they discovered that there were many young ladies who also served as National Service personnel in the more deprived villages further away from Daboase.

Coming from the cosmopolitan twin city with a heavy influence in homegrown music, dance, and regular entertainment, Kojo and his friends decided to organise a beauty pageant during what was called the "National Service Week."

The Sinister Village Beauty Pageant

"There were four of us boys, and the real reason we did that back then was not to commemorate the National Service Week. We figured there were so many ladies doing their national service outside the Daboase township and in the surrounding villages. So we decided to devise a way to bring them all together and undertake an official census of the ladies."

There is a seemingly sinister laughter in his voice as he reveals this. "So, the highlight of the 1997 National Service Week for us was the beauty pageant we called *Miss Daboase National Service*," he adds.

Years before this event, Kojo developed a love for the English language, with a particular admiration for the works of English dramatist, William Shakespeare. At St John's School in Sekondi, he showed interest in the debating club and became a member. When a vacancy occurred for head of the debating club, Kojo Frempong made a smooth transition into it, becoming the principal debater for St John's School.

After one of many impressive readings and recitals of the works of Shakespeare in school, Kojo's friends showered him with adulation and called him "Shakes," a shortened form of Shakespeare.

The boys of Daboase who organised the beauty pageant for the National Service ladies realised they needed a well-spoken and articulate person as Master of Ceremonies.

Shakes was the unanimous choice for the glorious evening.

The event was the small town's first beauty pageant put together by relatively sophisticated late-teen National Service personnel. Kojo was only too happy to display his oratory skills.

The nickname "Shakes" took on fresh meaning from that day. During all the years Kojo Frempong worked at Skyy Power FM, he was mostly known simply as Shakes.

Shakes never once considered working at a Radio station. There were really no radio stations in Sekondi-Takoradi to inspire a dream, apart from the state-controlled FM station operated by the Ghana Broadcasting Corporation that started in 1994.

That prospect occurred only when Skyy Power FM came in late 1997 to spawn a thousand dreams in independent broadcasting.

Becoming a Pioneer in Private Radio

"I was thrilled, I was blown open, I was ecstatic," says Kojo Frempong, describing the moment he first heard of the possibility of working at Skyy Power FM. He felt the thrill and ecstasy, even though he was nowhere near being offered a job.

The possibility of working with a new radio station was suggested on the evening the beauty pageant took place at the small town of Daboase.

One of the judges for the night came from Takoradi. He was enthralled to see and hear how Kojo Frempong steered the program as the Master of Ceremony. Towards the end of the beauty pageant, the unknown judge from Takoradi approached Kojo Frempong.

"Have you ever done radio?" he asked. The question struck like a bolt of lightning, but Kojo managed to answer correctly.

"No," he said, shaking in his still shining shoes, completely unsure about the premise of the question.

"You were very impressive this evening. You speak well, and your voice sounds good. Some friends of mine are coming to open up a radio station in Takoradi, and it is going to be called Skyy Power FM. If you want, I can recommend you to them to see if you could work there."

That's when Kojo's emotion was let loose and he was "thrilled, blown open, and ecstatic."

As it turned out, the thrill and ecstasy was painfully premature and the journey to Skyy was a long way off. It almost didn't happen for Shakes.

A Man Bigger than the Moon and the Stars

The sleek gentleman from Takoradi who served as judge on the night of Kojo and his friend's beauty pageant didn't have a direct connection to the emerging Skyy Power FM.

He was rather a friend of a certain Kofi Gyetsua Ankoma, known in Sekondi-Takoradi by the three capital letters KGA. Before the establishment of Skyy Power FM, KGA had made a name in the city as a professional Master of Ceremonies. He even had more than a few high-profile gigs, including being associated with the national *Miss Ghana* beauty pageant. KGA has a large reservoir of self-confidence and enjoys wearing custom-made three-piece suits of varying colours with matching shoes. He was among the first employees at Skyy Power FM and would informally try to assess the capabilities of anyone wanting employment at the new radio station.

"I went to KGA's office two or three times, but I could not find him," says Kojo. "KGA was bigger than the stars, he was bigger than the moon. You couldn't easily set eyes on him," recalls Kojo, trying to paint a picture of the famed KGA.

"But by the time I met him, Skyy Power FM had finished recruiting, and here I was with the fantasy of working for Skyy Power FM. But KGA asked me to go and see the Chief Executive Wilson Arthur anyway."

"What is the Difference Between the East Coast and the West Coast?"

Kojo Frempong loves music, including that produced by American rap musicians from the American east coast to the west coast. It was one of the qualifications he hoped would stand him in good stead.

Despite his disappointment that Skyy had finished recruiting, Kojo went to Skyy, and when Wilson met him, he said, "Kofi Gyetsua Ankoma has asked me to come and see you for an interview.

"Who are you?" asked Wilson Arthur.

"My name is Kojo Frempong and I went to Achimota School in Accra and St. John's School in Sekondi. I have also just finished my national service in Daboase," said Kojo.

Kojo didn't know it then, but two things out of his answer sounded good to Wilson: that the young Kojo went through his alma mater, St John's School, and also that he just finished his national service at Daboase, the closest town to Ateiku, the village where Wilson was born.

Wilson didn't give anything away, but instead asked a killer question after Kojo indicated he loved music, including hip-hop and rap music. It was about the American hip-hop and rap music scene.

"What is the difference between east coast rap and west coast rap music?" asked Wilson Arthur.

For most people, the question is, first of all, meaningless, because it required exquisite familiarity with the subject to even begin to understand it.

Kojo Frempong had that exquisite familiarity.

At this point in the interview, he brims with excitement to tell the story and is so alive describing it that you would think the experience happened in the last 24 hours.

"The answer I provided for this question is literally what made Wilson Arthur decide to hire me," he says, the sense of pride he felt about this more than 20 years ago undiminished.

By the middle of 1997, Tupac Shakur (2Pac) and Notorious B.I.G. (Biggie), both considered the most influential rappers of all time, had been murdered in drive-by shootings. The crimes were an off shoot of the American east and west coast gangsta rap music culture.

For Wilson Arthur, the fact that Kojo Frempong understood the question was by itself a win.

"I explained to Wilson that American east coast music carries a more aggressive sound while west coast hip-hop is more laid back. I spoke of some of the actors like Tupac, Snoop Dog, Dr. Dre..."

Wilson was both impressed and stunned, not just at Kojo Frempong's knowledge, but also at the quality of his language and diction. But he still maintained his poker face, as he had no good news for Kojo.

"We have finished hiring. You go home and we will get back to you," said Wilson.

One week later, Kojo Frempong got a call from Wilson Arthur.

"We got somebody from Accra who has about ten years' experience in radio, but we've had to let him go so we can accommodate you."

Kojo Frempong had no idea who the person was until fifteen years later. "The guy met me in Accra at a function and said, do you know I was booted out of Skyy because of you?"

"Oh, I couldn't have imagined it was you," said Kojo Frempong, while trying to sound as humble as possible.

Before he met the gentleman from Accra who missed out on being employed at Skyy, Kojo Frempong had proved himself at Skyy and later with Joy FM and TV 3, making national headlines by winning awards in broadcasting.

Joining the Pioneering Team at Skyy

While in the wild, with no immediate prospect of working for Skyy, Kojo Frempong listened to the station and loved what he heard. He knew the presenters were first class and appeared to be experts in presenting the various programs. Jam Master Caesar (JM Caesar) was one of those he admired. Kojo Frempong refers to him as *The Funky Bean Counter* for the fact that JM Caesar is actually a professional accountant, the only such professional he knew who could calculate complex but boring figures and at the same time talk smoothly, knew rap music, and succeeded as a radio presenter with class.

Any confidence Kojo had before he joined Skyy evaporated once he walked around the studio and offices, seeing the faces of the people whose voices he heard on air.

"The only professional work I had ever done before Skyy was working at the harbour as a labourer. And now, I was in the midst of stars like KingB, Uncle Opia, JM Caesar, and Kwesi Fletcher. It was both intimidating and surreal."

Of course, it was only a matter of time before Kojo Frempong himself got so good on radio that someone else at Skyy admired him greatly. "I was intimidated by the high quality and proficiency of Kojo Frempong," says Yaw Korankye, who later became programs manager at Skyy.

Yaw Korankye, KingB, and JM Caesar became like Kojo Frempong's older brothers, helping him to navigate the rest of his late teens, even as he learned to flourish as a celebrity on radio.

Kojo is full of high praise for all his colleagues and friends at Skyy, but he singles out KingB, saying: "KingB is one of the most well-put-together human beings I have ever dealt with. He is like a chest of drawers; everything opens perfectly and everything is neatly tucked away, and even everything he says is measured."

"What really strikes me now, looking back, was how much goodwill we had for each other. Every time someone else was on air, you willed that person to do well, to succeed, and you took pleasure in listening to the person. We were one solid team, a family. We ate together, we played together," recalls Kojo.

Ewurama Smith, who worked in the newsroom at the time says, "I learned to eat really fast because of Kojo Frempong, because Kojo could eat twice as fast as most of us."

Mealtimes were always competitive. First of all, it was never formal. A couple of colleagues may go to the city and bring delicacies like *waakye, jollof*, or *kenkey*. Sometimes, it was bowls of *fufu* and delectable goat soup.

Once the food arrived, no one tried to find out who it belonged to or who was allowed to eat because the unwritten rule was clear: any food around the studio could be eaten by anyone in the vicinity. It was always consumed with fervour on a first come, first served basis. Wilson Arthur the Chief Executive himself would also join the reckless crowd to grab as many morsels as possible.

Those unscheduled mealtimes at Skyy brought a lot of fun and laughter.

In spite of the speed at which Kojo ate with the rest of us--including the volume--he maintained a stick-like figure during all his time at Skyy.

Kojo Frempong's ability to shine on radio was easy to see. Within months of joining Skyy Power FM, Kojo Fremong became a lead commentator during the 1998 African Cup of Nations football tournament in Burkina Faso.

That was the first time Kweku Ackaah-Boafo, a practicing lawyer and sports enthusiast, met him. Like a prophet, he told Kojo Frempong, "Young man, you have a wonderful future. Please keep it up!"

Kweku Ackaah-Boafo's title has since changed. He is now *Justice* Kweku Ackaah-Boafo because he works as a High Court Judge in Ghana.

Ackaah-Boafo became one of our colleagues at Skyy on the sports desk as an analyst and commentator. I interviewed him for this book and his memory paints an enchanting picture of Kojo Frempong's star quality.

Returning from England after being away for a year, lawyer Ackaah-Boafo tuned to Skyy Power FM in his car to listen to football commentary on the ongoing African Cup of Nations. That is where he first heard Kojo Frempong on radio, giving a brilliant, live commentary.

"His language was apt, it was precise, and the fluency with which this young man was speaking was so impressive," says Ackaah-Boafo.

"The next day, I decided to go to Skyy and look for the owner and the young man whose commentary I heard. I was introduced to Kojo Frempong, and as he spoke, I recognised his voice. I was amazed because he was so young and just an A-level graduate."

That is when, like a blessing, Ackaah-Boafo said, "young man, you have a wonderful future. Please keep it up!"

Kojo absolutely flourished at Skyy, manifesting sagacity as host of the *Jolly Breakfast Show* and the late afternoon program, *Drive Jam*, where his knowledge of various genres of music came in handy.

Moving on from Skyy Power FM, Kojo Frempong went to *Joy FM*, and later *TV3, Viasat One TV, and TV Africa.* Along the way, he picked up the best TV Show Host in 2014 and 2015 at the *Radio and Television Awards.* Afterward, Kojo Frempong went for a Master of Public Administration degree from the Kennedy School of Government at Harvard University in the United States.

No matter how far he goes in life, Kojo Frempong says there are a few things that he would not change, including his love of Takoradi and the strong foundation in life that he had at Skyy Power FM.

"I spent the first 16 years of my life in Takoradi, and I will never trade it for anywhere in the world," says Kojo Frempong, adding, "not even Perth, Australia. Takoradi is this place like no other in Ghana; we are given to the hustle, and we acknowledge it! The hustle is real!"

As only Kojo Frempong would, he quotes William Shakespeare toward the end of the interview saying: "All the world's a stage, and all the men and women merely players. They have their exits and their entrances; and one man in his time plays many parts, his acts being seven ages."

Beside the permanent bond of love he shares with his former colleagues at Skyy, Kojo Frempong says, "The leadership that Wilson Arthur provided us in terms of how to do radio was par excellent. I would not trade my beginnings in radio for any other teacher, not even the BBC. Wilson would often say, 'just get it done and have no inhibitions.' He never passed on his fears to us, and that allowed us to be liberated. To him, it was as if everything was possible."

Kojo Frempong's emotions are high when he says, "going back in time fills me with so much pleasure, and I appreciate the opportunity to have worked with all of you, and to have worked in that great entity called Skyy Power FM in Takoradi."

"We've kept those bonds from Skyy, and we know that if anything happened to any of us, it happened to all of us."

Long after the interview, and before I wrote this chapter, I could feel myself agreeing with my former colleague.

Ambition Meets Confidence and Courage

When you are used to long distance flights around the world, short flights can feel a bit unsettling. I had one such short flight with my wife from London to Amsterdam on a snowy day in January 2010. We arrived in London from Perth, Australia, the day before. Heavily jet-lagged, we still had to hop over to Amsterdam.

The plane took off from London, and the familiar steep climb through the clouds occurred before levelling off for a steady flight, but a steep descent started before any comfort in flying set in. It left me no time to reflect on the prospect of meeting a friend I had not seen for more than a decade.

After disembarking at Schiphol airport, Samuel Kwesi Fletcher walked through the nearly empty arrival hall to greet us in a warm embrace. He was the friend I was hoping to see.

After spending time with him over a few days, it seemed obvious that Fletcher was essentially still the same man I knew at Skyy Power FM back in Takoradi, but quite a lot had changed in his life. He had become a husband and a father of three handsome boys. He also now speaks Dutch like a native.

The last time I saw Fletcher was in August 1998 in Takoradi when we were both working for Skyy Power FM. Together with a few others, we constituted the backbone of the newsroom. With his many talents,

Fletcher was also the legendary host of the flagship morning show called the *Jolly Breakfast Show*, the Saturday musical show *Aba Fresh*, and the *Sunday News Review* talk show.

An Opportunity to Study in Europe

Fletcher had been investigating the possibility of studying in Europe. Eventually, he made the decision to leave Skyy Power FM for further education in The Netherlands. He told no one, except me. I respected his decision not to announce his exit, guarding the information he gave me with the same protection a journalist gives to his sources of information.

The night before Fletcher left, I knew the next morning's show must be hosted by an under-prepared employee.

The newsroom would also be limping.

News Review, the top-ranking political talk show on Sundays would have to be produced and hosted by someone else who would likely also be under-prepared.

That someone was me.

Morning arrived, and empty spaces where Fletcher would usually appear raised questions: *Where is he? Is he ok? Could we reach his emergency contact to find out? How come no one knows anything?*

I was Fletcher's closest friend and colleague, and I provided answers consistent with the best version of what I knew, while at the same time balancing my loyalty to my employer on one hand, and loyalty to a friend and colleague on the other.

That is how Fletcher's year-long work with Skyy Power FM ended. A few days after Fletcher left, he called my 2G mobile phone from Amsterdam to say he had arrived safely. Then he apologised for leaving me in a fairly vulnerable and unsupported position. He was genuinely apologetic, hoping that his decision would not ruin our professional relationship and friendship.

The Story from Day One

Fletcher is a good storyteller with a great memory, so I knew I was in for a treat when I called to interview him for this book. As close as we were, I didn't know how his association with Skyy Power started. So, I ask him to start from the beginning.

"Do you know Wakiki?" he asks.

My mind flings straight to William Nyarko, a hard-nosed investigative journalist who used to work for Ghana's leading private newspaper *The Ghanaian Chronicle*. When I was reporting for the same newspaper between late 1996 and 1997, William was doing a much higher level of journalism that won him the *1997 Best Investigative Journalist of the Year* award in Ghana. He repeated the feat for the same prize in 2001. All that memory comes back to me in a flash, and I feel like I am in a trance, remembering the so-called "inky fraternity" we shared.

"Yes, I know Wakiki," I say. "Wakiki is William Nyarko of *The Ghanaian Chronicle*," I confirm to Fletcher.

"Ok," says Fletcher, adding, "William Nyarko and I used to go to Ghana Institute of Journalism from Taifa in Accra. He introduced me to Kofi Amofah Acheampong, and Kofi Amofah introduced me to Wilson Arthur, the owner of Skyy Power FM."

Months after interviewing Fletcher, I reach William Nyarko and say, "I interviewed Fletcher as part of a book I am writing, and Fletcher traced his exploits back to you."

"Wow! Fletcher, Kofi Amofah, Taifa, etc." It was his way of acknowledging that what goes round comes around, confirming the relationships from the past that still meant a lot to him.

"Kofi Amofah Acheampong knew Wilson Arthur at the time he was operating Music Paradise in Accra," continues Fletcher. "I visited him in the middle of 1997, and he said to me that he had a friend who was going to open a radio station in Takoradi. Because he believed in my abilities, he encouraged me to take up the opportunity to work there."

Coming To Skyy Power FM

"I was hungry and ambitious for success, and I knew Takoradi very well, so I accepted the challenge. In fact, Kofi Amofah helped me to prepare my first CV for this job," recalls Fletcher.

Fletcher met other ambitious young men in Takoradi who Wilson brought from Accra to work with Skyy. Two of those were Root Eye and Michael Griffiths. Strong friendships among them developed quickly. Fletcher was practically a native of Takoradi with some of his family members living there. For a time, both Root Eye and Michael Griffiths lived with Fletcher in his home.

"When I met Wilson in Takoradi with my application, he accepted me right away and made me start working, even before the station launched," says Fletcher.

"Because I was willing and determined to succeed, I was ready to do anything for this project."

Kwesi Bediako was one of the friends Wilson Arthur made when he arrived in Takoradi to establish Skyy Power FM. Bediako operated *Global Designs*, a computer graphics design service. He was the one who designed and printed large posters announcing the coming of the new radio station.

Fletcher helped to raise other signposts for the new station.

"I raised all the initial directional signposts for Skyy at that time," recalls Fletcher.

Wilson Arthur's Old Car

Anyone who knew Wilson Arthur at that time also seems to harbour a story about his old VW Golf. Fletcher remembers his experience with the old car.

"Wilson had this old VW. It was a Golf 1 or Golf 2, I can't even remember which type it was. It was a broken car, so I was always trying to fix it and use it a little in town and it would break down again, and again," recalls Fletcher.

As I listen to Fletcher bewail the old car, it reminds me of the country singer Dan Seals who expressed nostalgia about an old yellow car: *"Somewhere in a pile of rubber and steel, there is a rusty old shell of an automobile,"* he sang, ending the chorus with *"and if the engines could run on desires alone, that old yellow car will be driving me home."*

I thought perhaps Wilson should have kept the old car and built a small museum for it at Skyy House. That car had its own story, for like Dan Seals' old yellow car, *"there was no road too winding and nowhere too far"* for all the journeys it took.

Fletcher himself had a Mazda, and he employed someone who drove it for him as a taxi. Uber was not a business idea back in 1997.

"I used my taxi to do the rounds to raise all the signposts," recalls Fletcher. The few weeks of test transmission and other preparations for commercial broadcast soon evaporated and the real show time arrived.

It is Show Time!

Programming for Skyy Power FM took on full shape with the morning show, the *Jolly Breakfast Show*, at the apex every weekday. Nana Fynnba Derby, who joined Skyy from the University of Cape Coast, was trained to host the show. She had some experience at ATL FM, Cape Coast University's campus radio. She was endowed with poise and a good voice, along with impeccable English.

With all the assistance she had with an excellent production team and music selection, the morning show was a big hit. Fletcher, in the meantime, was in charge of news and current affairs with the help of Maame Efua DeGraft Aidoo. The two of them were schoolmates at the Ghana Institute of Journalism. I was still at the periphery of Skyy at this time, and it would take a few weeks before I formally joined Skyy on a full-time basis as deputy news editor, working closely with Fletcher and Maame Efua.

A couple of weeks after the *Jolly Breakfast Show* started, Kwesi Fletcher offered to tell a joke on the program. Wilson Arthur agreed and then listened to the joke live on air. That was all Wilson needed to work out that Fletcher had a lot more in him than meets the eye.

Wilson decided Fletcher must have a permanent role on the morning show. It was a crucial and strategic decision because it took just a few more weeks before Nana Derby took up an opportunity at the Cape Coast University as a teaching assistant. Nana Derby's *Jolly Breakfast Show* became Kwesi Fletcher's show through and through. Becoming a permanent part of the morning show before

Nana Derby's departure allowed Fletcher to reinvent the show in his own image.

Fletcher's Life Before Skyy

The work at Skyy was Fletcher's first job after completing the Ghana Institute of Journalism. But this was preceded by his experience with acting and drama.

"My interest in drama started through my friend, Pius Mensah, who was a member of *Kubekrom*, a drama group for the Centre for National Culture," he says.

His interest continued to grow during his time at the school of journalism. He even produced his own low-budget movie called *Come Back Lucy*, and he made friends in the film industry, including Nat Banini, Regina Amanorbea Dodoo, Fred Amugi, Edinam Atatsi, Mina Otoo, Anastasia Lomotey, Kwesi Koomson, Samuel Nai, Veronica Quarshie, Kenny McCauley, Bob Smith the diabolo man, Sheila Nortey, and Brew Riverson, Jr. These were all big names in the Ghanainan movie industry at the time.

Fletcher carried all that history on arrival at Skyy. His association with the film industry is also why he was already known in Takoradi before Skyy made him even more popular.

As a journalist, Fletcher is a serious-minded person, but he also possesses an instinctive ability for showmanship and entertainment. He can switch from moderating a mirthless political talk show with politicians in one moment to doing a stand-up comedy with jokes that leave audiences in stitches, especially as master of ceremonies for live musical concerts and beauty pageants.

In contrast, I knew how to work only around the dictates of strict news and current affairs. Fletcher absolutely had the ability to be present and active at three or four parties at the same time, while I struggled to make my presence known at one low-keyed event. I would play chicken most of the time, while Fletcher would walk through fire without being burned just to get results he believed in. Every time it happened, I looked at him with admiration, wondering where he got his courage from.

Driving the Jolly Breakfast Show

Fletcher brought all that flair and quality onto the *Jolly Breakfast Show* after Fynnba Derby's departure. Having already recognised Fletcher's abilities, Wilson added to it by helping to produce the morning show, especially with an exquisite selection of music, while the small newsroom supported the show with information.

"I didn't have a problem with courage. What I needed more was content. For a morning show that started just after 6 am and ended at 10 am Monday to Friday, it was crucial that besides music, it should include information that is rich, interesting, and informative. That information should also be beneficial, but often, there is a need not just for local news and information," says Fletcher.

"You remember at that time, it was very difficult to get information on the Internet," he says, and then he reminds me how Kojo Frempong and myself used the old dial-up Internet to find information. "You and Kojo Frempong were the two people who used to bring some information from the Internet."

Of course, every success Kojo Frempong and I had in finding information on the Internet was always a painful exercise. The sluggish dial-up Internet connection took a long time, and when we finally got the information, we had to save it on a floppy disc that made a lot of vexatious hissing noise while saving. Somehow, every single day was special for the *Jolly Breakfast Show*. "You can't have a bad morning on the morning show," we used to say.

Humour and Jokes Every Morning

Along with all the other ingredients, Fletcher kept the show alive with humorous jokes. Over time, members of the public would call to give exclusive jokes to Fletcher. Fletcher would, in turn, add his own spin in retelling the stories, leaving listeners laughing for hours.

Fletcher would later share feedback from the people who gave him the jokes. They are often amazed how Fletcher turns it around to make it better and funnier. Fletcher got so good at the antics that he earned the nickname, "The Humour," given to him by Michael Griffiths. The jokes segment became so popular and attractive that it was sponsored by Aquafresh and MacClean toothpaste produced by Reiss & Co.

In the early days, the work at Skyy was a continuous seven-day gig. So, besides hosting the morning show from Monday to Friday, Fletcher also came in on Saturday to present *Aba Fresh*, a show that unearthed new music. And then he showed up on Sundays as well for *News Review*, a news analysis program that I later hosted for many years.

It was Fletcher who discovered Tony Osei-Gyasi and brought him as a panelist to the program. Tony Osei-Gyasi remained permanent on the program for many years through which he and Captain Sowu confounded listeners with quality analysis and a deep understanding of various subjects.

Sweating for a Start-Up

In true start-up fashion, Fletcher, along with some of the other employees, especially those in the marketing department, worked to bring income by looking for adverts nationwide.

"Kofi Amofah Acheampong, the guy who introduced me to Wilson, was also an advertising agent, and I would contact him to see what adverts he could pass on to us. I was going round, even as far as Accra, looking for adverts," says Fletcher. "I remember visiting all the advertising agencies in Accra, including Media Magic, Media Whizz Kids, Icon, Media Number 1, etc."

Fletcher had big dreams and found numerous ways to make himself unstoppable. Like many of the talents that passed through Skyy Power FM, he moved on to a radiant future.

Amsterdam's university *Vrije Universiteit* was his first stop where he earned a first degree in Social Sciences and a master's degree in Policy and Communications. He took his talent to the *European Networking Group* as Media Relations and Events Manager, after working briefly with IBM Netherlands as a Community Relations Officer. Next, the *Commonwealth Telecommunications Organisation* beckoned. For three years, he worked as Manager Corporate Communications and International Events, traveling the world over as part of his work.

Finally, Fletcher decided to move back to Ghana and ultimately ended up with the *Volta River Authority*, a crown jewel in the nation's power generation industry. For about a decade, he has worked first as the organisation's head of Corporate Communications and then Manager for Corporate Social Responsibility. He has visited Takoradi many times and made stops at Skyy Power FM, his old stomping ground.

Before the interview with Fletcher ends, I shoot a question at him.

"Did you know Yusuf Garaad Omar became the foreign minister of his country?"

For a period of two weeks in March 1998, Yusuf Garaad Omar and Anthony Howson, both from the BBC, trained us in Radio Journalism at the British Council in Accra. This was just five months after Skyy started.

To promote better radio journalism on new private radio stations around Ghana, BBC World Service and the British High Commission sponsored the program to train journalists from stations including Skyy Power FM and Joy FM. Kwesi Fletcher and I were there for Skyy, while Fred Chidi, Kweenu Haizel, and Ofoe Diogo represented Joy FM.

Yusuf Garaad Omar from Somalia had a wealth of experience with the BBC. Decades after our classroom interaction, he was on the news as having been appointed as Somalia's Foreign Minister.

As part of the training, a field trip took us to the ancient slave castle in Cape Coast. Shocked by the atrocities evident, Yusuf Garaad said, "if this happened in Somalia, those who did it could not possibly set foot in Somalia again."

The experience is one of many thousands of strands that tie us in the newsroom together.

"Back then, we knew everything we accomplished was going to help in our future. We learned a lot of lessons at Skyy that bring us many benefits today," says Fletcher.

For Fletcher and the many dozens who made history in Ghana's Western Region, Skyy Power FM and Takoradi remains a place full of stories and events that influenced their trajectory in life.

12

A Dormant Talent Discovered

"Almost everybody Wilson Arthur picked for Skyy was right from scratch. He has a gift for picking the right people for the right job, and I don't know how he did it."
— *Kwete Quaynor, one of the pioneers of Skyy Power FM*

The only reason Kwete Quaynor would spend a long time in any shop is if he were looking at a music collection on display. He lived in Cape Coast, and while visiting Accra in late 1995, he found a music recording shop called Music Paradise.

It was the best music shop he had ever seen. As it turned out, he spent an awfully long time carefully looking through the collection, taking in the various artists, studying the albums and individual songs, as well as reading every printed word on the CD covers.

"I can't recall how long I was in the shop for," says Kwete, "but at some point, I could see a movement in my peripheral vision." He continues, "This gentleman walks up to me and says 'I have been observing you. You seem to have a good taste in music.'"

Wilson Arthur Finds a Talent

The gentleman who walked up to Kwete Quaynor was Wilson Arthur, the owner of Music Paradise, who would go on to build Skyy Power FM. Kwete Quaynor would also go on to become the third host of the flagship morning show, the *Jolly Breakfast Show*.

"I was not pleased with the interruption from this gentleman at the shop. Every effort he made to talk to me just increased my annoyance, because I just wanted to be left alone to check out the music collection, but I could see this shop owner was not going to give up," recalls Kwete.

"I was young, cocky, and hot-headed. I tried to say as little as possible as he talked to me."

The unwelcome situation for Kwete at Music Paradise soon got worse, as he was not prepared for what felt like a bomb dropped by Wilson Arthur. First, Wilson Arthur said, "you have a good voice; your voice will sound good on radio."

Kwete was startled.

"It sounded strange that someone I didn't know would take notice of my voice," says Kwete, trying to reproduce his feelings from 25 years before.

"I will be setting up a radio station in Takoradi. Would you be interested?" That was Wilson Arthur's breaking news and a question that once more startled Kwete. He would learn much later that he became one of the people who heard about the establishment of a private radio station in Takoradi-- before it happened.

Not Taken Seriously

Kwete was now curious, but also totally unconvinced. Somehow, he remembered to show some good manners. He mumbled something in response to Wilson Arthur, saying quite sheepishly, "that is something I have never thought about."

"In reality, though," he tells me in the interview, "I didn't really take him seriously. I did not take him seriously at all. I met someone for the very first time and within minutes, he told me I am good material for radio. Who does that? There was no way I was going to take him seriously," says Kwete, a blast of disbelief in his voice.

"You know, this was the formative years of private radio in Ghana, and the idea of being on radio was so new and unfamiliar. I honestly thought Wilson was bluffing, or at best, he was just trying to be a frontman for some rich person who had the plan to set up a radio station in Takoradi; or maybe he was just throwing his weight about. I thought to myself, *who are you, and where are you coming from?*"

*K*wete speaks as earnestly as possible to convey exactly what he felt in the presence of Wilson Arthur at that music shop, back in late 1995.

"Wilson gave me his contact card with his phone number. He asked me to stay in touch. I didn't give him my number because I didn't take him seriously, and that was it," says Kwete.

The Kwete Quaynor We Knew

Kwete's narration fits the man my colleagues and I got to know very well as a member of the Skyy Power FM family in Takoradi. He is good looking and has every reason to feel good about himself.

He is funny, intelligent, and would easily get emotional about anything he really cared about. Kwete has sufficient self-confidence and would not allow himself to be misled into thinking what he believes to be impossible. That is why he was not moved at all by Wilson Arthur in the few minutes they interacted.

This feisty young man returned home to Cape Coast and tried to forget the man he met at Music Paradise in Accra.

He soon became a freshman at the University of Cape Coast.

Despite dismissing Wilson Arthur, his words kept playing back in his mind, especially the observation that Kwete had a good voice for radio.

"Even though I didn't take him seriously, I found myself thinking about it, and his words woke up an interest in me that I never knew was there," recalls Kwete.

Discovering His Own Talent

At the University of Cape Coast, Kwete found out that the Atlantic Hall operated a small campus radio called Atlantic FM (ATL FM), where students volunteered their time to play music and read out information from the newspapers about significant events around the country. Mostly though, the small FM station focused on entertainment and student affairs.

With his new-found motivation from the owner of Music Paradise, he approached ATL FM and expressed his interest. To his surprise, he was accepted after an on-the-spot audition. Afterwards, Kwete would go to the campus station at least once a week for his own rookie gig on air.

He mainly played music, and when he talked, his schoolmates would tell him how good he sounded. Fynnba Derby, now a full professor of criminal justice at Virginia State University in the United States, was one of the friends Kwete made at ATL FM. They both ended up at Skyy Power FM as pioneers of the first commercial radio station in the Western and Central Regions.

The informal experience at ATL FM stood him in good stead to present all manner of programs during his years at Skyy, apart from being the host of the high-stakes morning show.

Finding Faith in the Man from Music Paradise

Kwete was finally convinced that Wilson Arthur of Music Paradise had extraordinary insight into the capability of individuals, their skill and talent, even though the individual may be unaware.

Later in his professional life, Kwete would retain a permanent respect for Wilson. As he says, "Wilson has the rare ability to recognise talent as soon as he sees it."

"Almost everybody Wilson Arthur picked for Skyy was right from scratch. He always had something that led him to the right people. He has a gift for picking the right people for the right job, and I don't know how he did it," reflects Kwete.

A trip to Takoradi, and to 37 Windy Ridge

One weekend during Kwete's second year at the University of Cape Coast, he and some hot-headed friends decided to go to Takoradi for fun. Takoradi was only a 45-minute ride in a taxi they hired together. "It was my first visit to Takoradi," says Kwete.

"I know someone who is involved in a new radio station just up the hill at Windy Ridge," one of the hot-headed friends said when they arrived in Takoradi, around the Monkey Hill area. They all agreed to stop by this new station, but only briefly. The station was test transmitting on 93.5 FM at the time. Kwete later learned that the station's name was Skyy Power FM.

"We arrived in the taxi, and our friend got out to go and see the person he wanted to see," recalls Kwete. "We sat in the taxi, thinking he would be back in a few minutes. Ten minutes later, our friend was still in the building. Meanwhile, our taxi driver was getting agitated and warned he would have to charge us more money for taking extra time," says Kwete. "Being the exuberant one among us, I decided to follow our friend into the building."

When he entered the office, he met a man who immediately said, "Hey, I know you!"

"No, you don't know me," shot back Kwete. "I am here to find our friend who just entered this office."

"I know you," insisted the man, his gaze still fixed on Kwete.

"No, you don't, you can't know me. I just arrived from Cape Coast with my friends in a taxi, and one of them has come in here," said Kwete, hoping the man would shut up.

"I know you," the man said for the third time.

"I met you in Accra…" said the man.

"Where in Accra?" asked Kwete.

"At Music Paradise in Adabraka," answered the man.

Kwete had been visiting his Aunt in Accra when he went to Music Paradise. His Aunt's house was close to Music Paradise so all he said to the man was, "it could be true."

Kwete, at this point of the interview says, "Phillip, to God, I had completely forgotten meeting this man."

"You came into the shop; I talked to you about an FM station; can't you remember?" said the man, who was now close to grieving that Kwete seemed not to remember at all.

"You see, you didn't take me seriously," observed the man from Music Paradise.

Kwete's whole world came crashing down.

"To be honest, I didn't," he confessed.

The Great Epiphany

Kwete Quaynor's second face-to-face meeting with Wilson Arthur was one of the greatest epiphanies in his life. It is so seared in his mind that it is one of the memories that still gives him goose bumps when he recalls it; and it is evident in the way he tells the story with passion in my interview with him.

Kwete had totally dismissed Wilson Arthur's declaration that he was planning to build a private radio station in Takoradi and would give him a job if he were interested. And now, he has just run into the man once more and didn't even recognise him. Wilson, on the other hand, picked him out straight away and spoke with far more clarity than Kwete could handle. He was now staring in the face of Wilson Arthur, humbled and a little ashamed for not trusting and believing his words from more than a year earlier.

Kwete punctuates the interview once more, saying, "Phillip, if you know me, I have a big mouth and I am so blunt, but for once, I could not find the words to respond to this man."

"This is the radio station I was telling you about. It is real. It has happened," said Wilson Arthur.

Kwete's exuberance and hot-headedness evaporated, revealing the real young man who had so much to learn in life, including humility.

"So, would you be interested in working here? We are test transmitting and will be launching soon," said Wilson Arthur.

Kwete stammered, as he tried to answer the question as responsibly as possible. He knew he could not afford to make any more mistakes in responding to Wilson Arthur.

"Yes," he said, a little unsure, as he thought about how he could possibly mix his schooling with working for Skyy FM in Takoradi.

Wilson Arthur's next statement made Kwete's heart sink.

"We have this guy from the BBC who will be running training and orientation for all the presenters on Monday. I want to see you here on Monday."

It was Friday, and Kwete started sweating.

He pauses the interview and urges me to picture the scene.

"Phillip, imagine; all this is happening within ten minutes." he says. "All I wanted to do was find our friend who had come to this office and was taking too much time to return. Then I ran into this man again and within a matter of ten minutes, he had turned my life completely upside down to the point of offering me a job on the spot. Everything was happening so fast, so fast that I didn't even have time to think through it."

The Opportunity of a Lifetime

The job offer was as easy as that, but Kwete's circumstances didn't allow him to accept it. He could not turn it down either.

"Err… I am a student at the University of Cape Coast, so it is going to be a little hard coming and going back and forth," said Kwete.

Wilson Arthur had an answer and even a solution.

"My brother lives in Cape Coast. He comes here every day, so you can join him. Link up with my brother in Cape Coast. Give me your number, I will give it to him. Let him know where he can pick you up in Cape Coast. I want to see you here on Monday. We are going to have fun."

Wilson was referring to Kennedy Arthur, his older brother whom we all called "Big Bro." The interaction was happening on Friday, and Wilson Arthur was effectively saying Kwete should join the Skyy crew on Monday.

Returning to the waiting taxi with his friends, Kwete could not fully explain the interaction he had with Wilson Arthur at the station. His friends thought he was making lame excuses and rebuked him for wasting time. He could feel in his bones that the trajectory of his life had just changed.

Getting Rolled into Skyy

Back in Cape Coast, Kwete made the call to Kennedy Arthur on Sunday night to introduce himself. "Yes, my brother told me you will be calling, and I have since been waiting for your call," said Kennedy Arthur. Kwete knew everything was moving too fast, but now, the speed had gone supersonic.

"I am leaving for Takoradi at 5:30am tomorrow morning. Are you still coming with me, and where should I pick you up?" asked Kennedy Arthur.

Interrupting the narration again, Kwete tells me, "it had still not occurred to me what I was stepping into."

"Somehow, I said yes to Big Bro," recalls Kwete.

He told Kennedy Arthur to pick him up from one of the three major entrances to the University campus. The two strangers in Kennedy Arthur's BMW arrived back at 37 Windy Ridge before 6:30 am on Monday.

Kwete was introduced to the team. He didn't know any of them except Maame Efua DeGraft Aidoo, who he knew years before in Cape Coast. "Because everyone else at Skyy was new to me, I had to be polite and be a gentleman," he says, causing me to laugh. His reference to needing to be polite reminds me of Kwete's troublemaking nature, despite his noble looks.

If there were ever an advertisement for a professional arsonist, Kwete Quaynor would be the first to apply for the job. And if he were to be offered such a job, he would do it with great delight, and for free.

He is among the colleagues who would sometimes walk into the newsroom and deliberately bang on a desk, kick a chair, or even remove a pile of papers from the printer for no reason other than to attract attention or cause annoyance.

He would do this at a time those of us in the newsroom were scrambling to put a bulletin together for the top of the hour. Many of our other colleagues, including Kojo Frempong, Yaw Korankye, and Kwame Dzokoto exhibited similar traits.

Over time though, those of us at the newsroom developed a hardened exterior and successfully restricted everyone from coming to the newsroom, unless they arrived while announcing they would not cause any disturbance. Such antics which were constantly on display became a fulcrum around which constant laughter and banter were generated.

The training and orientation at Skyy for all the new employees took a full week.

"Everyone seemed to know what they were doing. There were those who would be reading the news, being on the morning show or the late afternoon program. I didn't know what I would be doing, and I was not told where I would fit in the structure," says Kwete.

"At the end of training and orientation, I assumed that I didn't make it and my service was not required for the new station. I thought it was a waste of time, but I still approached Wilson Arthur to thank him for the opportunity, after which I would return to Cape Coast for the last time."

"No, you are not going," said Wilson after Kwete started saying his goodbye. "You will be working with the morning show team."

"So that is what happened," recalls Kwete. "No heads up, nothing. I started without realising I had started professional broadcasting."

On the Microphone and the Console

The agony of mixing full time university education with early morning work on a radio station's morning show was just about to start.

For almost the entire duration of his time at University of Cape Coast, Kwete Quaynor made the daily trip between Cape Coast and Takoradi to work at Skyy. Even for us who worked directly at Skyy, we almost forgot that he actually did not live in Takoradi.

He would arrive very early in the morning and after the *Jolly Breakfast Show* midmorning, he would travel back to Cape Coast to attend lectures. Occasionally, he would even sleep in the studio overnight, including some weekends. He was the only one working for Skyy who did not live in Sekondi-Takoradi.

Kwete Quaynor ended up anchoring a variety of programs, including music programs and sports. But he was best known for becoming a long-term host of the *Jolly Breakfast Show* after Kwesi Fletcher left Skyy for Europe. Kwete's most vivid memories at Skyy, though, had little to do with the sensitive microphones and complex consoles. It was the quality of relationships we had at the workplace that made the workforce function like a family.

He looks back over 25 years and is especially impressed that the people Wilson Arthur employed were mostly ordinary girls and boys who exhibited passion for their work and were hungry to learn. "I know people who had already made a name in broadcasting who approached Wilson for a job, and he said no. He chose a lot of raw material, and yet, look at the quality he had. Everyone he picked turned into gold," says Kwete, almost philosophically.

Everyone Gets a Raise, Except Kwete Quaynor

As relationships, even in a family go, one day, Kwete became bitterly disappointed with Wilson Arthur and his brother Kennedy Arthur. It was months into the operations, and they had decided everyone had worked hard enough to deserve a pay rise.

When Kwete received his pay slip, however, it showed the same wage as the previous month. Already armed with information that everyone had the raise, he asked Wilson and Kennedy why he didn't get a raise.

"But you are only working part-time, so, no. We are not considering part timers for a raise at this time," he was told.

Kwete felt crushed!

"I was so disappointed and in pain that tears started welling up in my eyes. I felt like all my hard work was not appreciated at all, and I made up my mind on the spot to leave and not come back again."

"I told a few of our colleagues who were present. I already had my bag packed and was on my way out, but like the family that they were, they all came together to comfort me. They even offered to top up my salary from their own pockets. But for the fellow feeling they showed, I would have left Skyy that day, and of course, it would have been a mistake on my part," says Kwete.

Enduring Memories of Skyy

By this point in the interview, Kwete is both relaxed and worked up as he recalls the invigorating memories that he offered to tell some personal and intimate stories to illustrate the raw human dynamics at the workplace. He tells the stories with care to illustrate just how close Skyy was to being a real family.

"One of our colleagues started dating a lady in the city, but the lady did not disclose that she was married," says Kwete. "Wilson got to know, so he called this colleague into his office. I was there, and Wilson gave him a heartfelt piece of advice that I have never forgotten."

"Wilson said, 'I can confirm the lady you are dating is married, but I know she has not told you. So I am urging you as your friend to break off the relationship now.'"

Kwete says Wilson followed up by saying something truly profound: "Apart from the fact that it is not morally acceptable, if you take somebody's wife, someone else will also take your wife in the future."

Kwete returns to talking to me, saying, "It was so subtle. I was not the one Wilson was talking to, but it sent shivers down my spine. And that is how Wilson had everybody's back at Skyy."

"The bond we had was so strong. It was so much so that we did not even feel like complaining at all about whatever we were receiving as remuneration. People held us in high esteem, and we had a rare sense of job satisfaction that overshadowed everything else."

Kwete remembers Wilson as having a real hands-on approach to the work in connection with all of us. "He takes interest in every person, and as soon as he sees you are a little bit free, he will call you into his office and start having a chat with you, wanting to know how you can improve or talk about any issues or challenges you are facing. The lessons you learn working with Wilson Arthur are priceless. He was the boss, but he was like a brother; a big brother," explains Kwete.

Kwete is so on the roll with the memories that he shares another personal story concerning himself. I left that story out of this book, but it is available on the original audio interview with Kwete online.

Kwete's enthusiastic and lively retelling of his experiences at Skyy was mesmerising and has been carefully preserved, not just in this book, but in his own voice--the voice heard on Skyy for many years.

Still looking back, Kwete says, "for some reason, all those Wilson picked... we all became like family. Within a short period of time, it felt as if we had known one another for ages. You would remember: we would eat together, go out together--we did everything together."

Talking about the employees of Skyy like a family unit, he says, "we were almost always together. Everyone knows where someone is at every point in time. I don't know how Wilson could pick us from different backgrounds, different places to make one big family. It is as if he knew we could all get along."

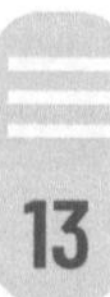

From Skyy Power FM to the White House

"I just choose to see the lighter side of things because I personally don't get anything from getting agitated or angry or brooding over stuff. The lighter I make the situation, the better I am able to handle it. So good or bad, you'll probably see a smile on my face."

— *Naa Adoley Thompson, reflecting on her time at Skyy*

In June 1994, Walt Disney Pictures released the original animated musical drama *The Lion King*. The film, watched by millions around the world, went on to become the highest grossing film of that year. Naa Adoley Thomson was only 15 years old when she watched the movie in the same year it was released. And she watched it over and over again, long before Skyy Power FM was established. Naa Adoley felt at the time that *The Lion King* was the greatest movie ever made.

She is now a mother and has watched *The Lion King* with her children more times than she can count. Long before motherhood arrived, *The Lion King* was a tool she used to rescue the first children's program that went live on air at Skyy Power FM.

Stepping into Skyy Power FM

Shortly after Naa Adoley turned 18 years old, she walked to 37 Windy Ridge where Skyy Power FM was undertaking test transmission. She met Wilson Arthur to discuss the opportunity of working with the station. But there was a problem.

All the essential positions had been filled, including those for presenters on all the programs that had been drawn up. There was no slot left for her. However, Naa Adoley's confidence and manner of speaking impressed Wilson Arthur so much that he offered her the role of a reserved presenter.

She was assigned to understudy Maame Efua DeGraft Aidoo.

Apart from being a journalist in the newsroom who would read the news bulletin, Maame Efua was also going to host the *Skyy Spicy Lunch* afternoon program. Commercial broadcast started early in the morning on 5 October 1997, and Naa Adoley's place was simply to hang around, help with reception duties, listen to what she was told to do by others, and generally watch the Skyy Power FM ship sail on.

The end of the first week of broadcast came. It was Saturday and just about every presenter had their turn in the studio to announce themselves and deliver their individual programs. Naa Adoley wondered when she would ever get the opportunity to speak into the microphone live in the studio.

The next program on that Saturday was due to start at 2 pm. It was the *Skyy Kiddie Time,* a program designed to feature children.

It was to be hosted by someone who loved and understood children and knew how to motivate and bring the very best out of them live on radio.

The person chosen was a gentleman who lived in Takoradi. He had a track record of organising children's programs off air. Skyy did not employ him directly; instead, he was to come in every Saturday to run the program.

Wilson Arthur wanted to get a taste of what the first children's program would sound like, so he kept checking the time. Naa Adoley also looked forward to it. Her ears were getting finely tuned to the full output of Skyy in the few days the station had been on air.

At 1:45 pm, the gentleman who was to host the *Skyy Kiddie Time* was nowhere to be found, and Wilson Arthur panicked. It was now 2 pm on the dot, and there was still no sign of him.

The only option left was to play music to fill the slot, as it was clear the host of the children's program was not going to show up, but at 2:01 pm, Wilson made a dramatic decision.

Fixing his gaze on Naa Adoley, Wilson said, "the guy has not turned up; you are going to host the children's program. Find some good music, get in the studio, and make the children of Sekondi-Takoradi feel happy."

Naa Adoley accepted the challenge.

Lion King's Hakuna Matata to the Rescue

She was well aware of the richness of Skyy Power FM's music library with many thousands of CDs that no radio station in the country had yet dreamt of.

The CDs were also well arranged so that it was easy to find a chosen genre of music. Within seconds of entering the library, Naa Adoley picked up a beautifully illustrated CD, showing a lion standing on top of a hill in the glow of golden rays of a rising sun.

The CD was *The Lion King Original Motion Picture Soundtrack*. Moments later, the radio sets used for monitoring in the office could be heard blaring the classic, bouncy, and euphonic song, "Hakuna Matata."

When Naa Adoley introduced the program, it sounded as if *Skyy Kiddie Time* was a deliberately well-designed program being executed by a well-trained presenter from the all-new Skyy Power FM.

That is how Naa Adoley set sail with *Skyy Kiddie Time* on Saturday, 11 October 1997 when Skyy was only six days old as a commercial enterprise.

A Problem-Free Philosophy

With the novelty of private broadcasting at its peak, just about every radio set in the entire Sekondi-Takoradi metropolis was tuned to Skyy.

In those days, people listened to the radio with the same devotion displayed when watching their favourite TV program. It was not uncommon to see families, including children, listening intensely to the radio together.

"*Hakuna Matata*" continued to play, evoking the emotions people associated with watching the movie. As listeners were drawn to the distinctive song, Naa Adoley's velvety voice chimed in. She sounded as if her voice was singularly made for radio, the quality and smoothness of her language unmistakable.

Most impressive was the fullness of her confidence as she came across like a professional radio presenter who had practiced her craft for years. She sounded happy and upbeat, speaking directly and lovingly to children, reminding them why their parents and guardians were the best people in their lives. She described herself as an "auntie" to all the children, calling herself Auntie Naa Adoley.

She announced to adult listeners that children of Sekondi-Takoradi have a new home on Skyy Power FM every Saturday on the *Skyy Kiddie Time.*

"Skyy Kiddie Time was always the best time of my week. I always looked forward to it," says Naa Adoley in an interview for this book, 24 years after her Skyy Power FM experience in 1997.

"I loved that show through and through," she says.

More than just her effectiveness as host of a children's program, Naa Adoley demonstrated a personality that is both positive and easy going. She was never angry. She knows only how to be happy, and this shone brightly through *Skyy Kiddie Time.*

"I just choose to see the lighter side of things because I personally don't get anything from getting agitated or angry or brooding over stuff. The lighter I make the situation, the better I am able to handle it. So good or bad, you'll probably see a smile on my face," says Naa Adoley.

When she says those words in my interview with her, I feel it fully summarises her personality. It is as if she continuously echoes the sentiments in "Hakuna Matata;" with no worries, standing up only for a problem-free philosophy, even when she is surrounded by chaos.

From Skyy Power FM to The White House

From the day she stepped into Skyy Power FM, Naa Adoley appeared to be destined for something great. As her life unfolded to reveal what she became, it all seemed effortless.

She was born in Takoradi and lived in the vicinity of Skyy Power FM in the suburb of Windy Ridge. Her decision to walk to Skyy and express her interest in working there seemed casual, but underneath, she had willpower that was as strong as steel. She believed Skyy had come to represent the best of Sekondi-Takoradi and decided she must be part of it.

There was always something in her character that conceals her determination, with the only thing visible being her friendly manner.

When she completed University of Cape Coast, she found a path to the United States after saying goodbye to her beloved Skyy Power FM and Sekondi-Takoradi. Years after being in America, she saw a black man called Barack Obama ascend the presidency and settled into The White House.

Not long after, she picked up work as a public servant, working for the US federal government. Her work, as she says, involved "finding innovative and more efficient ways of awarding complex government contracts."

She became a member small group that initiated and implemented the strategy for the transformation.

That team worked from the White House.

For a good period of time during the Obama administration, the White House was Naa Adoley's place of work. She would occasionally run into President Obama and Vice President Joe Biden on the compound, but well outside the well-known Secret Service ring of steel around the leader of the free world.

She says the noise of the president's Marine One, the world's most sophisticated helicopter, taking off and landing was something she got used to.

No, her work never took her into the actual Oval Office. Only a few people actually got that close. As she explains, the White House is actually a sprawling complex, far more than what is shown on TV when reporters do a live stand-up, using it as a background.

"The West Wing, where the president works, is actually small, and most people who work in the White House have their offices in the Eisenhower Executive Office Building, and that is where my office was; that's where I worked," says Naa Adoley.

Oval Office or not, she still called a portion of the White House compound her workplace, and the journey that took her there started from Skyy Power FM at 37 Windy Ridge in Takoradi.

A Program In the Image of Naa Adoley

On 18 October 1997, the gentleman who was originally billed to host *Skyy Kiddie Time* turned up to host the program. He arrived on time, well prepared. Naa Adoley was also prepared to host the program.

The gentleman started expertly outlining to Wilson what he was going to do on the program. Wilson was barely paying attention. Halfway through his presentation, Wilson said, "thank you for coming," and then he delivered the blow. "Naa Adoley did a fine job last week. I want her to continue hosting the program until further notice."

As Naa Adoley recalls the memories long after two decades, she also remembers how it felt.

She says, "Wilson was so impressed with what I did because I basically, excuse my language, pulled it out of my butt. Even the "Hakuna Matata" song, I just pulled it out of nowhere, you know. Everything was so organic, and I guess that is what impressed Wilson."

The *Skyy Kiddie Time* Naa Adoley helped to inaugurate got even better with time. "I kept adding flavour every week, and the kids just loved it," she says.

When Yuki Ampofo later joined the program and started hosting it herself, there was no deviation in quality. The quality was sustained even when one of the young former participants on the program, Nelly Lomotey, graduated to the point of hosting the program herself. She and Yuki Ampofo perfectly reflected the sparkling spirit with which Naa Adoley started the program.

The fun and innocence beamed whenever *Skyy Kiddie Time* goes on air is infectious and easily melts the heart. It could cause soldiers in a brutal combat to declare a ceasefire, if only they listened to the sweet and intelligent children that Naa Adoley, Yuki Ampofo, and Nelly Lomotey guided on air during many inspiring discussions and conversations about their young lives.

It was as if these three young ladies went to a special institution where the only subject taught was how to host a children's program on air in the most radiant and cheerful way.

They spent time with children on radio every week for years in a professional setting and never once made it feel like work.

Enduring Friendships

These young ladies in their individual interviews revealed that they benefited a great deal from their association with Skyy as well as producing and hosting the children's program.

They all tell of the close friendships they formed at the workplace. They all describe those relationships as being nothing but family. That family, even though mostly now dispersed across the world, is still an enduring tapestry of deep friendships.

KingB is one of the first generation of Skyy Power FM presenters who also now lives in the United States.

"I can go to Atlanta without telling KingB, and go sleep in his house with my family. And he does the same. When he comes to Florida, he doesn't have to call me and tell me. He comes and knocks on my door and sleeps in my house. My husband knows him and my kids call him Uncle Kingsley," says Naa Adoley.

"It is the same with Yuki," she adds.

"Yuki came to visit her cousins in Arkansas. She called me, got on the plane to Florida, and my kids called her Auntie Yuki. We all had features and characteristics we liked amongst each other. It was just a good experience all in all."

Reflecting more on her working life at Skyy, she says, "we learned a lot, especially for kids like Yuki and me. I especially wanted to be famous, but that Skyy experience, as much as I enjoyed it, I learned that a huge responsibility comes with being famous. Now I know, so I love my private life."

She adds: "I really wish that at one point in the future, we could all get back together to relive that experience just for a week or so... that would be just so much fun!"

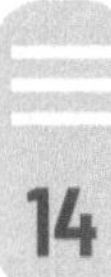

14

Kofi Kinaata's Memories of Skyy Power FM

"Skyy brought a lot of artists that we did not know to Takoradi. My childhood memories would be incomplete without Skyy"
— Kofi Kinaata on how Skyy Power FM influenced and inspired him on his way to becoming a popular musician in Ghana

Perhaps the most significant thing that has come out of Sekondi-Takoradi in the 25 years since the establishment of Skyy Power FM is the hugely talented young man called Kofi Kinaata.

His birth name, Martin King Arthur, evolved into Kofi Kinaata, with "Kinaata" being a Takoradi-style amalgamation of *King* and *Arthur.*

He has become one of the biggest and most popular singers and songwriters Ghana has ever produced. In what seems like a relatively short career, Kofi Kinaata has captured the adoration of Ghanaians to the point that it is possible to run the risk of exaggerating his impact and influence.

"Kofi Kinaata is the A.B. Crentsil, the Paapa Yankson, the Kwame Ampadu … he is all the music greats that Ghana has ever produced in one person. He is the guy setting the standards," says Root Eye.

Root Eye is a music star in his own right, having contributed to Reggie Rockstone's historic Hiplife album *Makaa Maka* in 1996.

Root Eye was also one of the first presenters on Skyy when it launched in October 1997. Winston Amoah, who also worked for Skyy Power FM and later Joy FM in Accra, put it in a simpler way: "I'm happy to have seen Kofi Kinaata in my lifetime. Great guy."

Nana Kwesi Coomson is a close confidant of Kofi Kinaata. In a Facebook post on 26 February 2021, he wrote:

"Anyone who has been in the Showbiz Industry for more than a decade will attest to the fact that it is rare for a typical Showbiz brand to be admired in equal measure by both the young and the old, corporate and street, affluent and not-so-affluent, the church and the ghettos, parents and their children, CEOs and janitors. The Kofi Kinaata brand should be studied; theories should be developed around how he did it."

As of the middle of 2022, Kofi Kinaata has accumulated a blinding list of awards for his creativity in writing pulsating music loved by everyone, from business executives to janitors.

The Trifecta in the Making of Kofi Kinaata

It turns out that there is a laser-straight line between Skyy Power FM and the stratospheric rise of Kinaata and his music. But that line is only one of three in a triangle. There is the fundamental influence of his parents, particularly his mother, and then there is the long-standing history that Ghana's Western Region, represented by Sekondi-Takoradi, produces a constant stream of talented people in music and entertainment.

The combined energy and influence of three different forces created Kofi Kinaata: parental influence, the power of private and commercial radio stations, and the unique cultural and musical legacy of Sekondi-Takoradi.

Nevertheless, success was guaranteed only because Kinaata was willing to focus, take calculated risks, and work hard to reach the height he has attained.

A Talent Rooted in Genes

The foundation of Kinaata's aptitude for music is wholly genetic. "The music thing is from my Mum," he says in my interview with him, adding that it goes further than that.

"I was told my great, great grandfather was a musician back in their village. He used to play the locally made guitar and sing along."

He also remembers his mother constantly singing lullabies to him.

"My mum sang those songs, and as a kid I thought everyone knew the songs, but later I realised they were mum's songs. My Mum composed them all herself. She had about ten lullabies for me, for my senior brother and for my senior sister. That is what my Mum does. She has a very good voice."

Like a reflection of Paul Simon's song *Under African Skies*, Kinaata heard his mother's "very good voice" ringing around his nursery door, forming his first memories. Also shaping his earliest memories were melodies and rhythms he heard from an old radio set at home.

The Family Radio Set

When Skyy Power FM started commercial operations in October 1997, Kofi Kinaata was only seven years old, living in Effiakuma, a suburb of Takoradi. His family owned a little radio set, and every morning it was tuned to *Twin City Radio*, a public broadcasting service operated by Ghana Broadcasting Corporation

That was before Skyy was established.

"I remember they used to call it FM, FM," says Kinaata.

One day, it appeared to him that the value his family attached to the radio set increased. They stopped tuning into *Twin City Radio* and switched to a new station called Skyy Power FM. The station also started broadcasting 24 hours, so people tuned in, and almost never tuned out.

Every small shop, and businesses operated in kiosks around Kinaata's neighbourhood tuned-in to Skyy. They turned up the volume to the maximum, and no one ever complained about the volume being too loud.

It is possible to walk a kilometre or more through an entire neighbourhood and all the while hearing the transmission of the same radio station from multiple radio sets in different shops and homes.

"Everybody started saying Skyy, Skyy, and no one seemed to talk about *Twin City Radio* anymore," recalls Kinaata.

As an impressionable seven-year old, he took note and found listening to Skyy Power FM a lot of fun. With deep emotions, he says, "one person I remember is Uncle Opia."

Uncle Opia, who died in 2006, was a beloved broadcaster whose radio broadcast around 5 am on weekdays was designed to help families wake up their children and listen to some good advice on radio before going to school.

"A child at my age will not pay attention to what is on the radio, but because I loved music, that was the only place I could turn to for music," Kinaata explains.

"My parents were more interested in the news, but I always waited to enjoy the songs they played," adding, "I was into Skyy Power because they brought a new phase to entertainment. They played all kinds of music, especially hiplife which attracted me a lot."

While developing his love for entertainment by listening to music on Skyy Power FM, Kinaata was also drawn to the carefree life in the company of other children in Effiakuma.

Playing football with his friends came to him naturally. He became so good at it that his family and friends thought he had the potential to turn into a professional player.

In one song, he tapped into his continuing love for football:

"The actual fact is I am an Arsenal (football club) fan, so I have no fear of a broken heart," he rapped in one of his songs called *Single and Free*.

The reference to Arsenal Football Club is purely out of service to music because in real life, Kofi Kinaata is a fan of a different football club: Manchester United, according to Nana Kwesi Coomson, who also acts as Kinaata's public and media relations officer.

In those days at Effiakuma, children developed a form of resilience by testing their physical strength through frequent fist fights without provocation. It was also a form of sport, a kind of no-rules boxing in which each child learned to fight to win or courageously acknowledge defeat.

Kinaata ended up in some of those fights. He developed a reputation for fighting as a little boy, which worried his mother.

"I was like the black sheep in my family, always causing trouble. My mum would always complain. She told me that if I bring money home because of boxing, she won't take it, and she asked me to become either a footballer or a singer," recalls Kofi Kinaata, the accomplished singer-songwriter.

Back to His Roots in Music and Entertainment With Skyy

Music was always Kofi Kinaata's first love. After his tumultuous teenage years, he naturally drifted back to it--with the help of Skyy Power FM.

More than playing music on radio, Skyy Power FM was now bringing musicians to Takoradi from other parts of Ghana for different music festivals.

One of those festivals was held at the front carpark of Skyy Power FM as a free, open-air show. Kofi Kinaata knew he could not miss the live music concert so heavily promoted on radio. Besides, Skyy Power FM was only two kilometres from Effiakuma, where he lived.

"My dad would not allow me to go. After he left the house, I asked my mother, and she also didn't want me to go, but I sneaked out and went. I enjoyed myself so much that I did not realise it was getting really late," says Kinaata.

That night, he walked the two-kilometre distance, and by the time he returned home, it was early morning at dawn. Neighbours were already awake doing their house chores.

"When I returned, my father was very angry with me and a few of the neighbours physically restrained him from punishing me. Instead, he brought out a pen and paper and wrote an agreement for me to sign, forcing me to make a commitment that I will not go out at night without his permission. And then he also signed it," relates Kinaata.

"My father is a preacher and also a strict disciplinarian and doesn't like to talk too much," he added.

The written agreement did not stop Kinaata from patronising numerous outdoor entertainment events regularly organised by Skyy Power FM.

"Skyy brought a lot of artists to Takoradi. They brought Kwabena Kwabena, Okomfo Kwadee, Akatakyie, Nana Kwame… they brought everybody, and whenever Castro arrived, it was like homecoming," recalls Kofi Kinaata.

"My childhood memories would be incomplete without Skyy," he adds, with a trace of emotion in his voice.

Music and Entertainment Made in Sekondi-Takoradi

While looking up to Skyy Power FM as an inspiration for high quality entertainment and music, he also started to recognise Sekondi-Takoradi and Western Region as the root of rhythms and a rich environment for developing his talent.

Everywhere he roamed in the city, he was reminded that it was the home of great Ghanaian musicians, including C.K. Mann, Paapa Yankson, Gyedu-Blay Ambolley, and A.B. Crentsil.

"You cannot talk about good music in Ghana without talking about Sekondi-Takoradi and Western Region. We have a legacy of good music, rhythms, and melody in the Western Region," says Kofi Kinaata.

Rap for Pride at Melody

An important event in Kofi Kinaata's journey occurred when he applied to take part in a competition called *Kasahare* (or rapid talking) to decide the best rapper. "All the participants were rapping in Twi, but I decided to rap in Fante language, the type we speak in Takoradi, and that was my big break because everybody discovered that I had the talent to be among the very best in Ghana," he says, recalling the euphoria that greeted his performance.

"I was not paid a lot of money, but I didn't mind, because as far as I was concerned, I was there to rap for pride, and to show I have the talent and I was ready to work hard for success."

Before this dramatic discovery, Kinaata says he had a friend who was also a singer. The friend once took him to a studio to record a track after which the sound engineer realised that Kinaata had a lot more talent than his friend. "The engineer took me aside and said I should come alone next time, because he can see that I have a lot of talent to make it big," recalls Kinaata.

The Rest is History

Kofi Kinaata, more than anyone else, knows his rise to fame came through a lot of learning and hard work. He says, for example, that he was proficient in rap music and when he started writing music, he did not know what a chorus was.

Unafraid to acknowledge this, he wrote a song called *Onnyi Chorus* (*which in Fante means,* music without chorus) to illustrate how uninformed he used to be, except the song itself, crafted to showcase his inadequacy, became a hit on its own. With each composition and song, Kinaata found new followers of his work, and his rise to fame shows no sign of slowing down.

In 2016, he was recognised as the songwriter of the year. Almost every year since then, he has accumulated multiple awards, almost too numerous to specify. As fellow musician Root Eye suggests, Kinaata is well on his way to becoming "all the music greats that Ghana has ever produced in one person."

Composing a Song for Skyy Power FM

"So you composed a song exclusively for Skyy Power FM to mark its 20th anniversary?" I ask Kinaata in my interview with him.

The question takes him aback because the song he composed for Skyy, unlike any of his other songs, was not made available online or on any streaming platform.

As if remembering something he had forgotten, he says, "yes, I made that music for Skyy. It was a gift for Skyy Power for their anniversary; for the role they played in developing music and entertainment."

In Kofi Kinaata's heart and mind, his motivation to compose a song for Skyy came from a deep-seated appreciation about what Skyy Power FM meant to him, how it shaped his memories and inspired his innate love for music and entertainment, and in the process, helped with the development of the Western Region.

Skyy Power FM meant that much to him, and he unleashed his full memories in the song, laced with praise and admiration, singling out the Chief Executive, Wilson Arthur.

"Asaay, Memories," he exclaims in the song right at the beginning. His fondness for Skyy Power FM since his childhood is unmistakable throughout the song.

Skyy, Mr. Wilson Arthur, Ayekoo!

(Ayekoo means well done in Ghana).

Some of the words of the song he made for Skyy are are follows:

From 1997, I'm telling you what I've observed…
When I wake up in the morning, I hear "Skyy Power"
Skyy Power FM, 93.5, Western and Central and the whole of Ghana
says
Congratulations and well done!

Such is the impact of Skyy Power FM in a city known for its culture and music that one of its songwriters and celebrated musicians was inspired to sing and acknowledge its historic contribution and influence. No wonder, for as Kinaata says, "my childhood memories would be incomplete without Skyy."

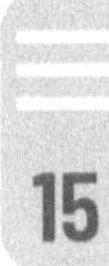

15

The Silent DJ

"I have never mentioned my full name at Skyy. Only some of my classmates in school knew it. Nobody at Skyy knows it. I had a lot of trouble with the name when I was in school, so when I came to Skyy, I told people my name is Ato Parry."

At Skyy Power FM, we knew him only as Ato Parry, and we even shortened the name to "Ato P." He is a member of the small gang Wilson Arthur brought with him from Accra to start the radio station.

Ato Parry now lives in Italy.

Before speaking to him for this book, I interviewed Papa Tony Ashun-Codjiw. Papa Tony and Ato Parry were schoolmates at Sekondi College; long before Skyy was established.

A Character Almost Unknown

"Even in school, we were not always sure what his full name was," says Papa Tony. "Ato Parry's real name is long and complicated. You know kids in Sekondi-Takoradi and how we can tease each other, especially in school. When Ato first mentioned his name in class, we laughed so much that he didn't mention his full name anymore. Even the teachers thought the name was a mouthful," recalls Papa Tony.

"Parry is his surname, but he has three other names with the initials, R, A, N. As a result, we started calling him RAN Parry *(pronounced run-Parry)."*

Papa Tony, who now lives in Calgary, Canada, remains one of Ato Parry's best friends across the Atlantic. He sympathised with all the teasing Ato Parry put up with, but he also couldn't help laughing as he recalled the history of it all.

"So what is your full name?" I ask Ato Parry.

His immediate reaction, captured in a light laughter, confirmed there was some riddle to it.

"My full name?" he asked, as if to confirm my question. I didn't respond, using the silence as an indirect pressure to let him talk.

"My full name…hmm, only some of my classmates know it. I have never mentioned it, and nobody at Skyy knows it. Everyone knows me only as Ato Parry. I had a lot of trouble with the name, so when I came to Skyy, I told people my name is Ato Parry."

In the Fante language, Ato (*or more accurately, Ato Kwamena*) is an automatic name for a boy born on Saturday. Since he was born on Saturday, he decided to go for simplicity.

After some coaxing, Ato Parry finally pronounced his full name - but he mumbled it a little bit, so I could not guarantee I got it right even on the recording. When he sensed my heightened curiosity about it, he declined to repeat it. The joke was now on me as he laughed saying, "if you didn't get it the first time, you won't get it again."

It was many weeks after the interview that Ato Parry told me his full name: *Ridley Ashcroft Noble Parry*.

The Very Quiet Achiever

The years Ato Parry kept his full name under wraps even after he became a popular figure on radio is an illustration of his whole character: he is smart, cautious and at all times volunteers to say far less than he knows. He is never in a hurry to demonstrate his talent or knowledge.

He is a very quiet achiever.

Ato Parry worked with Wilson Arthur at Music Paradise in Accra, together with Wilson's nephew, Sammy Arthur and KingB, Wilson's school mate and childhood friend.

He saw the very baby steps leading to the creation of Skyy Power FM. "The guys at Vibe FM were Wilson's friends, and they were always talking about making radio. They came to our shop all the time to collect CDs and Wilson was always going to the studio at Trust Towers," says Ato Parry.

"I got to know Wilson when I finished Sekondi College. My Uncle invited me to work in his shop and also learn how to fix computers. He enrolled me into a computer school close to Wilson's music shop," said Ato Parry.

Music Paradise was located in-between the two places Ato Parry would go, and as a result, he would walk past Music Paradise everyday.

Ato Parry Discovers Music Paradise

"I really love music, you know," says Ato Parry. One day, I was walking to work with my friend and we heard this nice music playing from Music Paradise, so we went to the shop to ask about who was singing, to find out who the artiste was. There I saw Sammy Arthur and Wilson."

Ato Parry believes he and his friend did not get the best welcome or anything close to excellent customer service upon entering.

"Because the shop was small, when there are more than five or six customers at a time, there was always a risk that someone might take away some CDs without paying for it. Wilson said this had happened before."

He continued, "Wilson looked at us with some suspicion and told us to stand outside for sometime until they called us back in to serve us."

"We just left, because they seemed to think we might steal something from the shop, but we are not that kind of people," said Ato Parry. A few days later, the love of music lured Ato Parry and his friend back to the shop.

"We were the two guys you told to stand outside the shop," Ato Parry and his friend told Wilson Arthur on returning. "We are not bad boys; we just want you to record some music for us."

The transaction took place.

Ato Parry recalls that he paid for the recording; but it took multiple visits to the shop before the cassette was handed to him. When Ato

Parry got home and played the tape, the songs did not include the ones he specified.

"At first, I was annoyed because I felt I had been cheated. But the more I played the songs, the more I liked them. My friends also listened to the songs and liked it. That is when I realised that Wilson really knows music and he also had a huge collection of music."

He told Wilson that he was very impressed and continued visiting the recording shop, and soon, he became friends with Wilson Arthur.

"Wilson told me I have a good heart (that I am a good person) and he would like to work with me because I also know music."

"I agreed, because I love music."

From that point, Music Paradise was run on a part time basis by four men; Wilson Arthur, KingB, Sammy Arthur and Ato Parry.

"I learned a lot during this time," says Ato Parry. "The three people I worked with all knew music, and I learned from all of them."

Ato Parry became a skilled DJ. Wilson Arthur would deploy him and Sammy Arthur to play at different social events in Accra for a fee.

Later, when he had to choose between working for Wilson and his Uncle's shop, he ultimately chose to stick with Wilson.

"Because I was busy working at Wilson's shop and failed to pay close attention to my uncle's business, he fired me."

Knowing Wilson Arthur for Real

Ato Parry discovered the relentless entrepreneurial spirit Wilson Arthur possessed while working with him. It started with a short-lived music and entertainment magazine called *Trendi*. Wilson came up with the idea and started publishing it.

"Wilson used to read music and entertainment magazines from overseas, so he decided to publish a local one for Ghana. He wrote the articles himself and KingB did the typing on the office computer. Wilson made me the marketing officer and my job was to take the magazine all over Accra to sell," recalls Ato Parry.

"The articles for the magazine were too much for KingB alone to type, so I brought a young lady called Violet to help. Violet was working as a secretary in my Uncle's shop."

"The first edition of *Trendi* magazine had American musician Keith Sweat on the cover," says Ato Parry, "and the second edition featured Ghanaian new music sensation, Reggie Rockstone."

In a separate interview for this book in August 2021, Ralph Menz of *adFocus* also remembers helping Wilson Arthur to market and sell *Trendi* magazine at the time. The magazine was discontinued as soon as Wilson decided to build Skyy Power FM.

All the manpower, talents and efforts that went into running Music Paradise had all now moved to Takoradi to support Skyy Power FM operations.

"When we all left Accra, Wilson Arthur handed Music Paradise to Mark Okraku Mantey." Okraku Mantey himself was a music producer who later became a politician and served as Ghana's Deputy Minister of Tourism, Arts and Culture.

"At one point, Wilson didn't want to take me to Takoradi immediately because of lack of accommodation, but I told him that I am a Sekondi-Takoradi boy, and could find my way around. At that time, my father was one of the bosses at Social Security and National Insurance Trust (SSNIT) in Takoradi so I could stay with him."

Helping Others Go on Air

One of Ato Parry's outstanding contributions is that he taught many of the presenters how to use complex studio equipment, including the entire range of studio craft.

"Ato Parry really helped me to learn how to use the machines," says Aba Moses who believes she came to Skyy Power FM as a total greenhorn. "He took me to the small production studio near the newsroom and patiently showed me how to operate the console, the microphone and how to use the big CD players."

"I had the voice and everything, but it was Ato Parry who chose the music for me and helped me with operating the equipment," says Abena Bondah who used to present *Skyy Spicy Lunch*.

Root Eye, who was already a musician before joining Skyy, also remembers the valuable coaching he had in studio craft from Ato Parry.

"He showed me how to open the microphone to a proper level and then have the confidence to speak in between tracks without talking over the lyrics," he said in an extended interview.

Almost Dead Silent on Air

The time came for Ato Parry himself to take to the airwaves on his own program called *Highlife Mix*.

Highlife Mix featured a more modern form of Highlife including Hiplife, and Ato Parry played it with a distinctive style of mixing the songs like an accomplished DJ. His reputation grew quickly, and musicians across Ghana were sometimes desperate to offer Ato Parry some money so he could play their songs. The practice in the industry is known as "payola."

"Sometimes, representatives of musicians would send me a CD with some money to play their songs on *Highlife Mix*. I made so much money that at one point, I didn't touch my salary for more than six months. I am sure I made more money than any of the presenters at Skyy."

I cannot recall Ato Parry speaking a full sentence on air during his own hugely popular music program, except for perhaps an odd announcement.

The only thing I barely recall him mentioning is his own name, Ato Parry, but that was later shortened to *Ato P*. "Michael Griffiths is the one who called me Ato P, and I liked it," he says.

The power and appeal of the music he played meant he could get away without talking, making himself a genuinely accomplished *silent* DJ. What he held back from saying on air, he made up for in the way he mixed and played music.

Ato Parry's *Highlife Mix* program preceded *News Review*, a current affairs program I hosted every Sunday, from 1pm to 3pm featuring Captain Sowu, Tony Osei-Gyasi and others.

Kojo Antwi's album, *Superman* was new and Ato Parry played the tracks *Sikadam* and *Afofanto* and mixed them with such sweetness, it kept listeners glued and ready for the hard-hitting current affairs and political analysis program that filled Sekondi-Takoradi after lunch.

Ato Parry welcomes me to take over from him with my panelists by playing Skyy Power FM's well known jingle: *"the power of news, the power of information, the power of music; Skyy Power!"*

Ato Parry unleashes his power through music, while I take over to release more power through news and information, including eliciting deep analysis from Captain Sowu and Tony Osei-Gyasi by asking piercing questions derived from exhaustive research.

Like many of the presenters, Ato Parry was close to Wilson's wife Adwoa Amofah, who was also our boss. In his case, he knew her from Accra when he was working for Wilson Arthur's Music Paradise.

"One week after I joined Music Paradise, Adwoa Amofah came from London," says Ato Parry. "She is a very good woman and Skyy would have been impossible without her. Wilson is a lucky man to have her in his life."

More than 20 years after leaving Skyy Power FM for Italy, Ato is particularly proud that he is possibly the one who started *Highlife Mix* style which included a tasteful mixture of Hiplife and some aspects of Ghanaian traditional Highlife which proved to be wildly popular.

It is quite an achievement for a man who played on radio without talking, and instead, allowed his competent DJ-ing skills to speak for him.

16

The Irreverent Ato-Kwamena Dadzie

"When you have something to tell someone, you think it through and weigh the pros and cons about how the person will feel... I don't do that. I just dive in and tell you what I have to tell and then get on with life. I don't care whether you are hurt or you are going to cry to your mother..."

– Ato—Kwamena Dadzie, Ghana's most irreverent journalist who started his career with Skyy Power FM

The first time I saw Ato-Kwamena Dadzie, his thick spectacles reminded me of my grandfather. I used to examine the old man's glasses, believing no one could possibly see anything through those thick glasses.

As Ato walked into Skyy Power FM's offices at 37 Windy Ridge in Takoradi, I instinctively overlayed his face with my grandfather's and wondered how the lanky young man was able to find his way around with the three-pound weight of glasses resting on his nose. Besides, he also looked like he had not had a full meal for several weeks.

It was 1999, and he came fresh from the Ghana Institute of Journalism (GIJ) and was seeking to undertake his internship with us at Skyy. When Skyy gave him the chance, I was happy for him. I thought the opportunity would at least help him to eat well and start to look as well-fed as the rest of us.

The Real Ato-Kwamena Dadzie

The real Ato-Kwamena Dadzie emerged soon after he was accepted into Skyy Power FM, and his true identity had nothing to do with his looks or thick glasses. He is a native of Western Region and grew up in Essikado, the little historic town that is part of the Sekondi-Takoradi metropolis.

Ato arrived at Skyy with an impeccable recommendation. We learned later that he graduated top of his journalism class. It is impossible to know Ato and not fall in love with his brilliance and all-round cheekiness. One of our colleagues, Elloeny Amande, describes him saying, "Ato is a guy constantly in the middle of a prank."

Wide Open Space to Make Mistakes

When it was time for Ato's class at GIJ to undertake an internship, most of his mates chose print or broadcast media stations located in the national capital. Being the son of a poor single mother, Ato had other unique circumstances.

"My mother was selling *bofroat*, and throughout GIJ, I was practically homeless. We were moving from one uncompleted building to another in the suburb of Adenta. Besides, you often need good contacts in order to get yourself accepted in the most prestigious media houses in Accra as an intern," says Ato.

Bofroat is a fried and delicious doughnut-like treat in Ghana, but women who prepare it for sale would usually make very little income. That was the life Ato and his mother lived. As a result, Ato says he went to the less fancied *Ghana News Agency* for his internship.

He also went to *Radio and TV Magazine* (RTV), a small magazine whose publisher was Robert Mills. At RTV, Ato met the editor at the time, Kofi Asmah, who later became a successful lawyer in Ghana. "Around this time as well," says Ato, "I heard about a new radio station in Takoradi called Skyy Power FM."

Ato grew up in Sekondi-Takoradi, so he says, "I thought going to Skyy Power FM for my internship would be a nice opportunity to go back home for a while. I told myself that Skyy would be a nice place to cut my teeth because it is an environment familiar to me with a smaller radio station than Joy FM in Accra."

What Ato says next impresses me: "The room for mistakes at Skyy would be larger, and the room for learning would also be larger."

His words immediately remind me of the fact that Ato can be very strategic and wise in his calculations. In this case, he recognised that a large room and wide-open spaces to make mistakes (and from which he could learn) was something valuable. As I listen to him, I can hear old Dixie Chicks' 1998 music, *Wide Open Spaces*.

"She needs wide open spaces, room to make her big mistakes," says a portion of the song.

On arriving at the wide-open space of Skyy Power FM, Ato says he met Esi Gyan, a beloved former colleague who lost her battle against cancer in March 2014.

"I met Esi Gyan at the reception, and she seemed angry about something. Suddenly, I found this woman to be a challenge, a hard nut to crack," recalls Ato.

"This woman didn't seem to laugh, but I told myself that I am going to make her laugh her heart out when I start working for Skyy. As I sat down to talk to her, I tell you, Phillip, I fell in love with Esi Gyan on the spot," recalls Ato, adding "I told her this before she died. I told her that I loved her."

The love Ato had for Esi Gyan was a love that we all shared at Skyy. The entire workforce operated like a family and Ato walked in and took his place as he got to know everyone else.

"I Was the Happiest Intern"

Ato's first memory of Skyy is dominated by the two people he first met: Esi Gyan and veteran journalist, Kwesi Mould. The two are probably the ones Ato loved the most. They are also the ones we lost to death, apart from Uncle Opia and Samuel Ansah.

With the approval of Wilson Arthur, our senior editor Mr. Mould welcomed the new intern into the newsroom. That was when I met Ato, the young man who would add so much value to Skyy news and current affairs with his brilliance, hard work, and wit.

"Even though Mr. Mould was much older than the rest of us, he was very nice to all of us. We were like his children; he could even be our grandfather. If he didn't have grey hair, you would think he is our age mate," observes Ato.

Mr. Mould, whom we loved dearly, was a special man who put a smile on our face everyday. "One day," says Ato, "Mr. Mould told our colleague Maame Efua DeGraft Aidoo that the way she read the news was 'belligerent.'"

I remember the incident very well. Maame Efua and I used to present the major news together. She had a beautiful voice for radio and presented other programs at that time. For some inexplicable reason, Mr. Mould expressed the view that her manner of reading was "belligerent." We were baffled and challenged Mr. Mould, while defending the quality of Maame Efua's reading.

We pounced even more when we realised his defence was weak and porous, so we told him that he is the only one we knew who had a belligerent personality. He gave up instantly saying, "you are all small boys," while laughing it off. From that day on, we told Mr. Mould almost daily that he was a "belligerent man," and he would always laugh. Over time, calling him "belligerent" became a sign of how much we loved him and how much he loved us back. He encouraged us to challenge him and welcomed our views and feelings, but not without a healthy resistance.

Our relationship with Mr. Mould was so cordial that we called him "Oldie Mouldie" or "old Mr. Mould," and he felt happy about this. One day, as part of our usual pranks against Mr. Mould, Ato got Ewurama Smith and the rest of us to put together a short poem that we thought would irritate the old man.

Part of the poem read:

Old Mr. Mould

Always trying to be bold

Try him, and you will be told...

The poem was printed and posted in the newsroom. When Mr. Mould read it, he just dismissed it, saying, "you children are always making trouble."

"Mr. Mould did not carry any airs whatsoever. He was very practical, down to earth, and took us in his fatherly arms and shepherded us along the way in so many ways," says Ato.

Ato and I recall one story Mr. Mould shared with us when he worked as a newspaper editor in Nigeria.

"An important person died, and the publisher asked me to write a tribute on his behalf which I put on the frontpage of the newspaper. I added a photo of the publisher, but the photo showed him laughing heartily which didn't match the message," said Mr. Mould. "The publisher was very angry with me," he said, "because the photo made him seem like he was celebrating the death of the deceased."

It was one of the many stories he shared about his experience in journalism. He used it to teach us the need to use good judgement in producing stories with appropriate photos and illustrations. Ato and I have a good laugh as we recall the story. "I have never forgotten the lesson in that story, including other experiences Mr. Mould shared with us in the newsroom," says Ato.

"I was the happiest intern at Skyy," he says, adding, "I was learning a lot and I had the freedom to do a lot of things; it was a very serious learning experience and the work at Skyy really shaped me in so many ways."

"Since Skyy," he continues, "I have not worked anywhere else where the friendship and camaraderie is as close. Skyy was like a family. A bunch of young people in their formative years met together over a common dream and formed a family of their own. It was like a clan. I have not experienced that in any other organisation over the last twenty years since I left Skyy, I am telling you, and it started from day one! No one outside Skyy would think I was an intern. I was accepted and treated equally," recalls Ato.

"A Rather Staid Newsroom at Joy FM"

In 2001, Ato left Skyy for Joy FM in Accra. He took along his brilliance, hard work, and wicked humour. In the national capital, all his qualities were magnified, especially his irrepressible spirit to make those in power uncomfortable.

"The contrast between Skyy and Joy was too much," says Ato, recalling his first few weeks at Joy FM. "The newsroom at Joy was so staid, quiet, and boring. One day, I just got up and shouted,

'You people, don't you have fun? This place is too quiet. Let's make some noise!'"

I could imagine how everyone in the newsroom would have reacted. I knew many of those colleagues at Joy FM from the early days, including journalists like Kofi Owusu and Matilda Asante. Apart from being Western Regional Correspondent for Joy FM for many years, I ended up working there physically in early 2007 after my days in London, before moving to Australia.

(On a sad note: while writing this chapter, I received the heartbreaking news of the passing of Elvis Kwashie in December 2021. Elvis was one of the editors at Joy FM and later became the General Manager for Joy brands).

I imagined the folks at Joy FM would have discovered that they had among them a crazy young man they imported from Skyy Power FM in Takoradi. Inevitably, Ato changed the culture in Joy FM newsroom in the way only he could.

Over time, Ato was given what was an ordinary slot on the Joy FM morning show to present newspaper headlines. The segment saves you from having to go to a news stand yourself to read fresh front-page headlines.

Ato-Kwamena Dadzie, however, turned the slot into a national theatre of comedy. Not only that, but he also offered a unique analysis that drew attention to important national issues. He did it by scolding and ridiculing everything and everyone, especially those in power.

He had a way of exposing a lack of common sense among those in power, persuading many listeners that the country has many idiots as leaders. He did this almost every morning, and, inevitably, he made more than a few enemies. The more enemies he made though, the more humorous and irritating he became.

When he roasts leaders on radio, it is accompanied by a distinctive laughter which carries the impression that he is a person wholly comfortable in his own skin, with not a care about the world or what someone thinks of him. It is an aspect of him that endears him to those who know him well. On the other hand, if you only knew him from a distance and also happened to be the butt of his jokes or uncharitable words, you feel pain that no strong pharmaceutical pain reliever can cure.

Ato eventually adopted the phrase, "Ghana's most irreverent journalist," and for many years wrote a blog online that attacked and ridiculed irresponsible leadership.

Prior to that, he wrote a stinging satire in Ben Ephson's *Daily Dispatch Newspaper* under the pseudonym J. A. Fukuor, a deliberate misspelling of the name of then president, John Kufour.

The sharp-shooting articles were revised and compiled into a book called *Pretending To Be President*, published in 2010. He trolled President Kufour relentlessly in his articles and made the president's supporters uncomfortable.

Ato-Kwamena Dadzie as a Professional Referee

Years after he left Skyy Power FM, another would-be journalist arrived at Skyy claiming to know Ato. The person brought along a resume which stated that Ato-Kwamena Dadzie agreed to be a referee. Ordinarily, I would hire anyone in a heartbeat if they got a recommendation from Ato. I looked through the application and other documents and could not see any sign of an employee with promise, so I called Ato for a private conversation.

Once I mentioned the applicant's name to Ato, he said, in his characteristically frank manner: "Don't employ that person, you will regret it." And being Ato, he said it with a good measure of disdain, adding, "this person can't write even one good news story."

That is all I needed to hear because I trusted Ato's professional judgment implicitly.

As I spent nearly two years researching and writing this book to tell stories like these, I got to the point where I started looking forward to getting the book published. Having interviewed almost one hundred individuals for the book, I felt it was worth telling it in all its glory, through the eyes of dozens of boys and girls who grew up to become men and women of substance.

I made an arrangement with my wife (a reasonably uncomfortable one) that in the event I don't live to see it published, my wife should contact Ato and hand over the entire manuscript, including all the original audio interviews, because I believe he is the only one I know from Skyy who could also tell the story in written form. That is how much regard I have for Ato, after all the years of working with him and getting to know him so well.

There are really no accurate words or phrases to describe Ato. Every attempt to describe him drives you into inaccuracy, but I will try anyway:

Ato is one of the most irritating and irreverent journalists Ghana has ever produced. He is also one of the funniest and friendliest people, and he has a volume of intelligence that is way too large, even for his big (and these days, bald) head.

The Diplomacy Barometer

In the context of our newsroom operations, I have been told by many people that I am harsh and direct on the job. I wanted to draw a sharp contrast that I believed existed between Ato and me in this area. I decided to use the example of one of our colleagues, Kwame Adu-Mante.

When I interviewed Adu-Mante, he told me that Ato is honest to a point where diplomacy for him is a nonexistent concept.

So I say to Ato, "Kwame Adu-Mante says you called him an empty coconut before showing him how to report on the year 2000 general elections."

I wait for his reply.

"Kwame Adu-Mante has stories to tell, some of which I don't remember," says Ato. "The way I live my life, I just say things off the cuff at the spur of the moment and I immediately forget. That is why I never think of anybody as an enemy because I just say what I think, and other people are free to tell me what they think and I just move on…" says Ato.

He continued: "I remember there were times I spoke to Kwame Adu-Mante harshly and I taught him a few things, but I have no recollection of the details. For me, if it is not a pleasant memory, I discard it. You can see I have a big head, but it doesn't mean I have unlimited memory space."

I was already laughing, but I still wanted the point to stick, so I say, "compared to you, I am a pretty shiny five-star diplomat."

"I agree," he says and disarms me rather easily.

He continues, "when you have something to tell someone, and you think it through and weigh the pros and cons about how the person will feel… that is the process that makes the conversation stick in your head. I don't do that. I just dive in and tell you what I have to tell and then get on with life. I don't care whether you are hurt or you are going to cry to your mother."

Taking a little time to calibrate more, Ato says, "regarding the things I hear Adu-Mante say, it is more likely, than not, that I said them."

Clearly, Ato chose his words carefully. He indicted himself but still left some room for escape in a humorous way.

A Fun and Lively Learning Environment

In many ways, the Skyy Power FM newsroom was like a perpetual classroom. We were always learning by talking, discussing every topic, and questioning everything. We read a lot of books and consulted the dictionary about once an hour.

Some of the books we cherished most were professional handbooks on journalism. One such book was the 1993 Edition of *BBC Producers' Guidelines*. I can't remember how we got that in our newsroom, but it was a fine guide for every journalist in the areas of accuracy, straight dealing in programs, impartiality, taste, decency, as well as conflicts of interest.

Another such book was *Writing Broadcast News - Shorter, Sharper, Stronger* written by veteran international journalist, critic, and trainer, Mervin Block. His book advocates fidelity to excellent broadcast news writing that is simple, short, sharp, and strong.

This was one of the books that helped us to always keep in mind that broadcast news stories should be meaningful, well grounded, relevant, informative, interesting, occasionally entertaining, most definitely factual, and properly attributed.

After years of not writing news for radio and television, I am sure I lost some of that *shorter, sharper,* and *stronger* writing skill. I found out while writing this book.

My wife Gabriella and our 10-year-old son Zion were my domestic editors for the first draft. Together, they would point to my recklessly long sentences.

Most of the ridiculous lines they deleted were those I wrote with ease. As Mervin Block would say, "The more you know about writing, the harder it is to write. The less you know, the easier it is."

The years we spent learning in the Skyy newsroom, in addition to reading good books, reminded us of just how much we didn't know.

Ato Tries to Stir Controversy

The most controversial thing anyone told me as I researched this book came from Ato-Kwamena Dadzie in answering a rather bland question I posed regarding the uniqueness of Sekondi-Takoradi. It was in the context that Skyy Power FM could happen only in that city.

"People in Sekondi-Takoradi are generally easy-going. What makes it so special?" I ask, hoping for some insight from a boy who grew up in the Twin City. "I think it should have something to do with the sea," he says almost boringly.

"Phillip, I think the sea has a way of humbling you. If you stand by the ocean, you know you are nothing. You are a speck. You are even smaller than a speck of sand in this huge universe."

It sounds philosophical and I pretty much agree with it, but still I expect more.

"Look, frankly, look at this country, right? Those people we say are boastful--I am not going to mention any tribe--but they don't have the sea. There is no sea near where they are, so they think the world belongs to them."

I feel awakened a bit at this point, trying to listen more attentively.

"When you wake up and you go and stand by the ocean and you hear how almost every week the sea has taken away a friend of yours, or some fisher folk went to the sea and didn't return but died on the high seas--I think it has a way of humbling you. With that humility also comes a sense that, well, let me look at the lighter side of life because anything can happen."

Again, deeply philosophical, and I continue listening.

"You are an Ewe, right?" Ato asks me.

"Yes," I say, with no idea where he is going with this.

"Have you ever seen an arrogant Ewe?" he asks.

I am caught off guard, because, all of a sudden, it dawns on me that Ato is about to draw a controversial and dangerous tribalistic contrast, so I am stern in my reprimand.

"Hey, hey, Ato--don't go there! Don't go there," I say, my voice revealing a seriousness that is almost equal to ordering a ceasefire during a heated battle.

There is a long-standing mutual respect between Ato and me. I have always felt that he respects my views. He is not a pushover in any way, but I have had a few occasions in which I gently and diplomatically re-adjusted him when he appears to be heading in a direction I think is unhelpful.

He feels quite comfortable with a level of controversy that I naturally shy away from, so I stand my ground and firmly push back. He laughs it off and, to my relief, ceases going in that direction.

In a professional setting, Ato and I, together with all the amazing men and women of Skyy Power FM in Takoradi formed a permanent bond of friendship. In the newsroom, we engaged in passionate discussions and arguments over many fine points in journalism.

Throughout our whole life, the one outstanding thing is that we never considered ourselves complete. We took our work seriously, but not ourselves, knowing we were, always and still, simply works-in-progress.

Mervin Block, one of my favourite authors, puts it best when he says, "If you ever consider yourself a finished product, you're finished."

So Ato-Kwamena Dadzie and I, together with all the great men and women we worked with are not yet finished. We are just starting off with a long road ahead of us. And a lot of stories and history behind us.

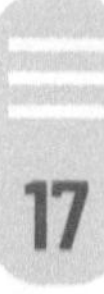

I Came to Skyy as a Greenhorn

"The kind of English, the level of English they were speaking terrified me. How can I go and compete with these ladies, especially Fynnba Derby?"
— *Aba Moses, one of the pioneers who started a career in radio at Skyy with no experience.*

On 6 October 1997, Uncle Opia, a broadcasting legend in Western and Central Regions, arrived at the home of Aba Moses. The day he came was also the day the new radio station commenced commercial broadcasting, having only just finished test transmission over the previous month.

Uncle Opia's mission was to get Aba Moses into the studio that morning for a live radio broadcast. But Aba Moses had no idea, and neither was she prepared. She was not expecting Uncle Opia's arrival, and she had never experienced what it is like to speak live on radio.

Opia arrived in a Skyy Power FM-branded minivan, and Aba Moses told him she was preparing to go out for an appointment.

"Change of plans," said Uncle Opia. "You are coming with me to Skyy. I have been looking for you for a while. We need to work today; get ready and let's go."

With some consternation, Aba Moses stepped into the minivan. Within the hour, Uncle Opia was going to put her live on air, but she had no idea.

Childhood Love for Radio

Aba Moses had a delightful and honeyed relationship with radio sets since she was a young girl. It started with her father's iconic *Sanyo Akasanoma* radio set.

Just a few decades ago, that radio set, proudly assembled in Ghana's industrial city of Tema, represented the full height of technology in Ghana. Each morning, Aba Moses had the responsibility of tuning the *Akasanoma* radio set to either BBC live from London or Ghana Broadcasting Corporation's GBC Radio 1 or Radio 2 from Accra. She enjoyed that little morning routine.

It took considerable skill for young Aba Moses to carefully rotate the dial and get the clearest possible signal through the old, constantly crackling short-wave frequency.

Every radio set evokes fond memories of her father as well as the absolute magic of being able to hear euphonic music and voices on a wireless set, broadcasting from up to thousands of miles away. Her love for radio became constant and permanent.

The Blessings of Harmattan

Harmattan is a weather condition that occurs annually all over Ghana and West Africa between November and February. It is characterized by cold, dry, and dusty winds, with a dramatic drop in humidity.

For some reason, the condition during this period allows FM radio frequency to travel much further. Some radio enthusiasts discovered that with extra-long antennas, they could pick up faint Joy FM signals in parts of Sekondi-Takoradi, especially at higher elevations. Joy FM was the first successful private and commercial radio station operating out of the national capital, Accra, and it was a station loved by many.

Aba Moses loved Joy FM. The signals from the station in Takoradi were never stable, and it was impractical to sustain any clear transmission.

Sometime in September 1997, Aba Moses engaged in an almost futile attempt to tune into Joy FM from Takoradi, only to be greeted by the clearest sound she had ever heard on radio.

What Aba Moses tuned into was the test transmission of Skyy Power 93.5 FM. The radio set she had at the time was analogue and didn't show the glorious digital information. She kept her dial there, fully mesmerised by what she was hearing.

Then she heard an assuring voice on the set.

"This is the test transmission of Skyy Power 93.5 FM," said the smooth, baritone voice.

It was the voice of Uncle Opia, instantly recognisable to Aba Moses. She was familiar with that voice from Uncle Opia's years on Twin City Radio as an employee of the public broadcaster, Ghana Broadcasting Corporation.

Uncle Opia was the finest thing that had ever happened to *Twin City Radio*. He was a much-loved broadcaster, an expert in the Fante language, exceedingly funny, unassuming, and approachable. He commanded respect and admiration like no other personality in the Western Region, and he represented the conscience of the city. He was also celebrated as the unofficial Mayor of Sekondi-Takoradi.

No one has ever entertained the thought of being better than Uncle Opia in what he does and how he does it. And now, this legend has crossed over from *Twin City Radio* to the all-new Skyy Power FM.

History with Uncle Opia

Even though Aba Moses had no particularly sterling skills to bring her into Uncle Opia's orbit, she remembers him assisting her to undertake some basic media marketing services when he was at *Twin City Radio*. That is how she got to know Uncle Opia face-to-face.

Somehow, she felt Uncle Opia would encourage her once more if she made a move to become part of the sensational new Skyy FM.

Apart from Uncle Opia, other voices featured during the Skyy FM test transmission included those of Michael Griffiths, Nana Fynnba Derby, Maame Esi Mark-Hansen, and Maame Efua DeGraft Aidoo.

The more Aba Moses listened to the Skyy Power FM test transmission, the more she loved it. And she was convinced the station was going to be one of the most progressive forces Sekondi-Takoradi had ever seen.

Her desire to be part of the new station also grew, but she would quickly tell herself the quality she heard was too far above her skills and abilities.

"The kind of English, the level of English that they were speaking, terrified me. It really terrified me. How can I go and compete with these ladies, especially Fynnba Derby?" says Aba Moses in reflection. And she adds, "I also remember Michael Griffiths' fine voice, saying, 'this is Skyy Power FM.'"

The Courage of a Woman

A battle continued to rage between Aba Moses' feelings of inadequacy and her great yearning to be part of this new sophisticated radio station.

In the middle of one of her many contemplations, an idea struck her, after which she went straight to the Sekondi Post Office and purchased stationery to write what her heart was telling her.

After about an hour standing on one of the counters at the Post Office, she finished writing an application for employment at Skyy Power FM.

She did not post the letter.

She took it straight to the Skyy Power FM premises at 37 Windy Ridge.

The Man in Boxer Shorts

"When I arrived at Skyy, I met a guy in boxer shorts--not knickers, but boxer shorts and a t-shirt," recalls Aba Moses.

"I greeted him and he responded very nicely and immediately said to me, 'I like your voice.'"

Meeting someone at the premises who immediately said, "I like your voice," was a comforting experience.

The only problem was the gentleman in the t-shirt and boxer shorts did not appear to be a person whose opinion would count for anything when a decision was to be made on whether or not Aba Moses could be employed.

The compliment was worth something, but not a whole lot, she thought. But she was very wrong.

"I heard about this station, so I have brought my application," said Aba Moses to the man in the boxer shorts.

"Are you sure?" asked the boxer shorts man.

"The man then started speaking in Fante, so I also switched from my rusted English to Fante," says Aba Moses.

In response, the man said in Fante, "hey, you have good control over the Fante language, I am happy. I am looking for such a voice, and this is what I need, so come!"

The man in shorts was Wilson Arthur, the co-owner and Chief Executive of Skyy Power FM.

The Unconventional Interview

Back at 37 Windy Ridge, the man who makes and approves most of the important decisions at Skyy--the man in a t-shirt and boxer shorts at that moment--ushered Aba Moses to the reception.

He asked Aba Moses to wait for Uncle Opia.

Uncle Opia was to be the one who would interview Aba Moses to determine her suitability as a presenter. Aba Moses waited and waited. And she waited some more, but Uncle Opia didn't show up.

So, Wilson, still in his boxer shorts, came back to Aba Moses with a task that constituted an effective interview.

Her application was written in English to request employment as a presenter in Fante language. Wilson brought back Aba Moses' application with additional sheets of paper and a pen to make a request.

"I am not sure when Uncle Opia will come, so I want you to translate your application letter from English to Fante," said Wilson.

At that instant, Aba Moses learned that it is not wise to judge a man's characteristics, position, or authority by his boxer shorts.

"To be frank, I am not good at writing Fante or translating something from English to Fante, but at that point, I found the courage and boldness to do it," recalls Aba Moses. She continues, "the man looked at my work and he was happy. The man could not read Fante himself, I could tell, but he was happy."

Shortly after, Uncle Opia came, read her application and the translation from English to Fante, and was pleased with Aba Moses.

She was told to go home and expect to be contacted.

Not Called, Not Forgotten

Aba Moses returned home, hoping that she would be called and offered the job. Days passed with no word from Skyy. The days turned into weeks, and then she knew it was over.

Satisfied that she had done her best, Aba Moses stopped thinking about Skyy and what could have been an adventure of a lifetime.

Then the dream walked right back into her home, in the form of Uncle Opia on the day Skyy started commercial operations.

Uncle Opia and Wilson Arthur had actually made up their minds to employ Aba Moses shortly after her interview, but they did not tell her. They also didn't have any clear plan in place to contact her.

Aba Moses' letter had only a post office box address, not her residential address. And she did not have a phone contact. Mobile phones at the time were new and expensive. Wilson Arthur and Uncle Opia were extremely busy, fully occupied in the weeks and days leading up to the start of commercial operations.

Everything was in a state of flux, made worse by the fact that up to 90% or more of Skyy FM broadcast was going to be in English. Somehow, there was some expectation that Aba Moses would come back by herself to find out whether she would be employed or not.

She never showed up and only half expected to be contacted by Skyy.

As Monday, 6 October 1997 approached, Uncle Opia started getting desperate to find Aba Moses. If he didn't find Aba Moses, then the entire Fante program would be run all by himself.

The Last Hour Dash

Just hours before the first Fante program went live on air, Uncle Opia remembered a snippet of the conversation with Aba Moses during her interview.

She had made a passing reference to the area in Sekondi where she lived. Armed with this minute recall, Uncle Opia went to the area and literally spoke to some of the residents, asking about "the fair lady who lives around here."

That is how he rediscovered Aba Moses. And that is how Aba Moses started to believe once more that you get what you want only when you keep trying.

A Step into the Deep End

As Aba Moses would soon learn, the persistence she needed to survive in radio is orders of magnitude more than the courage it took her to write an application for employment.

Despite being completely green, Aba Moses was the key person needed to start off the Fante language programs on Skyy.

Aba Moses didn't know she was considered that valuable as she stepped out of the minivan with Uncle Opia at the station. It was around 9:00 am on that day, only an hour before the first Fante program went live on air.

Uncle Opia took Aba Moses to the studio, and that is where Aba Moses' most agonising and excruciating experience in radio started.

"You Are The Most Important Person When You Speak"

"When he took me to the studio, he made me sit right in front of the microphone. And then he said, "Ewuraba [young lady], we are about to go live on air," recalls Aba Moses.

"I felt like I didn't even understand what he meant. And he continued by saying we are going to talk about the unhygienic conditions around the Sekondi-Takoradi metropolis."

"People are reckless in throwing rubbish everywhere, and it is about time we carried out public education to promote better environmental hygiene," Uncle Opia said, summarising the essence of the program.

And then, as he was about to open the microphone to introduce the program live on air, he told Aba Moses to prepare.

"It was only at this time that it occurred to me he was expecting me to speak on the subject as well. He could see that I was very nervous" says Aba Moses.

Uncle Opia opened the microphone and immediately turned it off, saying to Aba Moses, "young lady, I know your family name is Moses; now what is your first name, so I can introduce you properly?"

"I had to quickly think on my feet. Then I said that I am a Thursday born, so you can call me Aba - let's use Aba Moses, and then he promptly introduced me. Then he turned off the microphone, realising that I was overcome with fear," recalls Aba Moses.

Uncle Opia went into full inspirational mode, his personal version of the "I have a dream" speech that Aba Moses will never forget.

"Look, this is radio. This is an opportunity for you to excel. What I need from you is to be bold. You have the voice, you have control of the Fante language, and what I need from you now is to be confident. Do not be afraid that people are listening to you. When I open the microphone, you will be the most important person speaking, so relax and kill that fear."

Opia opened the microphone again, and all that Aba Moses recalls is that she was able to stumble through and deliver.

Maame Efua DeGraft Aidoo To the Rescue

A week after the heart-stopping experience, Uncle Opia fell sick and could not work for many days, so Aba Moses, who was still only getting used to speaking on air, had to present all the Fante programs, including reading the news and various announcements, without assistance.

"I arrived at work in the morning only to be told Uncle Opia is unwell, and I had to do everything. I nearly fainted," says Aba Moses.

Her first solo presentation, including the news, was a flop, after which she descended into something close to depression. It was all so easy for everyone to see, including Maame Efua DeGraft Aidoo, who was deeply empathetic.

"Maame Efua DeGraft Aidoo called and spoke to me privately. Even though she was so much younger than me, she was earnest and encouraging," recalls Aba Moses.

Maame Efua's pep talk was deep.

"Auntie Aba," she started. "I don't know your background but I can see that you are a good woman. You have a fantastic voice. Your command of the Fante language is just fantastic. I am not saying you are not educated. I know you can do this."

The encouragement helped Aba Moses to succeed in radio beyond her dreams.

Feeling Tipsy on Air

There is no known record that any presenter was ever discovered drunk while on air. But Aba Moses says at least on one occasion, she was sufficiently tipsy while sitting behind the console.

"I was interacting with listeners who were calling live on air, and my job was to promote Castle Milk stout." Castle Milk was a mildly alcoholic drink, about 7%.

As part of the promotion, Aba Moses would answer each phone call by shouting "Castle Milk stout," and the caller must respond, saying "seriously smooth."

Wilson Arthur was in the studio, supervising the promotion.

"Wilson brought six chilled castle milk stout bottles, and he encouraged me to drink a little bit with each call," says Aba Moses.

"During the program," Aba Moses continues, "Wilson asked me to read an announcement that turned out to be a joke. It was about a man who lost one shoe after running to catch a commercial vehicle that had been waiting too long for him to finish urinating by the roadside outside the city."

Telling the story in Fante, a language that is a delicate mixture of style and extreme humour, made it all the more amusing.

"As a result of being tipsy, and the story being humorous, I lost control completely and went into a fit of laughter. I was afraid Wilson would frown and urge me to control myself, but he made it worse by laughing even louder," recalls Aba Moses with mirth.

"Naa Adoley Thompson was laughing, Yuki also came and joined, and Ato Parry, too. I laughed on air continuously for several minutes. It was embarrassing, and I will never forget that day."

The episode is an example of how relaxed the work atmosphere was, despite the highly professional output on Skyy Power FM. Wilson Arthur, who was young with youthful tendencies, was like the director of a highly choreographed performance that people in Western and Central regions loved.

Paying Back Skyy With Philip Osei Bonsu

By the time Aba Moses moved on from Skyy, she had the confidence of the celebrated and legendary Yaa Asantewaa, a woman who, in 1900s, stood with a gun against the might of the British colonial masters in Ghana. Aba Moses achieved a high status in broadcasting that she never dreamt of.

Her next stop was *Spark Radio* in Dunkwa-on-Offin where she worked as Head of Programs. Aba Moses found a gem there called Philip Osei-Bonsu.

She describes him as "intelligent with a good radio voice, full of confidence."

"The first day I heard his voice on air, I called him, sat him down, and encouraged him to pursue a career in radio."

Osei-Bonsu was undertaking his national service in the Central Region, as an intern with *Spark Radio*.

"You are radio material. You are the kind of presenter Wilson Arthur needs at Skyy Power FM," Aba Moses told him.

Before Osei-Bonsu finished his national service, Aba Moses wrote a letter to Wilson Arthur, urging him to employ Osei-Bonsu, a boy who would go on to achieve glory in radio.

Later widely known simply as OB, Osei-Bonsu spent years at Skyy being completely retooled by Wilson Arthur. As of the writing of this book, Osei-Bonsu is the leading anchor for a political talk show on a radio station in Accra.

Unsurprisingly, Philip Osei-Bonsu has a chapter in this book. It is the result of Aba Moses feeling the need to pay back what she believes she owed to Uncle Opia, Skyy Power FM, Wilson Arthur, and many others who constitute an incredible tapestry of a radio station that could have been made only in Ghana's Sekondi-Takoradi.

Professor Nana Fynnba Derby

"I was in my final year at University of Cape Coast when I was approached to work for Skyy. Wilson Arthur and his brother Kennedy were the friendliest pair to work with. These guys were fun-loving and cracked lots of jokes. They could make you laugh all day."

— *Professor Fynnba Derby, the first host of the Jolly Breakfast Show at Skyy*

In 1994, the means to apply for the establishment of a private and commercial radio station did not exist in Ghana. Political firebrand Charles Wereko-Brobby submitted an application anyway. When the authorities did not respond after some time, he switched on his transmitter in December 1994 and called his station *Radio Eye*. Before the end of that December, authorities brought the experiment to a swift end.

Under pressure from ever-growing domestic and international calls to allow democracy to flourish along with private commercial radio, the government blinked, and in less than 12 months, Joy FM became the first private radio station to operate legally in Ghana's capital, Accra.

Doreen Andoh was among the early pioneers of the new radio station, and her name and voice became synonymous with Joy FM's flagship lunch time program called *Cosmopolitan Mix*.

By the middle of 1997, it was Sekondi-Takoradi's turn to experience its first independent radio station, envisioned by Wilson Arthur.

While Wilson was recruiting for Skyy Power FM, he thought about someone similar to Doreen Andoh to host the morning show.

After weeks of searching, Wilson Arthur and his brother, Kennedy, found Fynnba Derby. She was a university student in Cape Coast.

"I was in my final year at the University when I was approached by Wilson and asked to work for Skyy. They heard my voice on Atlantic FM (ATL), the campus radio where I had been volunteering as a presenter," recalls Fynnba Derby.

"It was a very good time to be approached with the offer. I was about to leave campus and try settling into the real world, which included getting a job, and so I was excited." She adds, "there was so much joy, and so much anticipation."

As part of the offer, Wilson Arthur said, "just let me know anything you need to help you make the transition from school to Takoradi."

Fynnba Derby responded immediately, asking, "would you help me transport my things from Cape Coast to Takoradi, please?"

Fynnba arrived in Takoradi, and for many weeks, she was part of the preparations leading to the launch of Skyy Power FM. In the process, she got to know many of the new presenters who were going to be her colleagues when operations started in the Windy Ridge suburb of Takoradi. Along with those colleagues, she also got to know Wilson Arthur and Kennedy even better.

"Wilson Arthur and his brother Kennedy were the friendliest pair to work with. These guys were fun-loving and cracked lots of jokes; they could make you laugh all day. It was fun to be with them," says Fynnba.

A Stint With the Public Broadcaster

Another station on which Wilson could have heard Fynnba Derby's voice was *Twin City Radio*, the state-owned Ghana Broadcasting Corporation (GBC) FM station in Sekondi-Takoradi. She was living in Accra when the station started test transmission in 1994. On hearing the news, she decided to go there and audition.

The determined young lady walked up to *Twin City Radio*, on the hill overlooking the Effia Nkwanta Regional Hospital. She had heard that the GBC outlet in Takoradi was starting to look like a boys' club because not a single lady had been auditioned for the English programs.

"It seemed they had completed their recruitment," says Fynnba Derby. That piece of news only strengthened her resolve to be the first and perhaps the only lady to be auditioned for English programs at *Twin City Radio.*

Up on the hill, Fynnba met Paa Kwesi Brew. Kwesi Brew was one of the big guns at the station. With zero fear, Fynnba Derby looked at Kwesi Brew straight in the face and said, "you were hiring people. I didn't know you were auditioning, but I am here to audition, if you don't mind."

The bravado worked.

That day, after some sort of audition, she went live on air with the boys, all six of them: Paa Kwesi Brew, Benji Kumassah, Eric Sampson, Jojo Graves-Woode, and Kwame Nsaidoo.

A Reputation Established

"As for Fynnba Derby, she is ready for Accra," said one of the top executives who visited Takoradi and heard Fynnba on air. He was referring to her talent, quality of voice, and work ethic.

The *suggestion* was that only the very best presenters were good enough to go on air in the national capital, Accra. Despite impressing some of the decision makers at GBC, the entrenched and suffocating bureaucracy meant she could not be formally employed.

When Fynnba heard that she was good material for Accra, she said "I was excited, I thought they were going to pay me." She laughs at this point, in reflection. "They did not pay me. I was a student at University of Cape Coast then, and was told GBC did not employ students," recalls Fynnba Derby.

Nevertheless, she spent many weekends, shuttling between Cape Coast and Takoradi to work at *Twin City Radio* as a volunteer, driven only by her love of radio.

Eventually, Skyy Power FM raised its shiny mast, and Wilson Arthur decided to employ her straight out of the university.

"When Twin City Radio heard that I was going to work for Skyy Power FM, they finally made me an offer as a presenter and producer," recalls Fynnba Derby.

The joyless memory of making weekend trips to work on a voluntary basis for a public broadcaster that was not in a hurry to employ her felt uninspiring. Despite the offer *Twin City Radio* made, Fynnba Derby turned it down. "It was too little, too late," says Fynnba.

"Skyy Power FM was starting. I thought it would be better for me to start with them and be entrenched. I knew I was going to do well at Western and Central Region's first private radio station," she says.

A Return to Academia

By the time I call to interview Fynnba Derby for this book, she has been a university professor in the United States for many years, living an academic life as far away from Skyy as possible.

Months into making history as the first host of Skyy Power FM's morning show, Fynnba returned to Cape Coast University as a teaching assistant. That was only the very first step on her trajectory to becoming a full professor of criminal justice at Virginia State University.

Before that, Fynnba Derby secured a Doctor of Philosophy and Master of Arts degrees in comparative sociology from FIorida International University in Miami. That was in addition to a Bachelor of Arts degree from University of Cape Coast, having taught advanced research methods, criminology and theories of crime, and contemporary criminal justice.

For two years between 2012 to 2014, Fynnba Derby served as President of the Virginia Social Science Association, Virginia's oldest association of academic disciplines.

In recognition of her academic work and achievement, she received a *McGraw Hill Distinguished Scholar Award* from the American Association of Behavioral and Social Sciences.

Fynnba Derby's Mark at Skyy Power FM

In the preparatory stages before Skyy started commercial broadcasting, Fynnba Derby recalls a memorable meeting with Wilson Arthur, when they were designing the breakfast show. They had agreed on the structure and the content of the daily weekday program. The one thing they could not settle on was the name for the program.

They thought about different names, but none seemed to take their fancy. Just when Wilson Arthur and Fynnba Derby seemed to have run out of ideas, she remembered a BBC World Service program called *A Jolly Good Show* presented by Dave Lee Travis. As soon as she remembered it, she felt a bolt of lightning go through her.

"How about we call our morning show the *Jolly Breakfast Show*?" she asked Wilson, a smile breaking across her lips, extending to the rest of her face.

The same smile reflected on Wilson's face.

"Yes?" said Wilson, as if he were asking a question. "Yes!" he said again, this time as a statement, feeling excited, as he repeated the name suggested by Fynnba Derby.

Wilson approved her choice of the name on the spot, followed by a muted celebration, the kind a mason would feel when he added the final brick to a designer wall under construction.

When the first morning show beamed out of Skyy Power FM studios, it was the voice of Nana Fynnba Derby making the exciting announcement:

"Good morning, Sekondi-Takoradi and Western Region. This is Skyy 93.5 FM. I am Nana Fynnba Derby, the host of your all-new Jolly Breakfast Show, live from 37 Windy Ridge. I am here with the entire team to serve you the jolliest breakfast show with the latest news, great music, and information…"

Fynnba recalls the talent and enthusiasm of other pioneering colleagues like Kwesi Fletcher, Root Eye, Michael Griffiths, JM Caesar, and KingB.

She singled out Root Eye, whom she remembers was already a star even before Skyy started. "Wilson kept telling us about Root Eye who appeared on a music album by Reggie Rockstone, so I was expecting a hugely built man," she says.

"He didn't look like the star we expected. When I met him, I was surprised, and all I said was 'is that him?'"

It wasn't long, though, before she discovered Root Eye's scintillating style on air.

"When Root Eye went on air, he was exciting and sweet, and like the rest of us, many people just fell in love with him. I remember he had a few nicknames, one of which was, the *Kingsbite man*," says Fynnba. Kingsbite is the name of a delightful milk chocolate, made in Ghana, and Root Eye chose to use the name for himself.

Despite her relatively short period at Skyy, Fynnba Derby left an indelible mark as the first host of the *Jolly Breakfast Show*. Many presenters have since hosted the *Jolly Breakfast Show* and would only now learn that it was originally Fynnba Derby's breakfast show.

"Perhaps I should find out the royalties I am owed," she says, jokingly, as she remembers the city where she used to speak to millions of people on a private radio station she helped to establish.

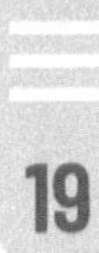

Godspeed, Olivia Esi Gyan

As a Skyy Power FM family, our hearts broke many times over before Esi Gyan was laid low into the gentle soil. The last time I spoke to Esi Gyan, she was in the United States receiving treatment, but she lost a fierce battle with cancer in March 2014. The rolling thunder of the sad news crushed each of us across the world.

A colleague who was living in Canada at the time, Ato-Kwamena Dadzie, called to tell me. It was a deeply painful conversation as we groped for comfort. Later, Ato wrote from the deepest part of his soul, saying, "Rest in perfect peace. God keep your sweet soul, Esi. Glad I got to tell you how much I loved you and I'd keep my promise."

Skyy Media released an official statement that said, "Esi Gyan, you will forever be remembered. Skyy Media Group is eternally grateful for your immense contribution in building the Western and Central Regions' most valuable media brand."

Professor Fynnba Derby of Virginia State University in the United States, a dear friend who also sought employment for Esi Gyan at Skyy Power FM, wrote a touching tribute for her funeral brochure.

Esi Gyan's husband, Daniel Adjei-Larbi, stricken with grief, together with their children, offered deeply moving tributes.

It was only a matter of time that Esi Gyan would be remembered in *Absolute Radio*, a book that celebrates the countless heroes and champions whose talent and hard work created a historic radio station in Ghana.

While writing this book, I reached out to Daniel Adjei-Larbi to let him know that his dear wife's name and memory would appear in this book.

Adjei-Larbi Joins the Skyy Family

Three years after Skyy started, Adjei-Larbi's work in the communications team at the Electricity Company of Ghana brought him to Takoradi. There, he became a close friend of the entire body of workers at Skyy, including Esi Gyan.

Esi Gyan was one of the pioneers of Skyy, working as our administrative manager at the time. Along with that role, she was also hosting a number of programs, reading announcements, and acting as a regular stand-in host for both English and Fante programs.

As Adjei-Larbi continued visiting Skyy regularly, he was smitten by Esi Gyan, and the two fell in love.

"I was on one particular program as a panelist, and Esi Gyan was the moderator. That is where we fell in love," he recalls. "I spoke to Wilson Arthur about my interest in Esi Gyan, and he encouraged me."

Esi Gyan became *Mrs. Olivia Esi Adjei-Larbi*, and their marriage was blessed with three beautiful children.

"You know, Esi Gyan was our sister at Skyy, and you became our brother-in-law," I said to Adjei-Larbi.

"I have always been part of Skyy," says Adjei Larbi in response.

I also ask him if he had something special he would like to say as his late wife's contribution to Skyy Power FM is acknowledged in *Absolute Radio*.

"Esi Gyan was part of the beginning in the humble days of Skyy. Skyy became a giant, and we cannot talk about the station's long journey without honouring those who planted the seed. Esi Gyan is one of those, so let me say thank you very much for remembering her in the book," says Adjei-Larbi with appreciation.

"Please Make Mention of Esi Gyan...my Sister"

As with many individuals mentioned in this book, Maame Esi Mark-Hansen had the chance to read the draft of the chapter that focused on her before it was published. Maame Esi, like many of us, was especially close to Esi Gyan, but Esi Gyan's name did not appear in the chapter that focused on Maame Esi Mark-Hansen.

As feedback, Mark-Hansen made only one request. "Please make mention of Esi Gyan, who was my sister," she wrote. Maame Esi wanted the memory of Esi Gyan to be preserved in *Absolute Radio*, because she was one of those who contributed to making history in the Western and Central Regions.

She could not possibly stand the thought about the possibility of Esi Gyan's name being air-brushed out of history, even if accidentally.

A Loss in the Family

We were all young when we met as employees of Skyy and became closer than friends. That is why Esi Gyan's death hit us all hard. It was a death in the family for which none of us were prepared. It was so personal to us all.

I was sitting behind the computer when I read Maame Esi Mark-Hansen's message, and then I turned to my wife Gabriella and my young son, Zion. They were my closest collaborators in putting this work together. They heard the original stories from me many times before they got written, and they have read through all the manuscripts and corrected many errors.

"We have feedback from Maame Esi-Mark-Hansen," I shouted across the home office.

"What did she say," asked Gabriella.

"She only requested one thing," I replied.

"What was her request?" she asked.

"She wants us to include Esi Gyan's name in the book because her name is not in the chapter that she read. I think she wants to be sure we don't forget Esi Gyan," I replied, matter of factly.

My words, rather than being just a fact, registered differently on my wife. She knew the story and the emotions it carried. She sighed and expressed admiration for the fact that Maame Esi Mark-Hansen so lovingly and thoughtfully requested the inclusion of our late colleague in the book. The raw emotion got to me at that point along with the painful memory.

I felt a huge writer's block and turned off the computer. My eyes felt wetter than normal.

So, to Maame Esi-Mark-Hansen and the entire Skyy Family:

This is the chapter our sister Esi Gyan deserves, marking a quarter of a century in which history was made in Ghana's Western and Central Regions through private radio.

Many Uncried Tears

"You and your children certainly continue to carry the burden of Esi Gyan's absence," I say to Adjei Larbi, recognising that *siblings* like us from Skyy would never know the deepest pain of losing a mother and wife.

Adjei-Larbi agrees, expressing thanks for the thought, while showing a remarkable fortitude in talking about his wife's memory.

By the time Esi Gyan passed, many of us were scattered around the world, from across Ghana to Europe, North America, and Australia.

"Those of us who didn't have the chance to attend the memorial for Esi Gyan never had a real closure," I say, hoping I am expressing the sentiments of my colleagues around the world. Again, Adjei-Larbi is magnanimous.

"I understand," he says.

Esi Gyan's Memory Lives On

In many different conversations with Adwoa Amofah at Skyy during the research stage of this book, she shares a simple, but exciting piece of news with me.

"You won't believe who just came to visit me," she says.

"Who? I ask.

"Dave. Do you remember Dave? Esi Gyan's son." she discloses.

"Wow," I say.

Moments later, she sends me a photo of Dave and herself. Dave is handsome, a gorgeous boy, who at 17 years towers above Adwoa Amofah. "I can see Esi Gyan's smile on his face," I write in a message back to Adwoa Amofah.

The photo of Dave and the signature smile bring back memories of Esi Gyan in real life. There is a particular photo of Esi Gyan used in her funeral brochure which reveals so much. It shows her with the broadest smile, the sort that precedes an infectious laughter that we all shared at Skyy.

That photo also holds an enchanting gaze with which Esi Gyan would look at me most kindly and ask, "how are you, Phillip?"

It is a gaze none of us at Skyy will ever forget.

It is in our collective memories and lives on in the lives of her precious children. Esi Gyan's life will remain a constant celebration through her beautiful children, years and years from now.

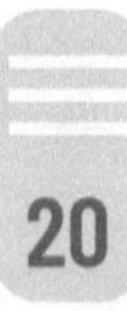

20

The Confidence of 17-Year-Old Yuki Ampofo

> *"The vibe in Takoradi was always big. We are funky, fun-loving and people loving, and people of Sekondi-Takoradi embraced Skyy Power. Skyy was like an extension of their own families. They welcomed the radio station and made it their own. That is what helped Skyy Power FM to succeed beyond our dreams."*
>
> — *Yuki Ampofo who joined Skyy Power FM at 17 years of age.*

The first encounter Yuki Ampofo had with Skyy Power FM was at Market Circle in Takoradi, the commercial nerve centre of the city. It is a very large roundabout within which a huge market was constructed, consisting of two-storey shops patronised by thousands of people daily.

It has occupied a special place in the lives of the people in the metropolis since its original construction nearly a century ago.

"I was at the Market Circle and came across this minibus with *Skyy Power FM* written on it," says Yuki, as she starts telling me her story. Yuki is referring to the old bright yellow and blue Skyy logo that clearly showed the name of the station with its frequency, 93.5 FM, emblazoned across the entire side and front of the van.

"I feel goosebumps on my skin as I visualise it," she adds, trying to describe the strong emotions she started feeling as I ask her to remember events that took place 25 years ago. "I don't know what came over me, but I was curious and approached the van to talk to the driver and the lone passenger," recalls Yuki.

Yuki, at 17 years old, had just completed Holy Child School in Cape Coast and returned home to Takoradi the previous week. It was the last half of 1997, and Skyy Power FM had just started test transmission. The new radio station's banners and other advertising material were all over the city, but Yuki was unaware. The one thing she was aware of was a strong urge to, as she puts it, "find a job, any job, to while away the time after completing secondary school."

Taking the Bull by the Horn

"You were so young, but so bold and confident in deciding to approach the minivan by yourself," I observe.

"I was alert to find a job, and I also believe in taking the bull by the horn," says Yuki in response. "The driver of the minibus was Sammy Arthur and the other person in the car was Kennedy Arthur, the older brother of Wilson Arthur," recalls Yuki.

Kennedy Arthur, a part owner of Skyy, was sitting in the passenger's seat of the minivan. He felt ambushed by the precocious teenager on the busy street where they had parked. Somehow, Kennedy Arthur had no choice but to answer questions posed in rapid fire by young Yuki.

"Who are you?"

"What kind of business are you doing?"

"When will you start?"

Yuki posed more questions after each answer, and when she finally understood Skyy was going to be the first private radio station in town, she made her own pitch.

"I just completed Holy Child School, and I am looking for a job. I would like to work for you," she said matter-of-factly.

Seeing the determination in the teenager's voice after fielding her questions, Kennedy Arthur was once more speechless. "Come to the office tomorrow, and my brother and I will interview you," said Kennedy Arthur, as he looked at the face of a young girl he would never forget for the rest of his life.

The job interview occurred the very next day, and Yuki Ampofo became one of the first employees of Skyy Power FM. She was hired to manage the new radio station's front desk at 37 Windy Ridge. She returned home and told her mother about being hired by the radio station. Her mother, justifiably, thought she was joking.

In Yuki's own words, her story at Skyy Power FM got only better from that day, and like the rest of Skyy Power FM's employees, it is a story with many lessons in life that she loves to tell.

The Opportunity of a Lifetime

A few years before I start writing this book, Yuki and I speak. She is on a business trip to Rwanda, representing a telecommunications company she worked for. Even back then, we could not resist talking about our shared experiences at Skyy. Now that I was formally interviewing Yuki and asking her to tell me her experience for posterity, she does not hold back.

"The time at Skyy was my first experience in the work environment. I learned how to use the computer at Skyy, and I learned how to manage the front desk. One of the things I remember Wilson for was that he imbibed in us the belief that each of us is a reflection of the company we worked for. Whether you were the driver, security man, or the administration officer, you were trained and empowered to sell whatever we had on offer," she says, adding, "Wilson effectively made everyone a salesperson at Skyy."

Yuki didn't stay as a front desk manager for long. She made speedy progress to become a permanent on-air staff member, demonstrating strong presentation skills and pure passion for the work.

"I presented our lunch time program called *Skyy Spicy Lunch* after Maame Efua DeGraft Aidoo left. Before that, I was doing many other on-air programs including *One-on-One* and the unique *Coast-to-Coast* program, apart from reading announcements daily. I also helped in the newsroom for some time."

Yuki says she observed that a lot of effort went into creating quality entertainment, especially for the regular outdoor programs that featured live band music. "We provided the platform for many artistes to perform throughout the city on a regular basis. Apart from that, even playing music in the studio on CDs was like an artwork."

"Wilson Arthur would often check to see our *music flow*. The *flow*, as he called it, is the arrangement of music to achieve specific tempo and rhythms to make listening a pleasure," recalls Yuki.

"Looking back, Skyy was an opportunity of a lifetime for many of us, and it helped us to value competence and excellence," says Yuki.

Old friends Meet at Skyy

"There were just a few people at Skyy when I joined. I didn't think I would know anyone there, but then I ran into Naa Adoley Thompson whom I knew from primary school."

"Later," says Yuki, "we were joined by Angela Oppong. Angela was my mate at Chapel Hill School". We lived five minutes from each other's homes. We grew up together and went to Holy Child College together in Cape Coast."

When Angela Oppong joined Skyy, she worked primarily in the newsroom and established a reputation as an effective news presenter.

Yuki remembers that much of the training was on the job and informal, but it was effective and produced excellent results. She says, "you couldn't be a loose fit or the weak link at Skyy. Everyone pulled together in the same direction, and you knew that your personal role did matter at work, and I learned that from Skyy."

"I learned how to be humble, to climb up the ladder from scratch and be able to run a show or host a program."

"We Were so Young, But Mature"

"You were one of the youngest, and yet, your output was first class. How did you do it?" I ask Yuki, trying to get more out of her. She responds with enthusiasm.

"I think that our background and upbringing also played a role. We came from homes that instilled in us discipline and passion, as well as respect for authority," she says.

"We had a good foundation from home. My Mum of blessed memory; I miss her every day. Mummy gave me the best training and propelled me for the life that I am living now. I believe that when you come from a background where you have been trained and made ready, there is nothing that is too difficult for you. If you come from a home where discipline is the order of the day, you will fit into any kind of environment or work situation."

She reflects on this more, adding: "after all, you have to listen to and obey instructions, and if you are not used to that from home, it would be difficult for you. Within our culture, when people notice you are unable to accept discipline, they tend to wonder if you have had assistance from any responsible adult at home."

Looking back, it is easy to see that Yuki had a trajectory that was so well set for success. Apart from that, she exhibited a level of maturity and empathy well beyond her years, especially in the way she treated children who featured on the *Skyy Kiddie Show* every Saturday.

"Wilson Aurthur would always ask us to prepare our flow. That means, to put the music together from beginning to end, building a specific rhythm and tempo that moves one track smoothly into another. Because of that experience, even now in my adult life when I listen to music in the car or at a party, or on radio, I can tell if the DJ is well trained or not."

"Because of my work at Skyy, I started higher education a few years late, but the advantage was that I entered university a mature, thinking human being. It made life easier for me to navigate," reflects Yuki.

"There was Never a Dull Moment"

"More than just a business, Skyy was a family," says Yuki.

"In the first two years, I didn't take any leave and never had a day off. I worked every day, including Saturdays and Sundays. Even on Christmas and New Year's day, I might spend a bit of time at home and then end up coming to the studio. We all just loved working there and being in the company of each other."

"The vibe in Takoradi is always big. We are funky, fun-loving and people loving, and people of Sekondi-Takoradi embraced Skyy Power. They gave us 100% of their support," says Yuki.

"For the people in Sekondi-Takoradi, Skyy was like an extension of their own families. We were a household name, and we were part of their lives. They welcomed the radio station and made it their own. That is what helped Skyy Power FM to succeed beyond our dreams."

Yuki also reflects on the close relationships formed at Skyy. "We did everything together," she says. "If I got invited somewhere, you can be rest assured that I am going with the guys at Skyy, whether it was a wedding or a party or anything else. We looked out for each other, and we relied completely on each other. We were committed to ensure each one of us succeeded."

"The experience we had at Skyy was lively, healthy and memorable, and I will always be grateful that I was part of that story," says Yuki Ampofo.

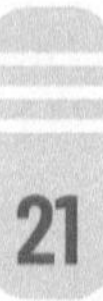

21

The Eloquent Emmanuel Sackey

"I learned that what a person says matters a lot because on radio, people listened and took you seriously. It helped me develop my self-esteem and confidence. I am very grateful for the opportunities at Skyy that shaped my thoughts, perspectives, and ideas about life."

— *Emmanuel Kodwo Sackey, who joined Skyy Children's program at 14 years of age*

I am ten years older than Emmanuel Kodwo Sackey, but on the day we met at the studios of Skyy Power FM, we struck up a friendship that continues to grow.

"When did we first meet?" I ask Emmanuel Sackey, a boy I have known for about 25 years as a result of my work with Skyy. True to form, Emmanuel Sackey has an answer that only he could produce.

"I met you first," he says, and I am a little confused, so I listen more attentively for clarification.

"I met you first, and by that I mean I met your voice. You had this baritone voice. It was always on-air during prime time news in Takoradi back in the day. The jingle was played before the news, and you would go like, '*this is Skyy Power News and my name is Phillip Nyakpo.*' So, to a large extent, I met you first. We were all in awe at the voice and the poise with which you read the news."

I take a deep breath after hearing Emmanuel. His words remind me of the power of radio and the overwhelming support Skyy Power FM received in Sekondi-Takoradi and the Western Region. As a journalist and news anchor that was on air every day, I was a beneficiary of the enormous goodwill, even in the eyes of a young teenager like Emmanuel.

So long lasting is the goodwill that after a quarter of a century, the now full-grown man in Emmanuel recalls the memory he formed with remarkable clarity. As a precocious teenager, Emmanuel himself, always in tip top form, became a star on radio as a panel member of *Skyy Kiddie Time*.

A Visit, Followed by a Debate

Shortly after Skyy started, several schools around the metropolis were given the chance to visit the station on excursions. During those visits, selected students would be asked to participate in *Skyy Kiddie Time*. When it was the turn of Ridge International School for the excursion, Emmanuel was one of the smart kids who was selected to participate.

"As part of the kids' program, Skyy organised a debate between my school, Ridge International and Chapel Hill School. I faced off with Kojo Ntow, a brilliant chap from Chapel Hill school who now works for the Ministry of Foreign Affairs in Ghana," recalls Emmanuel.

Naa Adoley Thompson, who was the host of the children's program, moderated the debate. "We were on radio for the first time in my life, and I had a good time," says Emmanuel.

Naa Adoley Thompson, thoroughly impressed with Emmanuel's performance, asked him to join *Skyy Kiddie Time* the following weekend, after which he got a permanent role on the weekly children's program.

During one of the rather hot debates during the program, I entered the studio with a script to read the news. I listened to Emmanuel speak eloquently before I presented the news. I was so impressed and moved by his cogent argument and good choice of words that I stared at him and asked: "Emmanuel, are you a child or an adult?" Everyone in the studio laughed.

At the end of the children's program that day, Emmanuel and I talked some more. We found out we lived close to each other at the Airport Ridge suburb in Takoradi, and our lifelong friendship commenced. Emmanuel was only fourteen at the time, and I was twenty-four.

Not Friends, But Brothers

"Fourteen is very young," I tell Emmanuel during the interview, as I reflected on the past. "How did a friendship between a fourteen-year-old boy and a twenty-four-year-old man happen?"

Again, it is vintage Emmanuel with an answer.

"I think that, firstly, you were very humble, Phillip, and you were engaging and affable. You took an interest in me and you would talk about things that my daddy would talk to me about," he says. Somehow, I felt like I wanted to meet the twenty-four-year-old man Emmanuel was talking about because I never thought about myself in the way he described.

"I think I was more comfortable talking to you about things and our conversations were very nice," says Emmanuel. "You encouraged me to learn, you encouraged me to stay focused, and you encouraged me not to be moved by fame. So, it was more like I found a big brother in you, or maybe you found a little brother in me. I think the fact that we also stayed in the same neighbourhood was helpful. We called our relationship a friendship, but it felt more like we were brothers. I didn't have an older brother, so it came naturally that I looked up to you in a lot of ways. You would often correct my English and suggest new words to use, and I am sure you've forgotten all that."

I am moved by Emmanuel's generosity as he recalls the quality of our friendship.

"I am listening to you right now, and I am thinking, *that is a nice story*, but when I was having those interactions with you, I don't think I was keeping it in my active memory to recall later," I say. I continue by telling Emmanuel my best recollections of our friendship.

"I was taken in more by just how intelligent and well behaved you were. I felt you held a promise and I felt you were highly conscious for a fourteen-year-old boy. I remember being able to have a conversation with you, so I recognised what you were, what you represented, more than what I was putting into you. Let's say, I saw your output, but I didn't see my input at all."

These were my true feelings, both then and now, but Emmanuel is not taking it easy on me.

"Well, that is how humble you are, Phillip," he says.

I believe most of what Emmanuel says, but my real perspective is that I counted it as a privilege to know and become friends with a young man who was so switched on in his thinking, attitude, and aspirations. I was compelled to simply add a little bit of fuel to his drive, the way numerous people have done for me in my life's journey.

Emmanuel used to work for the Danish Embassy in Accra as Senior Advisor for Private Sector Development. He is now the Head of Operations, Programs, and Partnerships for a development finance institution with a focus on providing access to finance for renewable energy and agriculture projects.

We certainly had a high-quality friendship that has proved to be even more valuable with the passage of time.

"It's true, we were like brothers, Emmanuel, but these days, with everything you have achieved, I feel like you are my big brother," I tease.

"If you ended up becoming a good-for-nothing fellow, I would have been very disappointed because as far as I could see, you were already something and you only needed to take the journey to permanently establish your value in life."

Voices of the Future

As a practicing journalist at Skyy, I was having constant confidential, off-the-record, and deep background conversations with senior public servants, lawyers, politicians, and business leaders. After those interactions, I would often sit or walk with young Emmanuel and have an equally scintillating conversation with a teenager who was clearly wiser than his years. That level of wisdom and brilliance is what Emmanuel and the rest of his friends brought to the weekly children's program.

Skyy Kiddie Time became my favourite program on Skyy because of the purity of the children's contribution, compared to the aggressive contributions on news and current affairs programs, much of which I managed.

The children didn't just sound innocent, sweet, and intelligent, they also radiated hope for their generation. By every measure, their supervised contributions on-air signaled that they were the authentic voices of the future.

Apart from this, my colleagues, Naa Adoley Thompson and Yuki Ampofo who hosted the program, also made it appealing. They would sometimes ask for my view on topics which the children could debate on-air.

Our Chief Executive, Wilson Arthur, also took keen interest, and it was the one program in which controversy, if ever there was any, was minimal. Nelly Lomotey, another teenager who was a panelist on the children's program, actually graduated to become a full-time employee of Skyy, as well as a permanent host of *Skyy Kiddie Time*.

"A Defining Moment in My Life"

"What are some of your vivid memories of the program?" I ask Emmanuel, trying to elicit some of the memories I would have missed. Without missing a beat, Emmanuel launches into a song that has always been associated with the children's program.

"Hakuna Matata; what a wonderful phrase!" he sings.

"That was the signature tune of the program!" I exclaim.

He ignores my excitement and sings some more: "It's our problem-free philosophy, Hakuna Matata!"

The song, one of the most popular in the 1994 Walt Disney animation film *The Lion King*, included the Swahili phrase, "*Hakuna Matata*," which means "no worries." We didn't know it at the time, but we were nevertheless moved by the power of that composition which always signaled the start of the children's program.

After singing happily, Emmanuel says, "being on Skyy was one of the defining moments of my life. I enjoyed the fact that I could share my views, that my voice mattered, and the fact that I had an opinion and people were willing and ready to listen. It helped influence most of the things I moved on to do and achieve in my life. I became more interested in reading, research, and engaging with people. I owe it to the exposure and the experience that was afforded me at Skyy Power FM."

"Sometimes, our debates on air got so heated that even adults would call in on the phone," recalls Emmanuel. "Often, Naa Adoley Thompson would remind them that we were just kids on radio, but the callers would say, 'but they don't talk like kids--they hold the discussions like adults.'"

Emmanuel tells me that the end of the children's program was sometimes just the beginning of a new discovery. "The magical moment for me was when we would go into the city after our show, and you would hear people talking about our program and having their own discussions and arguments about how we handled a topic on the radio. I even heard people say, 'that Emmanuel Sackey talks like an adult. Maybe he is an adult with a child's voice'. Those were the moments when I realised, wow, this is bigger than me, this is bigger than us, because our discussions lit up a debate in the public square."

"How was life for you in school after you became well-known through the radio program?" I ask Emmanuel.

"Back in school at Ridge International," he says, "there were two teachers who took keen interest in our radio show: Mr. William Oppong and Mr. Norman. During classes on Mondays, they would sometimes ask: 'who listened to *Skyy Kiddie Time* over the weekend, and what is your take on the debate Emmanuel and his friends had on radio?' That was very humbling and encouraging for me," says Emmanuel.

Outside school, he recalls that there were other activities involving Skyy in which he participated.

"We used to have street carnivals and football matches, and during that time, I would be among the stars walking with you, Naa Adoley Thompson, Root Eye, and JM Caesar. People would notice and point at me and say, 'aha, that is the small boy on the children's program.' All these are beautiful memories for me," he reflects.

Going even further, Emmanuel says, "I learned that what a person says matters a lot because on radio; people listened and took you seriously. It helped me develop my self-esteem and confidence. When

I went on to Presbyterian Boys School later in Legon, I became a member of the Editorial Board. Then in 2001, I won the International Poet of Merit award and traveled to Washington, DC, in the United States for the award. I look back and I am very grateful and feel very blessed for the opportunities that shaped my thoughts, perspectives, and ideas about life."

More than Just a Business Venture

"I am grateful and thankful that Wilson Arthur and his wife Adwoa Amofah, as well as his brother Kennedy Arthur, got together to build Skyy," says Emmanuel, adding, "the enterprise may have been a business venture, but it served a purpose way beyond that for the fact that it positively affected the lives of many people and I am just one of those."

"I can trace some of the most valuable lessons and traits I developed over the years to that business venture they started. Those were beautiful moments, Phillip," says Emmanuel, his voice filled with gratitude.

I agree with him and add my own perspective.

"Sometimes, we remember little and forget so much. That is why I felt strongly that a conversation such as this would help us preserve some of the memories in a special way."

I tell Emmanuel that if I get the time to write the book, the conversation we are having in audio will be published afterwards as part of the good memories worth keeping.

"We had to go to very faraway places in our memories; from our beautiful past, to bring it out," adds Emmanuel.

Among his last words at the end of the interview, Emmanuel says, "it is really good that you are doing this, Phillip, because it has brought back many happy memories."

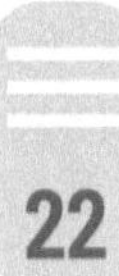

22

Skyy Power FM Was a Madhouse

"We didn't have time for formalities. We argued at the kitchen, on stairs, upstairs and downstairs, at the carpark and wherever we saw each other and decisions were made quickly. It is as if Wilson Arthur roamed the country to find and hire all the craziest people he could find. Oh, Skyy, what a madhouse! Somehow, it worked, and we all became like a family with close friendships for life."
— *Elloeny Amande who joined Skyy and distinguished himself in the sports department.*

"So, what work do you do these days?" I ask Elloeny Amande after we have been speaking for a while. I worked closely with Elloeny at Skyy from 1998.

In answering the question, he says he has his hands in a few things and then adds, "I also work as chief executive of Karela United Football Club."

"Chief Executive of what?" I ask, totally surprised. In a split second, I feel like Elloeny is speaking a language I have not heard before. I knew football was his passion, but I didn't think the lanky boy I knew would go as far as becoming the top executive for a major football club. I had also never heard of the name of the club he mentions.

Elloeny senses both my ignorance and incredulity, so he explains it all to me as gently as possible. "Karela United Football Club is one of the teams in Ghana's premier league, and I was appointed as chief executive in 2019. If you check the Ghana premier league today, you will see that Karela United FC is on top of the league," he adds.

I call Elloeny on 6 March 2021, which incidentally marks the 64th anniversary of Ghana's independence. The team, relatively new, was founded in 2013, long after I left Ghana. I check the league table online that day, and sure enough, Elloeny Amande's club is right at the top of the league table.

The discovery is symbolic and illustrative of the extensive changes that had occurred since our days at Skyy, when Elloeny worked in the newsroom and as a sports presenter. I have been away from Ghana for more than a decade and a half and progressively lost touch with events. Even though I have visited Ghana multiple times over the years, the more time passed, the less I knew about developments. Within that time, Elloeny became a well-known national TV sports presenter, studied to become a lawyer, as well as worked as a marketing professional firmly rooted in his passion for football.

The Teenager Makes an Appearance

Elloeny Amande came to Skyy at seventeen years old. Most of us were at least a few years older than him, so we protected and cared for him like a younger sibling.

In a separate interview, one of our colleagues, JM Caesar, reminds me that Elloeny came of age at Skyy and tasted his first alcohol in our company. The point of the story, though, is that Elloeny took the drink without realising it was alcoholic. We were out in the city eating at a restaurant. The drink, called *punch*, actually tastes like fruit juice, so Elloeny had his fill.

Shortly afterwards, we noticed the young man started speaking with more than his usual enthusiasm and then, slowly, logic evaporated from his sentences. When we realised what had happened, we took him home to his parents and explained the situation.

Elloeny survived, and since then, he has maintained a healthy fear of any liquid in a bottle, apart from water.

Creating His Own Chance

Elloeny joined Skyy through his own efforts, just a year into its operations. "I had just finished senior secondary school and started listening to Skyy. The power and influence of the station was sweeping the entire community, and I always told myself I wanted to be part of this," says Elloeny.

"I started to imagine myself talking on the radio and telling myself I can do this." Around this period of daydreams, Elloeny's family moved to the Airport Ridge suburb of Takoradi. "We lived close to the headmistress of the school attended by children whose parents owned Skyy Power FM, that's Wilson Arthur and his wife Adwoa Amofah," he says.

Through many different conversations, Elloeny convinced the headmistress to recommend him to Wilson and his wife for employment at the station. That is how he got an interview with the chief executive.

"You know Wilson Arthur is quite unconventional in his ways, so he interviewed me and then hired me on the spot," recalls Elloeny, still brimming with the decades-old echo of excitement.

"You can imagine my excitement," he says. "I went home and told all my friends and family. I told everyone. I was so excited, and then I started working with Skyy."

"I met you, Ato-Kwamena Dadzie, JM Caesar, Yaw Korankye, Kojo Frempong, and all these stars on Skyy. I was in a dreamland," he says.

"I came to the newsroom to learn how to write news stories, and I learned a lot, especially in the newsroom."

I remember just how fresh and green Elloeny was when he arrived. It fell to my colleagues and me to turn this teenager into a young reporter and teach him to develop a sharp nose for news and empower him to write with confidence and meaning. Our work was made easier by the fact that Elloeny was a quick learner.

Nonetheless, the newsroom was always a place of tension as we worked under pressure to deliver trustworthy news each day.

"What a Madhouse!"

As I think of asking Elloeny to share his memories of the newsroom, he drops a small bomb. "By the way, Phillip, you can be a snorty bastard sometimes in the newsroom." He laughs as he says this, adding, "I am sorry."

"Thank you," I respond without taking any offence, even as he continues laughing, a stream of memories of the craziness of the newsroom no doubt running through our minds.

"It was crazy in the newsroom, but it was good because it was part of a learning culture. You guys had a very high standard, you and Ato-Kwamena Dadzie. You had a very high standard."

"I remember you banned staff of the newsroom from fraternising with other Skyy employees while you were preparing the news bulletin. Dorothy Ward and Keziah Morgan, who are always nice and chatty, would get into trouble with you, Ato, and Mr. Mould if they are seen loitering or chatting with the other employees before the news is prepared."

At this point, it's as if the floodgates of Elloeny's memory open.

"I really, really, really liked my experience at Skyy. There was never a dull moment. Oh, what a madhouse, Skyy Power FM!"

"There was this underlying craziness. No matter how cool and collected you were, once you became part of that group, then you started showing your crazy side. I don't know if Wilson deliberately set out to recruit people of this sort. Even Yaw Korankye, who was very calm, discovered his crazy nature."

"You are right about Yaw Korankye," I say to Elloeny. "Yaw could have been a monk, and a good one as well, but the Skyy environment changed him, and he became worse than many others in teasing and making trouble for everyone."

"We had a very informal structure, so we held discussions and argued everywhere around the building to reach consensus on every issue. We argued in the kitchen, on the stairs, upstairs and downstairs, at the carpark, and wherever we saw each other, and decisions were made quickly. It is as if Wilson Arthur roamed the country to find and hire all the craziest people he could find. Oh, Skyy, what a madhouse! Somehow, it worked, and we all became like a family with close friendships for life," recalls Elloeny.

How the Journey with Sports Kicked Off

The most solid reputation Elloeny developed at Skyy was that he was an astute and passionate sports presenter together with Kojo Frempong.

"How did all that come about?" I ask.

"The irony was that I had not contemplated becoming a sports presenter. I wanted to be part of Skyy just to have the chance to speak on radio, but then Wilson insisted on putting me in the sports team."

"I grew up in an environment dominated by sports. In fact, Augustine Ahinful, a player in the Ghana national soccer team, used to live in the same storey building where I lived in the Takoradi suburb called Number 3. The influence was strong, so like most Ghanaian boys, I was crazy about sports, especially football. Wilson asked me which football team I supported, and I told him I supported Hasaacas, Kumasi Asante Kotoko, and Manchester United, and that was it," recalls Elloeny.

"I started working directly with Yaw Korankye and Kojo Frempong, who took the lead in the sports department. What we know today, as the Internet was new at the time, and we spent a lot of time reading about sports information around the world."

"The thing about sports is once you get into it and follow the endless stories from the dozens of teams, it consumes you. You find that you can't wait to see the next match your favourite team will play, and when they play, you are glued for hours. And then you start going beyond that to wanting to know everything about the personal lives of the players. All of a sudden, your whole life is dominated by sports, and that is what I experienced at Skyy, especially as a sports presenter who had to get the news first."

How to Nurse a Homegrown Trouble

Kuntu Blankson was part of the sports unit, and Elloeny says, "he was a good complement to our team because, whereas the rest of us had a strong bias for mostly the big stories on the domestic and international front, Kuntu was down to earth with details of developments on the local sports scene. Nothing happens on the local sports scene in the Western Region that he didn't know about. He had contacts with all the players, coaches, and administrators."

I know Wilson Arthur himself is also crazy about sports, and in the early days of Skyy, he accepted a role as part of the management of Sekondi Eleven Wise Football Club.

"That decision brought us some troubles, because Eleven Wise and Sekondi Hasaacas Football Club had a huge rivalry," says Elloeny.

"The intensity of that local rivalry is equal to what you see between Manchester United and Liverpool football clubs. The tension was bound to occur because Skyy, the most influential media house which was supposed to be independent and objective, now had its owner and chief executive in a management position with Eleven Wise football club," observes Elloeny.

"Kuntu was forthright in telling Wilson that it was a bad idea, but Wilson had made up his mind. Hasaacas was in the premier league at the time and Sekondi Eleven Wise were in the first division, so it was easy to see we were going to run into problems."

"Sure enough, we started having issues with Hasaacas supporters. They were hostile to us on many occasions when we went to cover their matches."

Because of Wilson Arthur's role, Skyy Power FM could not credibly escape constant accusations of taking sides with Eleven Wise against the interests of Hasaacas Football club.

Predictably, Wilson's foray into management with Eleven Wise didn't last, but his passion for football became even stronger. Years later, Wilson acquired his own football club based in Daboase, near Takoradi. Unsurprisingly, he named the club Skyy FC.

Complications that arose after Wilson Arthur decided to serve as a member of management for Sekondi Eleven Wise were a lot of drama. Looking back, Elloeny says, "it was good drama. I learned many lessons from those experiences that I am using now as chief executive of a premier league football club. I have an appreciation of the relationship between football clubs and their supporters, as well as the passion they show."

The National Reconciliation Commission Hearings

As part of our work in the newsroom, Elloeny and I worked closely together in reporting proceedings of the National Reconciliation Commission which started in 2002.

The Commission was established by the Parliament of Ghana to address abuses of human rights across the country for a multi-decade period from 1957 to 1993. That period was punctuated by military interventions in government and state institutions resulting in significant abuse of human rights, including some extra-judicial killings.

I was not prepared for Elloeny's reaction after I ask him about his memories in connection with that ground-breaking coverage.

"That experience was traumatic. You guys should not have let me cover that event," he says.

"I was not prepared to hear the cruelty of men against their fellow human beings. The deprivations, beatings, humiliations, and the killings. I remember particularly the stories of people who came and talked about how their father, mother, or relative was killed..."

"I was young, and I used to sit there hearing all these stories. I cried many times during the session. I remember Professor Henrietta Mensah-Bonsu and Archbishop Charles Palmer Buckle. The two of them who were part of the proceedings were always empathetic. They would hand out tissues and tell people to take their time and call for breaks. I used to wonder how the atrocities came about because these were Ghanaians against Ghanaians, the same people, people who grew up in the same community. Some of the victims actually knew the perpetrators and lived in the same neighbourhood with them. I used to cry; I used to cry during the hearing," Elloeny emphasises, his voice cracking with emotion.

Around the time of the hearings, I interviewed the Executive Secretary of the Commission, Professor Kenneth Attafuah in Cape Coast. He told me that the essence of the Commission's work was "to come to terms with the pains of the past and heal the wounds of many."

As Elloeny reflects on it all, he says, "I guess that whole exercise was important. From a personal point of view, it gave me a certain perspective on life. It built up a high level of empathy in me."

Elloeny's memory reminds me of a TV interview I did around the same time with Kwabena Agyepong, the son of a murdered High Court judge.

Kwabena Agyepong's father, Mr. Justice Kwadwo Agyei Agyepong, together with two other judges, Fred Poku Sarkodee and Cecilia Koranteng-Addow, were abducted and killed near Accra in 1983. Major Acquah, a retired military officer, was also killed at the same time.

At the time I interviewed Kwabena Agyepong, he was serving as the presidential spokesman for the then-Head of State, President John Kufour.

Kwabena had survived the pain of living without his father to become a successful individual; but as I carried out the intimate interview with him, I could see in his eyes the heavy remnant of the pain. It was evident in his voice as well.

Stories such as Kwabena Agyepong's were the ones young Elloeny Amande was exposed to without any psychological readiness as part of his responsibility at Skyy Power FM.

I am only a few years older than Elloeny, but as the news editor at the time, I can now look back and realise I had a responsibility to protect him from that raw exposure. It was a responsibility that I was not experienced enough myself to know at the time.

It took me almost twenty years to find out the effect it had on young Elloeny as he relates and re-lives the memory. I am only a little comforted that the project to research and write this book inadvertently provides the chance for Elloeny and I to reflect on it.

"I am sorry to know that the exercise and our close coverage had such a heavy impact on you," I say to Elloeny.

I add more, saying "you are an intelligent and sensitive person, and I am glad, as you said, that the experience, although painful, helped you to develop your personal ability to empathise with others."

As I reflect a bit more, I can't help but think that each of us is likely a complex collection of a billion pieces of memories, both good and bad and somewhere in-between.

A Look at the Legacy

The enduring memory of Elloeny's years with Skyy Power FM is the legacy he helped the station to establish. "Whenever I tune in to the many radio stations in Takoradi and hear their broadcasts, I feel that they all have Skyy to thank for being the trailblazer," he says.

Singling out *News Review*, a current-affairs talk show I hosted on Sundays, Elloeny says one of the panelists, Tony Osei-Gyasi, made a huge impact on his young mind.

I agree with Elloeny's assessment of Tony Osei-Gyasi. Tony possesses one of the sharpest minds I have ever known. He read so widely and became so informed that it seemed there was no subject he couldn't deal with. He is firmly grounded in history with a clear understanding of current affairs and how it shapes the future. Tony, as a panelist, deeply resented the political culture that manipulated people with hollow promises that are recycled every four years to keep politicians in office or bring new ones who are just as incompetent, ineffective, and selfish.

"Tony's contribution in analysing politics, economics, and the Ghanaian society in general, all enabled by the incisive questions, was scintillating," says Elloeny.

He compared *News Review* to *Front Page*, a popular talk show on Joy FM in Accra which used to be hosted by renowned broadcast journalist, Kwaku Sakyi-Addo. "I enjoyed News Review more than the *Front Page* program on Joy FM," he declares, adding, "you guys were the best."

The other weekly contribution on *News Review* which deeply moved people came from retired army captain Joel Sowu.

Captain Sowu, who had a front row seat on Ghana's history, accumulated a lot of knowledge, experience, and well-informed opinions on national issues, which he dished out generously within the context of a well moderated forum.

Elloeny says, "Skyy democratised radio with all the well-known presenters including Uncle Opia, Aba Moses, Thomas Dossah, etc. The presenters were all regular everyday people and spoke like the people on the street."

"Skyy, more than anything, gave people belief in themselves because the presenters on-air were people they knew and they felt a strong connection to them," adding, "Skyy also brought cohesion in the community through regular events and activities that brought the society together."

More than twenty years after he joined Skyy Power FM, Elloeny ultimately sums up his experience when he says that, "I really, really, really liked my experience at Skyy. There was never a dull moment." Of course, he also exclaims with many happy memories, "Oh, what a madhouse, Skyy Power FM!"

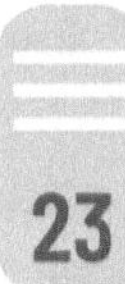

23

Joe Anim, A Foot Soldier for Ideas

"I tended to avoid mainstream news and concentrated on content that no one else was working on, including exclusive interviews with newsmakers. This made the Sapphire Report for Skyy special and desirable."

— Joe Anim, a contributor to Skyy Power FM's news and current affairs in the early years

Halfway through 1997, Joe Anim was working on the eighth floor of Trust Towers in Accra from where Vibe FM used to broadcast. He was the producer of the station's popular *Talk Shop* program hosted by Kwaku Sintim-Misa, better known as KSM, a name synonymous with stand-up comedy in Ghana. Before making an appearance on Vibe FM, KSM had spent years studying in the United States and subsequently distinguished himself as an actor, director, and talk show host on both radio and TV. Mid-1997 was a mere two years since the first independent radio station in Ghana, Joy FM, started operating.

Wilson Arthur was well known to Joe Anim. "Wilson was selling music CDs around that time in Accra, and he was often present at Vibe FM. He always took keen interest in the operations of Vibe FM and that is how I got to know him," says Joe Anim.

The Breaking News

It was on the 8th floor of Trust Towers that Joe Anim heard that Wilson Arthur was planning to build Sekondi-Takoradi's first private radio station. "I was not surprised to hear the news because Wilson Arthur had all the hallmarks of a person who could build and run a successful private radio station," says Joe Anim, recalling a 25 year old memory. "Wilson is an ideas-driven person, and he knows how to find, grow, and use talent," he adds.

I first encountered Joe Anim in 1998, months after Skyy Power FM's operations started. He came to visit Takoradi to discuss ideas to create content for Skyy Power FM.

In the period Wilson Arthur spent creating Skyy, Joe Anim continued producing *Talk Shop, Gospel According to Vibe,* and other programs for KSM. *Talk Shop* was the first monologue format talk show in Ghana. During that period, something even more significant happened between KSM and Joe Anim.

KSM established a private company called Sapphire Ghana Limited and Joe Anim became the first employee. The only currency Joe Anim loves to trade in his life is the currency called *ideas*, and he has never met anyone who celebrated it more than KSM. Sapphire was an ideas hub with Joe as head of programs.

"KSM is the best boss ever, because he lets you run with your own ideas," says Joe Anim. "When I have a business idea, I discuss it with KSM, and he tells me it is my idea and immediately empowers me to implement it."

Sapphire Report Comes to Takoradi

An idea for creating content for radio through Sapphire Ghana Limited brought Joe Anim to Takoradi. It was a kind of syndicated content creation, which at the time was a novelty in Ghana. The plan, as it pertained to us, was simple: develop exclusive news and interviews around Ghana for Skyy. He discussed the idea with KSM, who welcomed it enthusiastically, after which Joe Anim traveled to Takoradi to meet Wilson Arthur with the proposal.

"We prepared a document that explained it, so when I met Wilson, I explained it to him. Wilson understood it immediately and said *we are in for it*. He didn't even bother taking the letter. He was excited and positive about it and that is how the deal was done. What I liked about Wilson is that he is ideas driven, so we connect at the ideas level," says Joe Anim.

A short time after returning to Accra, Joe Anim started filing a deluge of exclusive news stories for Skyy under the brand name *Sapphire Report*. The nature and quality of his reports stood out.

"I tended to avoid mainstream news and concentrated on content that no one else was working on, including exclusive interviews with newsmakers. This made *Sapphire Reports* for Skyy special and desirable," recalls Joe Anim. "Wilson Arthur's vision for Skyy Power FM was solid. He knew how to get the people of Sekondi-Takoradi to buy in to the station with a huge listener base, and that is how I realised that I could be part of it by offering the *Sapphire Reports* to Skyy," says Joe Anim.

For a relatively new radio station, the *Sapphire Report* fulfilled the important need to provide exclusive and trustworthy news. Unlike the rest of us, Joe Anim didn't live in Sekondi-Takoradi, but his popularity increased in the city. Listeners who knew I played a major role in delivering news and current affairs on our station would tell me they enjoyed Joe Anim's *Sapphire Reports* which complemented our work in the newsroom.

"Technology was in its infancy, and had not evolved to the point we know now, so I went everywhere with my old 2G mobile phone," recalls Joe Anim. "I started phoning in my reports for Skyy with Maame Esi Mark-Hansen as the anchor in the studio. Those reports were broadcast just after midday on weekdays when Maame Esi Mark-Hansen would be hosting the *Skyy Spicy Lunch*," he explains, adding, "sometimes, I let Maame Esi do the interview herself directly after I had done the groundwork."

The days of being able to transmit hundreds of megabytes or even gigabytes of data over the Internet had not been realised. As a result, some of Joe Anim's reports for Skyy that were not time-sensitive were recorded on either cassette or CD and taken to the inter-city bus service in Accra to be sent to Takoradi. Joe would then call us with the bus details for us to get it for playback on air.

Often, though, my colleague Sylvia Odonkor in the newsroom would speak directly to Joe Anim on the phone to take his report. Based on the report, we were able to write our own news stories. Whenever there was important breaking news in Accra, we relied on

Joe Anim to give us both deep background and meaningful details. He was effectively Skyy Power FM's correspondent with access and good contacts.

An Unwelcome Taste of Fame

Joe Anim visited Takoradi many times during those years and was surprised that he had become popular with his syndicated *Sapphire Report*. This bothered him. More than twenty years later, he still recalls how uncomfortable he felt.

"I was never interested in becoming popular, and I never looked out for feedback. The way people talked about my relevance made it feel like there was a lot of exaggeration and I was not interested. I was only interested in finding relevant information and putting it out there for the benefit of the public," says Joe Anim, adding, "I started feeling the real impact of my work only when certain political leaders, including Goozie Tanoh and later President Kufour, indicated that they were aware that I was the source of trusted information on Skyy with the *Sapphire Report*. Even the management of a major resort like Busua Beach Resort near Takoradi gave me a whole bus to bring reporters from Accra to see their facility, just based on my reports. It was a real surprise to see the impact those reports made on people. That was when I realised that I needed to pay a bit more attention. From there, I added other dimensions to my report, including direct reporting from Parliament and the Office of the President."

As a result of the success with Skyy, Joe Anim moved on to establish a full studio in Accra, including a two-way phone system, where more in-depth news and analysis were produced for distribution. At that time, the production business became known as the *Sapphire Network of Affiliate Stations*, and John Mahama, who later became president of Ghana, launched that little enterprise in his then-role as Information and Communications Minister in the Jerry Rawlings administration.

"From that point," Joe Anim says, "I started doing stories on location and from the studio where I brought in a lot of different people to interview. For example, when Goozie Tanoh formed his political party as a breakaway from the National Democratic

Congress, he gave me an exclusive interview which was heard on Skyy in Takoradi before the rest of the country caught up with the details. I brought Fiifi Banson (Radio Gold and Peace FM), and Goozie Tanoh spoke exclusively to us."

Another major story Joe Anim did for Skyy concerned former president Kufour who had to address an important matter affecting his political party and the nation.

Says Joe Anim, "At the peak of the 2000 election campaign, I went to his house where the flagbearer granted me an exclusive interview on a controversial matter in relation to some tribal comments he was falsely accused to have made. The flagbearer knew that I had the ability to distribute the information nationwide. After the interview, one of his trusted advisors, the late Jake Obetsebi Lamptey requested the president to hold a press conference, but Kufour said he won't because he had already spoken to me."

"Joe Anim will take it nationwide," said President Kufour.

"I could feel the tension as people around the president started saying 'and who the hell is this Joe Anim anyway?'" recalls Joe Anim.

I understand why President Kufour appreciated Joe Anim's impact on Takoradi's Skyy Power FM. In those days, Sekondi-Takoradi was a stronghold of President Kufour and his New Patriotic Party. He was strongly represented there by the late Takoradi Member of Parliament Gladys Asmah, a woman made of steel whom President Kufour trusted with his life. There were a number of occasions when I would be interacting with Gladys Asmah and she would stop and receive a personal call on her mobile phone from President Kufour.

It Could Have Been Even Bigger

Looking back at his impact at Skyy with his *Sapphire Report*, Joe Anim says, "I believe I would have done an even better job and made greater impact if I paid closer attention to the overwhelming positive feedback I was receiving because of the reports I was producing. I was so shy about acknowledging my good works that I closed my mind to how I could have made an even greater impact."

"Skyy was such an effective platform championed by Wilson Arthur and his excellent marketing skills, and it made Skyy stand out, leaving a permanent mark in Sekondi-Takoradi and the Western Region," observes Joe Anim.

An Outsider and an Insider

In many ways, Joe Anim was both an outsider and an insider with Skyy. Even though he was never an employee, he had a deeper insight into the operations on Skyy, almost on par with those of us who worked there. He had the perspective that was a fusion of an insider and an outsider.

Observing the effectiveness of Skyy further, Joe Anim says, "Wilson connected Skyy to the community with numerous entertainment and events. He made the people own the station, delighting them with the newest trends in music including Hiplife introduced by Reggie Rockstone." One of Reggie Rockstone's collaborators on his seminal Hiplife album was a young man called Root Eye, whom Wilson Arthur brought to Takoradi to work for Skyy Power FM.

"Wilson was very smart in the way he managed and trained the raw human resource at Skyy together with creative content and first-class entertainment. He knew the presenters were all young and he motivated them and allowed them to explore their own talents and that brought out the best result," reflects Joe Anim.

Joe Anim is still relatively young, but he says, "I am retired, don't do media anymore except when there is an issue I feel strongly about, then I contribute. I have never been an on-air presenter; I have never wanted to be, right up to this time. That is in spite of the fact that I have done live reports and been a panel member many times during discussions on radio."

Far more than the modest way he paints his contributions, Joe Anim has helped to establish numerous radio stations around Ghana and unearthed dozens of talents in music and broadcasting. He discovered and brought two major talents to Skyy Power FM: the smooth presenter Abena Bondah and current affairs powerhouse Eric Ahianyo.

Always carrying a bag full of ideas, Joe Anim has also dispensed a stream of ideas for radio and TV programs around the country. "Almost every radio program I create are my own original ideas. The challenge I find is getting someone or a group of people to implement it the way I envision it," says Joe Anim.

A Selfless Desire to Celebrate Others

Along with generating profitable ideas for business and broadcasting, Joe Anim is in the business of discovering talent and celebrating people whom he believes have made significant contributions to the arts and entertainment.

Zapp Mallet, a Ghanaian legendary music producer, was one of the individuals who showed up on Joe Anim's radar. Zapp Mallet has an enormous body of creative work in music, including the pioneering of a new music genre in Ghana called Hiplife.

In March 2021, Joe Anim posted on Facebook: "If there's one person I will beg to produce a documentary of his life, it's Zapp Mallet. Talk about unsung heroes...He's not just 6 feet, 8 inches in height, he towers above many."

Nine months later in December 2021, Joe Anim put up another post after a major interview with Zapp Mallet appeared online. Samuel Attah-Mensah (Sammens) of Citi FM and Citi TV in Accra interviewed Zapp Mallett. Joe Anim's post on the subject read: "Sammens, thanks for this. I still maintain that this man needs to be celebrated. Zapp Mallet is a guru! He himself doesn't remember lots of the work he's done. He did all the Oman FM & Net 2 TV jingles for me, courtesy of Rahim Sinare, with his own voice..."

I agreed with Joe Anim that Zapp Mallet had a special place even at Skyy because when we started broadcasting, the euphonic and attractive jingles were one of the first things listeners fell in love with, and many of these were created by Zapp Mallet.

I refocus on Joe Anim, trying to recall and acknowledge his own contribution to Skyy FM, but he immediately turns shy and his enthusiasm vanishes. It leaves me afraid that he is going to end the interview politely, but prematurely. Instead, he asks that I ensure the contribution of Adwoa Amofah, Wilson Arthur's wife, is fully acknowledged in this book.

Identifying an individual who needs to be given credit for doing something outstanding is the only thing that energises Joe Anim at this point.

"Wilson himself will be the first to acknowledge that Skyy would have been impossible without the constant financial and moral support of his wife Adwoa Amofah," says Joe Anim, as he successfully deflects the attention I am drawing to his own contribution.

Given everything I know about Joe Anim, he will read this chapter one day and feel embarrassed that he has been placed on a pedestal. Predictably, he will call me to complain that he has been given too much attention, and I will say, "Joe, this is part of history that needs to be told." I will say it as gently as possible as a response to the old foot soldier who treats good ideas as a precious natural resource.

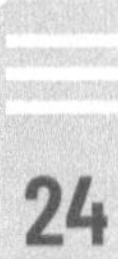

Socrates from Gliksten Preparatory School

"Skyy Power FM appealed to everyone, and it was a mystery to me. You don't often find radio stations that cut across like that, but Skyy had it. Adults loved it, children loved it. People in the formal sector loved it, and those in the informal sector loved it."

— Yaw Korankye, reflecting on Skyy Power FM's wide appeal across the Western and Central Regions of Ghana

Halfway through 1998, Yaw Korankye Antwi arrived in Takoradi to join Skyy FM, fresh from completing a degree from Kwame Nkrumah University of Science and Technology in Kumasi. Even though he goes by three names, "Yaw Korankye Antwi," he tends to introduce himself simply as "Yaw Korankye," leaving out "Antwi."

Either way, it made no difference to most of his schoolmates. "A lot of people actually did not know my real name," he says, adding, "you know, on campus, we all have crazy names."

Yaw Korankye's crazy name on campus was "Socrates," originally the name of an ancient Greek philosopher.

Another friend with a crazy name enabled Socrates' long journey from Kumasi to Takoradi and into Skyy Power FM.

That friend's crazy name was "Louis Farrhakan," originally the name of an American religious leader and political activist. This Louis Farrhakan, however, is a brother of Skyy Power FM's Chief Executive Wilson Arthur, who was also at Kwame Nkrumah University of Science and Technology with Socrates.

During his interview for this book, Yaw Korankye could not remember Louis Farrhakan's real name; proof that the "crazy" nicknames from school tend to be remembered more than real names.

Katanga Hall, Kwame Nkrumah University

The pride of Katanga Hall of the University of Science and Technology in Kumasi is a small, non-commercial campus radio station. It was called Conttato Radio.

For two years as a student, Yaw Korankye worked on a voluntary basis as the station's studio manager, program manager, and general manager.

He managed many dozen student volunteers, more than sixty at some point, and balancing the needs and demands of so many passionate students was hectic.

He describes the responsibility as heavy, saying he had to manage people and equipment at the same time.

Many students noticed Yaw Korankye's calm demeanor and effective leadership in his role. Two of the students Yaw Korankye groomed and managed at Conttato Radio transitioned successfully to work with Skyy Power FM in Takoradi.

Those two, Bob Gardiner and Joe Enuson, have also left a permanent mark at Skyy.

Another student who observed Yaw Korankye's effectiveness was Louis Farrakhan, whose brother owned Skyy Power FM in Takoradi. Louis Farrakhan recommended Yaw Korankye for employment.

That is how he arrived at Skyy Power FM and eventually became Programs Manager.

Meeting Uncle Opia Again

Yaw Korankye first met Uncle Opiah when he was a child in primary school living in Sefwi Wiawso, a town in the middle of a mountainous forest, almost 300 kilometres north of Takoradi. Uncle Opia had come to visit the Gliksten Preparatory School where Yaw Korankye was a student.

"Gliksten is the name of a British timber company that operated in Sefwi Wiawso, and my father worked there. The company set up the school for the benefit of children in that community, and they called it Gliksten Preparatory School."

Uncle Opia, who was working with Ghana Broadcasting Corporation's *Radio 1* came to record a children's program, which included performances by the children. Yaw Korankye was one of the children who performed.

"Uncle Opia addressed all of us children on that day, and because I was one of the main performers, I got to speak to him afterwards. It is something I remember very well," says Yaw Korankye.

Decades later, Yaw Korankye arrived at Skyy Power FM and ran straight into Uncle Opia. He recognised the old man immediately. Uncle Opia, however, did not recognise Yaw Korankye. He knew only that the young man was joining Skyy from Kumasi, where he had just graduated from university.

Uncle Opia, with decades of broadcasting experience from the state broadcaster, GBC, was the Programs Manager for Skyy at the time.

He was already well past retirement age but was enjoying the greatest admiration of his professional work from Skyy Power FM listeners. He was enjoying everything about his work except the internal and administrative role he still played as Programs Manager.

The plan was for Yaw Korankye to understudy Uncle Opia and take over as Programs Manager.

Just days after arriving at Skyy, Yaw Korankye suspected he was going to face some challenges in rubbing shoulders with the presenters, most of whom enjoyed celebrity status throughout the twin city. To succeed, Yaw Korankye deployed his greatest weapons: his humility and charm. His less noticeable quality, a deep sense of humour, would become apparent only later.

He carefully orchestrated a strategy of purposeful engagement with all the exciting and passionate young men and women he met running the show at Skyy.

"I don't lose anything by being humble; in fact, I actually learned a lot in the process because the team I met at Skyy was so warm and welcoming," says Yaw Korankye.

The Rules of Engagement at Skyy

Having aligned the rules of engagement at Skyy with his own values and character, Yaw Korankye launched his charm offensive only to realise success was going to be far easier than he anticipated.

"The much older Uncle Opia was very friendly and generous in teaching me everything about the programming at Skyy," says Yaw Korankye. One day, while he was still being taught the rudimentaries of programming on Skyy, he decided to tell Uncle Opia that he met him as a child when he visited Gliksten Primary school in Sefwi Wiawso.

"Uncle Opia certainly could not physically recognise me at this point because I was just a child back then, but he still remembered many details about the event and recalled talking to me," says Yaw Korankye.

"That single conversation drew us closer, and he became a man that I loved and respected. I learned so much from him, and he was happy to see me take up the responsibility as Programs Manager," he recalls.

Uncle Opia was a beloved figure, and his respect and love for Yaw Korankye was soon shared by everyone across the whole of Skyy. Perhaps one of the greatest personal achievements of Yaw Korankye at Skyy was that he commanded a lot of respect from all without ever demanding or asking for it.

His humility and sense of humour played a major role in this.

Taking up the Microphone at Dawn

Once the deal to work for Skyy was sealed between Yaw Korankye and Skyy boss Wilson Arthur, he was asked to go on air, but only at dawn, around 4 am on a program called *Skyy Christian Radio*. He enjoyed it, working directly with Akyen Aikins. The two of them succeeded Michael Griffiths who originally designed and ran the program from day one, with the permission of Wilson Arthur. It became a very popular program with the local pastors' network along with thousands of their devoted followers.

Yaw Korankye also replaced Kofi Gyetsua Ankoma (KGA) on the sports analysis program. KGA moved on to other programs. "Until Wilson asked me to do sports, I had never done it and didn't have much interest in it, but Wilson encouraged me, and with time, I was able to hold my own."

For a short time, Yaw Korankye presented the Skyy Power News as well, along with participating in a few other programs. It helped him gain a greater insight into the entire operation, enabling him to be a more effective Programs Manager. Looking back, he says, "I felt odd presenting the news and fluffed my lines often, so I got myself out of it quickly."

"I was Intimidated by Kojo Frempong and Elloeny Amande."

Skyy Power FM had a strong sports unit with presenters such as Kojo Frempong and Elloeny Amande, amongst others. The team was strengthened further after Kuntu Blankson joined Skyy. Kuntu presented sports in Fante at the time when more than 80% of Skyy's output was in English. But he helped the English sports production with his lifetime of contacts with sports people across Ghana.

From the early days, both Elloeny Amande and Kojo Frempong manifested talent and passion with analysis and a spirited presentation. "I thought Kojo Frempong, at that young age, was the best football commentator I ever heard on Ghanaian radio," says Yaw. This is the team that Yaw Korankye joined in his additional role as Programs Manager. Other sports presenters, including Eric Essel, Andrews Akavani, and Lawton Dadzie joined the team later

"In fact, I was intimidated by the high quality and proficiency of Elloeny Amande and Kojo Frempong," says Yaw Korankye. He meant this as a compliment to both Elloeny Amande and Kojo Frempong, two young men who would both move on to do great things in sports at a national level while winning awards and even managing a leading football team.

In delivering his compliment, Yaw Korankye manifests his humility by acknowledging that he was nowhere near as proficient as the slightly younger men he worked with.

Despite the occasional self-deprecation, Yaw Korankye is a well-respected workmate with an authority he uses to promote respect for everyone.

Sometimes, he plays the part of a father figure. This is exemplified in a story he shares regarding Kojo Frempong. "You know how we would often cram into JM Caesar's old car and go to lunch…" Yaw begins, trying to establish the context.

"Sometimes, we will drive past Takoradi Polytechnic where we would see a lot of students, including beautifully dressed ladies," he continues.

"Kojo Frempong will make remarks about how beautiful they are, and I would immediately tell him to keep quiet. Over time, when it got too much, I warned him that I would ban him from coming with us for lunch if he made another comment. He accepted my ultimatum and never made those comments anymore."

Of course, the rest of the boys at Skyy teased Kojo Frempong on how effectively Yaw Korankye made him shut up.

"I Was Never Much of A Celebrity…"

Yaw Korankye is very generous in reflecting the uncommon mutual love and admiration shared among what he calls "the Skyy Family." He is quick to point out that many of the other presenters had a much higher profile than him. "I was never much of a celebrity," he says.

"Paa Kofi Nyarko (Abronoma) appealed strongly to the whole of Takoradi," he continues. "At one point, he was the number one on the celebrity status chart. When Abronoma is in JM Caesar's car with us, we get fuel for free at the filling station. People in Sekondi-Takoradi were very generous to us. When we went to restaurants with Abronoma, it was always free food for us. Root Eye also had that kind of aura around him."

In further reflection, he says, "here are people who were celebrities, and the people of Sekondi-Takoradi would hail them wherever they go. At that time, Skyy had about 95 to 98% listenership, with the existing state broadcaster, *Twin City Radio*, hardly registering on the minds of people."

"Skyy Power FM appealed to everyone, and it was a mystery to me. You don't often find radio stations that cut across like that, but Skyy had it. Adults loved it; children loved it. People in the formal sector loved it, and those in the informal sector loved it."

Thinking about his years in Sekondi-Takoradi after more than 20 years, he says, "I consider Takoradi the best place I have lived. The years I spent in Takoradi were very remarkable."

The "L" and "R" Problem from Kumasi

One of the ways Yaw Korankye lit up Skyy when he arrived was to start calling everyone "Jack." When asked to explain why, he says, "in Kumasi, we call everyone Jack."

No one objected.

A more noticeable phenomenon linked to Ghanaians living in Kumasi and Ashanti Region is that quite a good number of them struggle to pronounce the letters *L* and *R* comfortably whenever it occurs in words, phrases, or even names.

So, for example, the name of one of Ghana's former heads of state, Flt. Lt. Jerry John Rawlings, can present some challenges for pronunciation.

Yaw Korankye, however, would jovially boast that even though he lived in Kumasi for a long time, he does not have that problem, or any other unique pronunciation variations identified with Kumasi and Ashanti Region.

The word *problem* is also a challenge in the context of the *L* and *R* problem.

Adwoa Amofah, wife of Wilson Arthur and one of the owners of Skyy, challenged Yaw Korankye, saying he has what others may see as a known deficiency in pronunciation. Yaw Korankye, in a typical

Skyy Family argumentative mood, also confidently challenged Adwoa Amofah to prove it.

Adwoa Amofah took a pen and paper and wrote the number 100 and asked him to pronounce it. He quickly said "*hendred*," (as in hen coop). Everyone laughed except Yaw Korankye. He pronounced it the way many Kumasi residents would without realising it.

There was much room at Skyy for mischief and banter. Once, Ato Kwamena Dadzie and I cooked up a plan that made Yaw Korankye embarrass himself on-air. We prepared one sports news article and intentionally inserted the word "proliferation," knowing he would falter in his attempt to pronounce it.

It worked, and the rest of the presenters, especially Paa Kofi Nyarko, had a marvellous time teasing him about it, even live on-air.

It is among some of the funny, but silly, stories that keeps the memory of the Skyy Family alive.

"When It Comes to Poisons..."

Yaw Korankye's sense of humour, even though concealed sometimes, comes out without warning. I had a personal experience with it while furiously editing a news bulletin for presentation. Yaw Korankye walked into the newsroom nonchalantly and started saying something that I couldn't care about. I tried to order him out of the newsroom as we often did with non-newsroom employees whenever they waltzed in looking for a chance to tease or make a joke. While slowly walking away, he paused and asked me a rhetorical question: "How can a short and small person like you sound so big on air?"

Without blinking, I shot back, "when it comes to poisons, the smaller the bottle, the deadlier the poison."

My retort stopped him in his tracks. Since then, almost every interaction between us is preceded by this old story.

In late 2005, Yaw Korankye and I were living in London and met in Tottenham. Our unique acknowledgement of each other was as follows:

Yaw Korankye: "when it comes to poisons..."

Phillip: "the smaller the bottle..."

Yaw Korankye: "the deadlier the poison!"

We laughed and hugged, enveloped by a thick fog of many happy memories.

An Environment of Brothers and Sisters

Yaw Korankye was enthusiastic in granting an interview for this book as we looked back at a quarter of a century of broadcasting and the roles we played along with dozens of other talented and passionate individuals.

"We had so much fun, and Skyy Power FM was an environment of brothers and sisters," he says. Uncle Opia is one of the four colleagues at Skyy who died before this book was prepared.

Yaw Korankye remembers all of them with fondness.

"Unfortunately, we lost our sister Esi Gyan and big brothers Kwesi Mould and Uncle Opia. We lost these three beautiful souls," he reflects, a tinge of sadness discernible in his voice.

But he also says, "The friendship we formed at Skyy has grown, and the bonds are getting even stronger with time. Bob Gee, Joe Enuson, Kwete Quaynor, JM Caesar, Paa Kofi, Yuki Ampofo, Ato Kwamena Dadzie, Elloeny Amande, Kojo Frempong... these are high-quality friendships of a lifetime," he adds, with a sense of pride.

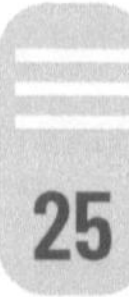

Root Eye: The Sophisticated Rastaman

"We just couldn't stay away from one another at Skyy. We were like brothers and sisters. We were more like siblings than friends. If you invited me to a party, you know that you are inviting the whole Skyy crew, because I am coming with my siblings. You are sure to see JM Caesar, Bob Gardiner, Maame Efua DeGraft Aidoo; everyone is coming. Skyy was more like a family house than a workplace."

— Root Eye, a singer and songwriter who joined Skyy as a presenter when the station started

Kwasi Nyarko Ofei found his voice as a singer and songwriter when he was in basic school. By the time the record of his first music came out, barely anyone knew his real name. His friends in school called him *Root Eye*, and it stuck with him. He went on to find fame as a musician, and later, as a radio presenter on Skyy Power FM in Takoradi. Root Eye became the name he carried along with his fame.

A major boost for Root Eye's journey occurred with another young man called Wilson Arthur.

"I met Wilson Athur on the eighth floor of Trust Towers in Accra where Vibe FM used to be," recalls Root Eye. "We went there for a general meeting in which Wilson Arthur and other people in the music industry were proposing the formation of an Association of Music Professionals in Ghana in early 1996. I was a young man at the time who was hungry for knowledge and information and Wilson Arthur won my heart and my admiration."

"A previous meeting on the same subject took place at Afrikiko nightclub in Accra," says Root Eye. "Wilson Arthur made impeccable presentations at both meetings, and I just loved him. I was like, 'who the heck is this?' He spoke with such brilliance, such intelligence and his argument was apt."

Starting Off with General Marcus

Before these meetings, Root Eye and another musician called General Marcus became friends. Says Root Eye, "General Marcus had a record deal with a company that operated in Jamaica, the United States, and Ghana, and he recommended me as a songwriter. Together, the two of us wrote songs and were also involved in distributing the CDs."

One of the shops selling their music at the time was Music Paradise, owned by Wilson Arthur. "General Marcus said he had given some CDs to be sold at Music Paradise, so he wanted to check and perhaps collect the proceeds, so we went into the shop together," relates Root Eye.

"I immediately recalled meeting Wilson on two previous occasions: once at the Afrikiko nightclub and later at the Trust Towers in Accra. Wilson disappeared immediately after those two meetings, and the two of us never spoke during those previous meetings. I knew Wilson but he didn't know me; and I also didn't know he owned Music Paradise," says Root Eye.

Root Eye listened quietly as General Marcus and Wilson Arthur discussed their business transaction at the shop.

"Just as we were about to go," recalls Root Eye, "Wilson Arthur enthusiastically told us that he was about to open a radio station in Takoradi and wished General Marcus could join him and host the daily reggae program. Pointing to me, General Marcus responded saying 'my friend here, Root Eye, is the best person who can fill that role,'" recalls Root Eye.

When Wilson Arthur heard the name, he was shocked and immediately asked, "is Root Eye the same guy who was featured on Reggie Rockstone's album?"

The answer was, of course, yes, and from that moment, Wilson and Root Eye formed a lifelong relationship. Even though Wilson Arthur was yet to build Skyy Power FM in Takoradi, the deal was that Root Eye was going to be a star on that radio station.

Becoming Part of Hiplife History in Ghana

Months before Root Eye met Wilson Arthur at Music Paradise, a new genre of music appeared in Ghana, called Hiplife. Hiplife is a creative fusion of world renowned hip-hop and the rich traditional Highlife music from Ghana. The genius who pioneered Hiplife was Reginald Asante Ossei, better known as Reggie Rockstone.

He was born in the United Kingdom to Ghanaian parents. They brought him back to Ghana where he learned the Akan (Twi) language and culture before returning to England and then the United States.

Reggie Rockstone's seminal album with the collection of the first Hiplife songs is called *Makaa Maka,* an Akan language expression meaning "I have said it, and I have said it" or more accurately, "I dare say it."

Root Eye was featured on that album, singing portions of the hit song *Sweetie Sweetie.* It was only later Root Eye himself would realise he had become, not just part of Hiplife history, but more importantly, one of the few historians of that genre of music in Ghana.

A set of unusual circumstances led to Root Eye's close relationship with Reggie Rockstone and his eventual appearance on the album.

"In 1994, Reggie Rockstone returned to Ghana from the United States and England to participate in the Pan-African Festival [PANAFEST] in Ghana. He came with another Ghanaian artiste called Freddie Funkstone. The two of them were part of *PLZ*, a small music group," says Root Eye.

Making Music with Reggie Rockstone

Root Eye says, "Reggie Rockstone's aim was to make a new kind of music by fusing the traditional Highlife music with the hip-hop music he had learned while living in the United States and England, but he could not find any music producer or sound engineer who could understand his revolutionary drive, because most of them only knew how to produce Highlife music."

"Before Reggie Rockstone's arrival in Ghana," continues Root Eye, "General Marcus and I had become friends with Rab Bakari (also called *DJ Rab*), a music producer from New York who lived close to my home in the Kotobabi suburb of Accra."

(On a sad note, Rab Bakari died in Ghana on 6 March 2022, while this chapter was being written).

One day, we went to a nightclub in the city where Reggie Rockstone and his friend Freddie Funkstone came to perform.

"DJ Rab was so impressed that he wanted to meet them, so I walked up to them and asked if they could meet my friend, after which we all ended up sharing the same table," recalls Root Eye.

As it turned out, that night had only just started for everyone.

"We all talked about music and Reggie Rockstone revealed how he had been searching for a producer who could understand the new music genre fusing western and Ghanaian traditional music. DJ Rab offered his expertise and that very night we went to a recording studio in Labone, and DJ Rab started creating sounds that demonstrated he knew what Reggie Rockstone wanted. We were so excited that we didn't sleep that night. We stayed up all night talking about ourselves and music. Our life together as friends started from there," says Root Eye.

Soon after that meeting, Reggie Rockstone started writing and recording different tracks for *Makaa Maka*, the album that made history as the first manifestation of Hiplife music.

Apart from Reggie Rockstone who was the primary artiste with production by Rab Bakari, contributions came from other talents. The contributors include Sammi B, Cy Davies, Samuel Kwame Bampoe, Alexander Tubman, Freddie Funkstone, Nananom, and Sydney Kofi Ofori. Legendary Ghanaian music producer Zapp Mallet also made significant contributions to complete the album.

"I observed the whole creative process, including the composition of the track *Sweetie Sweetie*" says Root Eye. "When Reggie Rockstone was putting this particular song together, I could feel and hear my voice in the song. Up to that point, I maintained a low profile about my own ability to write and sing, but when I heard the initial version of *Sweetie Sweetie*, I told Reggie Rockstone that I wanted to be part of it. Reggie then made me sing and he was so impressed that I wrote those lines. He was so excited and immediately declared in the studio that Root Eye is on this song."

Becoming a Radio Presenter

Root Eye's reputation as a singer and songwriter as well as a pioneer in Hiplife music was created with the release of Reggie Rockstone's *Makaa Maka* album. It was with that reputation that Root Eye and his friend General Marcus walked into Wilson Athur's Music Paradise shop.

It was also the reason why Wilson Arthur didn't believe it when General Marcus said his friend Root Eye was the same person who sang *Sweetie Sweetie* with Reggie Rockstone.

"Wilson was so happy and surprised to see me that he physically lifted me up and congratulated me, after which he asked if I would consider becoming a radio presenter on a new radio station he intended to build in Takoradi," recalls Root Eye.

After their dramatic encounter at Music Paradise in Accra, Wilson Arthur and Root Eye did not meet again until around September 1997 in Takoradi, when he finally built the radio station of his dream.

"I didn't have a mobile phone at this time, so Wilson Arthur sent a message through General Marcus, inviting me to come and check out the new radio station. The day I arrived in Takoradi is a day I will never forget," says Root Eye.

"Wilson and I spent a lot of time talking in the studio at 37 Windy Ridge, and I also got to meet other presenters who would later become like family. They include Kwesi Fletcher, Michael Griffiths, KingB, Naa Adoley Thompson, Maame Esi Mark-Hansen, and Kojo Frempong," recalls Root Eye.

"Later, Wilson took me into the city for lunch, and as we were driving around, he told me, 'Root Eye, I am going to make you a star in this city.'"

I was living in Takoradi at this time, and Wilson Arthur had told me about the famous Root Eye who will be joining Skyy. Under the spell of Wilson, I was also seriously considering joining Skyy myself, if it was going to turn out to be the credible media house Wilson was promising. I was trying hard not to fall for what I suspected was hype as preparations continued for Skyy Power FM to start operations. I eventually met Root Eye when he came, and the experience was, to put it mildly, disappointing. Root Eye didn't look anything like his reputation.

"People perceive me as a huge man with dreadlocks," he tells me.

The young man I met in 1997 was practically just a boy--slim, soft spoken, and his eyes still bore the signs of a boy who was still growing. There was only that constant glitter in his eyes that revealed he was highly creative and always learning.

Later, I wrote a profile about Root Eye for RTV, a pioneering radio and TV magazine in Ghana. I have a similar challenge as Root Eye in being mislabelled often as a "huge man." That, together with Root Eye's friendliness, led us to form a very close and permanent bond of friendship.

By the time Skyy Power FM started commercial operations, Wilson Arthur's prediction that Root Eye would become a superstar in Sekondi-Takoradi came true. I also became a member of the Skyy crew in the newsroom, earning the distinction as one of those who saw the creation of Skyy from the beginning.

Becoming a Star with Reggae Soundcheck

Root Eye's stardom on radio started the first day he went on-air when the station was still test transmitting.

He entered Skyy Power FM's impressive music library and focused on the reggae section.

"I looked into that collection and could see all my favourite CDs. I have been to Joy FM, Vibe FM, and Groove FM all in Accra, but Skyy, by far, had the biggest, the most organised, music library in Ghana at that time. I couldn't wait to share all this music with the public," says Root Eye.

"We had all taken part in a BBC training program at the station and Wilson Arthur insisted that I should play some music and entertain listeners. I felt nervous because I had never been on radio."

Ato Parry, who was technically astute in the studio, showed him how the mixer and microphones worked: how to fade in and how to fade out.

"We played good quality lovers rock reggae music for about thirty minutes without talking and finally, I found the courage to speak, and I said, 'Welcome to Skyy 93.5FM. I am sure you are wondering who is playing this music. My name starts with the letter 'R,' and at the end of each song, I will mention the next letter.' We kept going until I finished spelling *Root Eye*. I don't know how I got the idea to come out with that," he says.

Between the music and the spelling of his name by mentioning one letter at a time, Root Eye created curiosity and got the attention of listeners. He now said on air, "having heard me spell my whole name, you can now call in and tell me what my name is."

Listeners started calling to pronounce his name. The majority got the name right and many who called actually asked: "are you the same Root Eye on Reggie Rockstone's album?"

"This went on for about two hours," says Root Eye, "and, finally, I played *Sweetie Sweetie*, the song that I sang with Reggie Rockstone and told the audience that I was the same Root Eye, the singer."

Root Eye's quick thinking while under pressure in the studio made him an instant hit in Sekondi-Takoradi. His royal status on radio was established on that day, even before formal operations started in October 1997.

Working as Part of the Skyy Family

As Skyy started commercial transmission, Root Eye entertained listeners daily, from Monday to Friday, on his *Reggae Sound Check* program. He genuinely loved the music he played and the constant interaction he had with listeners.

The combination of being known as a musician and broadcasting daily on the extremely popular Skyy Power FM around the Western and Central Regions caused a tsunami of popularity that was impossible to measure.

According to Root Eye, his most vivid memories are about the closeness of our relationship. "Skyy was more like a family home than a workplace. My daily program was only two hours between 2 to 4 pm in the afternoon, but I always came early and hung around long after my program. The place was so exciting that none of us liked to stay home, even during weekends."

The dynamic environment also meant that we saw each other's strengths and weaknesses constantly.

Root Eye had a particularly bad habit, which many of our colleagues recalled with glee, in various interviews. Root Eye also talks about it with mirth.

"Most of the guys would often arrange to eat lunch around 1 pm everyday in the city, and the time was not convenient for me, as my program starts at 2 pm, but I would often take the risk and go out, hoping to return on time for my program," says Root Eye.

The result was that he was persistently late for his program.

He would run up breathlessly into the studio just before the top of the hour. Many times, Sammy Arthur would start playing some music for him before he waltzed in with a belly full of light soup and goat meat with Fufu he had just eaten in the city.

Yaw Korankye was Programs Manager, and it was his duty to speak to Root Eye about it, but of course he didn't have much success.

Root Eye sustained the habit of being late for so long that it was a surprise when he eventually decided to do something different. Rather than continuing to go out for lunch an hour before his program, he arranged for the food to be brought to him in the studio.

The arrangement created its own drama as he ended up having to eat during the first ten to fifteen minutes of his program.

"It was a top secret that during the first fifteen minutes of his program, Root Eye would be eating his lunch, usually Fufu and soup, and a choice selection of meat," recalls JM Caesar.

No one outside Skyy knew this because there was no evidence of the constant drama on air. The *Reggae Sound Check* Root Eye presented was of high quality.

Many listeners, especially ladies, would call in regularly, and among other things, they would say the sun shines brighter for them whenever Root Eye spoke on air.

On a typical afternoon, his happy booming voice on air would say, "this is the Kingsbite man, Mr Romantic, Root Eye. I will take you all the way to 4 pm today on this magical station, Skyy 93.5 FM. Let me serve you good people with this moving track from Buju Banton."

Buju Banton's song called *23rd Psalm* would start playing. The slow, piercing, and melodic instrumentals followed by lyrics originally written by ancient King David fills the air:

> *"It is so good to praise the Most High Jah every day…*
> *Goodness and mercy all my life*
> *Shall surely follow me*
> *And in Jah's house for ever more*
> *My dwelling place must be."*

Almost effortlessly, Root Eye who describes himself as "the sophisticated Rastaman," creates a meditative and joyful mood running for two hours straight. That is how Root Eye sets Sekondi-Takoradi on fire, five days a week, between 2 to 4 pm on his show.

The Family We Found at Skyy

When I first attempt to contact Root Eye to interview him for this book, I call him on an old phone number. It was picked by a young boy whom I later learn is fourteen-year-old Barima.

"My name is Phillip Nyakpo," I say, "and may I please speak to Root Eye?"

"Oh, he is no longer using this number," says the young man. He speaks so well and sounds relaxed.

"My Dad told me a lot about you," he says.

"He doesn't use this number anymore; he has given it to me. I can give you the number he is now using." Barima proceeds to give me Root Eye's current number and I thank him.

"Has your dad really told you about me?" I ask, quite excited to hear the voice of the son of my friend, especially when he is so friendly and polite.

"Yes," answers Barima. "He said you were friends at Skyy Power FM in Takoradi."

I left Ghana before Barima was born, and I have never met him. But listening to him tell me just on the spur of the moment about the decades old friendship between his father and me is moving. It feels special.

It reminds me how I have told my own ten-year-old son about Root Eye. I imagine that perhaps our sons would meet one day and share stories they heard from their fathers.

My imagination hinges on the persistently deep personal connections within the workforce at Skyy, and Root Eye emphasises it throughout my interview with him.

"Everyone at Skyy was a special person," he tells me. "We became like a family and even after we all moved on from Skyy, someone would always call every few months just to check on you."

"Skyy established an energetic and vibrant modern pop culture in Takoradi, Cape Coast, and through the Western and Central Regions, including regular events in Cape Coast, Takoradi, Tarkwa, and Axim," he adds.

"That vibrance extended into the economic life in Takoradi and there were numerous businesses which grew and expanded even nationwide because of Skyy. The fact that we operated like one strong family made it possible," says Root Eye.

As the interview draws to a close, Root Eye, the local radio superstar, the Hiplife music historian and artiste, is far more interested in talking about the close relationships we formed at Skyy.

"We just couldn't stay away from one another at Skyy. We were like brothers and sisters. We were more like siblings than friends," he says. "If you invited me to a party, you know that you are inviting the whole

Skyy crew, because I am coming with my siblings. You are sure to see JM Caesar, Bob Gardiner, Maame Efua DeGraft Aidoo… Everyone is coming. Skyy was more like a family house than a workplace," he reminisces.

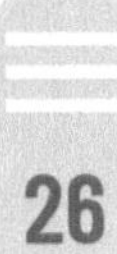

26

Bob Gee: A Decade-Long Morning Show Host

"If any radio station was to start and do the same thing that Skyy Power FM did in the past, it would still be the success template for them."

— *Robert Jimdim Gardiner (Bob Gee), former host of the Jolly Breakfast Show and the Local Chat Show on Skyy Power FM*

It was a day of national tragedy. My colleagues in the newsroom and I kept looking at the ticking clock and scrambled to put together a comprehensive news bulletin. We had the duty to tell the story that brought tears to millions of people across Ghana. Our own emotions were suspended as we took reports from other journalists in the national capital, Accra.

The breakfast show team, led by the anchor Bob Gardiner, rushed into the newsroom, and he addressed me directly. "Hey, Phillip, it's time for the news," the concern was palpable in his voice. I didn't even try to glance at him as I looked laser-straight at a printer that was malfunctioning exactly at the time I needed it to spit out pages of news that we had written.

The tension in the air felt thick.

Bob Gardiner walked back into the studio without another word. Just then, I noticed I might not have been breathing for what seemed like a whole minute.

In the Middle of the Storm

Suddenly, the radio set we use in monitoring our own station started blaring a sweet, soothing, and rhythmic music.

I was in a tunnel
And couldn't see the light
And whenever I'd look up
I couldn't see the sky

It was *The Storm Is Over Now* by R. Kelly. As the song bounced, A4-sheets of paper started flying out of the printer. It's the news I had to read as the anchor of the major bulletin that morning, the 10th of May 2001. I reached for the script and rushed into the studio which was just about 10 metres from the newsroom. Following closely on my heels was Eric Ahianyo, who brought along a Sony Mini Disc that had several voice-overs that we would be playing as part of the news.

Bob Gardiner was sitting in the morning show host's chair, relieved to see me. It was already past the hour for the news, adding to the tension and the rush for us all. Over the years, we developed a studio body language with which we could establish readiness for going live on air with the news. Our eyes locked for a moment, and we both knew we were ready to roll. Eric Ahianyo was standing behind Bob Gardiner, ramping up his last-minute technical readiness to play all the voice-overs on cue. The upbeat song by R. Kelly continued playing, soon to be faded out for the live news presentation.

But then I climbed the hills
And saw the mountains
I hollered help 'cause I was lost
Then I felt the strong wind
Heard a small voice sayin'...The storm is over

The storm on this gloomy morning was nowhere near over, and optimism was needed so badly. Skyy music culture was built to reflect the mood of the community most of the time, and on this tragic morning, the choice of music, its tempo, and the lyrics were apt. Like skydivers, it was time to jump out of the plane at high altitude, hoping our parachutes would work.

"Check with your time, it is exactly four minutes past eight. This is the breakfast show on Skyy 93.5 FM, and Phillip Nyakpo is all set with the major bulletin," said Bob, live on air.

Just then, he turned on my microphone and said, "Good morning, Phillip."

"Good morning, Bob," I responded.

From there, I was on my own, and like I did every morning, I launched into the news, reading it with as much professionalism, emotion, and seriousness as the content called for.

"The death toll from yesterday's violent clashes between supporters of Accra Hearts of Oak and Kotoko Football Club has risen to 125. The major hospitals in Accra are inundated with dead bodies and several hundreds of injured people. Meanwhile, President John Kufuor has called an emergency cabinet meeting this morning to discuss the tragedy.

Miss Elizabeth Ohene, the President's spokesperson who was at 37 Military Hospital spoke to reporters."

This was followed by Elizabeth Ohene's short statement on behalf of President Kufour. Next, we played a recorded live link-up with Stan Dogbe of Joy FM who was working closely with Komla Dumor in reporting the tragedy.

The rest of Bob Gardiner's *Jolly Breakfast Show* was all about the circumstances leading to clashes that resulted in intense grief for the entire nation. The newsroom and the morning show became amalgamated in delivering up-to-the-minute news and information as millions wondered how 126 people could lose their lives overnight during a game of football. The collaboration was also emblematic of how we operated as one unit at Skyy Power FM, our close bonds never breaking even under daily professional stress and strain. Through it all, Bob Gardiner was an outstanding team player. As Bob Gardiner himself put it, "the newsroom depended on the morning show, and the morning show depended on the newsroom."

Night Radio Always Comes First

Playing what is called *night radio* on Skyy Power FM is one of the ways most presenters graduated into becoming local celebrities. The real celebrity status is established when night radio players graduate and are given a slot on daytime radio.

Wilson Arthur, the gatekeeper at Skyy, is the one who ultimately agrees, first, that a person is promising enough to be given a chance even on night radio. Those who later got to know Robert Gardiner when he was at the apex of his radio game would never know that he used to play night radio. Most of those, the majority of listeners, know him only as "Bob Gardiner" or simply "Bob Gee."

Bob Gee arrived at Skyy as a graduate from Kwame Nkrumah University of Science and Technology (KNUST) in 1999. He had the advantage of being familiar with radio, having volunteered as a presenter with a campus FM station called Conttato Radio. It was a very smooth entry because the Skyy FM program manager at the time was Yaw Korankye. Yaw Korankye was also the campus radio's studio manager. He supervised Bob Gee at Conttato Radio. After completing university, Bob Gee spoke to Yaw Korankye, asking if he could get a chance at Skyy. Yaw Korankye in turn recommended Bob Gee to Wilson Arthur for employment.

"Wilson Arthur made me record myself so he could listen to it first," recalls Bob Gee. "In a way typical of Wilson Arthur, he took me on a drive and played the recording for both of us to hear in his car. I was not comfortable listening to my own voice," says Bob.

Wilson Arthur, however, was very pleased. "Your potential is as huge as the studio from which you recorded this," he told Bob Gee after they finished listening to the recording.

As a life-long mentor of many talented people in Ghana's broadcast industry, Wilson Arthur had a way of influencing those in whom he finds the talent and potential. Inevitably, employees with whom he had this sort of informal conversation quickly learn to believe more in themselves and start producing outstanding results. Over time, they generously attribute their own self-discovery to the coaching skills of Wilson Arthur.

With Wilson Arthur's approval, Bob Gee eased into the night radio gig. He was good at it, and not only that, Bob Gee had flair, and his diction, accent, and good grammar stood out. He worked so hard on sounding so good that when he spoke English, some listeners thought he was an Englishman raised in England. In addition, he had a real passion for radio, a combination Wilson Arthur often looks out for.

Soon, Bob Gee was moved to daytime radio, and not just on any program, but the late afternoon show, the *Drive Jam*.

The Host with the Longest Record on the Morning Show

Ultimately, Bob Gee's reputation as a radio presenter became so synonymous with the *Jolly Break Show* that the success he chalked on the *Drive Jam* just morphed into the morning show.

Most outstandingly, Bob Gee became the morning show host that lasted longer than anybody else. "I am the longest morning show host on Skyy Power FM," says Bob Gee, with a sparkle of pride in his voice. "I have hosted the program for about a decade. A number of people have been hosting it, but nobody hosted it continuously for as long as I did."

Bob Gee took over the ownership of the *Jolly Breakfast Show* from Kwete Quaynor. Kwete was combining hosting the morning show with his university education at Cape Coast University.

"I was at home one early morning when the Skyy minivan came over with the driver, Kojo Atta," recalls Bob Gee. "Boss Wilson Arthur says I should bring you to the studio right now to host the morning show, because Kwete is unwell and could not make it from Cape Coast this morning," said Kojo Atta to Bob Gee.

Bob Gee's breathing rate increased a bit because he felt a heavy mixture of fear and excitement. He jumped in the bus and the fifteen minutes' ride to Skyy Power FM studio at 37 Windy Ridge was the trip that kick-started his fame as a broadcaster. With the assistance of Wilson Arthur and staff of the newsroom, Bob Gee's maturity as a presenter was on full display during his first three hours on primetime radio.

Listening to Bob Gee tell his story is captivating, even though most of what he says was well known to me. I listen attentively, taking notes while watching to be sure the recording machine is working. I want to capture the first-hand account as narrated by the individuals I knew and worked with over many years at Skyy.

Having lived far away from Ghana for over fifteen years, sometimes the memories of the history we made together feels like pure fiction rather than true history. I remain quiet a lot and ask questions only for clarification or if I believe Bob Gee's response will enhance the story.

"Phillip, if you are not responding to me while I speak, I will think the call has dropped," cautions Bob Gee, completely out of the blue.

"Apologies, Bob," I say. "It is a habit I picked from interviewing people over the years where I kept quiet and made people talk until they got themselves in trouble," I add, and we both laugh in a manner reminiscent of the years we worked together at Skyy.

A Wonderfully Collaborative Environment

Bob Gee left Skyy Power FM after many years of service. He took his experience to Melody FM for a few years before branching into his own private business ventures. The *Local Chat Show*, which identifies news trends in music, was one popular program Bob Gee hosted with the help of Joe Enuson before he left Skyy.

He spent about five more years at the rival station, *Melody*, and then moved to Empire FM operated by the EIB Network for about a year before taking a long break from radio. During that time, Bob Gee hosted a similar program and called it *Chat Down Ghana*, which outcompeted the original program on Skyy. "It is your chat show that is killing us," Wilson Arthur told Bob Gee a few times when they would meet at different places in Sekondi-Takoradi. It was a friendly nod to the effectiveness of his former employee.

It has already been years since Bob Gee left the premier private radio station, but he still considers Skyy a home that holds some of his fondest memories.

"Skyy was still new when I joined after completing university. Despite the existence of the public broadcaster, *Twin City Radio*, Skyy enjoyed monopoly across the metropolis. Everyone listened and everyone wanted to identify with it. The daily impact it made was so huge that you had no choice but to listen to Skyy Power FM."

Bob Gee struggles sometimes to find the right words and phrases to describe the enterprise and its people which played the role of a local superpower. "The presenters of Skyy Power FM, for want of a better word, were demi-gods of the region," he says.

"You felt a sense that people identified themselves as belonging to a certain movement on radio sweeping across the entire Western Region, particularly Sekondi-Takoradi and also parts of the Central Region; Cape Coast specifically. It was a learning process, and it took a little while for some of us to get a real grip on what it was that we were doing because we were now learning all these interviewing skills, how to prepare for programs, and everything that went with being on-air. If any radio station was to start and do the same thing that Skyy Power FM did in the past, it would still be the success template for them."

"I remember we had a segment on the morning show called *Let's Talk About This*. It always centered on the hottest topic in the community or the nation, and people called in to express their opinions and views. Researching the right topic to motivate people to participate in discussions was itself a lot of work, and we always collaborated to make it a success every morning. We would raise issues on health and safety, business, and environmental concerns, working hand-in-hand with the newsroom. Sometimes the newsroom writes news based on interviews on the morning show and, also, some of the content of the morning show was based on news and current affairs generated by the newsroom."

A Fun and Playful Environment

Even though it was a naturally serious work environment, the playfulness with which all the presenters at Skyy approached their work was sometimes frightening, scandalous, and always unpredictable. First, there was the in-house newsletter we called *Skyy Power Inner News* (SPIN) generated by a few faceless people in the newsroom. It was never attributed to anyone, but everyone had a clear idea about the profoundly cheeky team that put it together.

The weekly publication contained simple gossips surrounding friends, family, and the office. These are then exaggerated, magnified, and stretched right up to breaking point. No one, from the chief executive to the security man in the complex, is spared. The stories are diced, sliced, and served on pages pasted on a special staff noticeboard for all to read. Sometimes, a little crowd would gather to read it aloud together and the resulting laughter is equally shared. The only thing bearable about SPIN is that it was always funny and playful, and SPIN continued as long as it did only because the workforce worked and related to each other like a family that deeply cared for one another.

Sometimes, the playfulness is accidentally taken into the studio in the morning, and it runs like a theme. By the end of the day, everyone is left laughing through the office. Bob Gee orchestrated a lot of these.

On public holidays and other occasions, each presenter is compelled to enter the studio and sing one line of a chosen song known to challenge the vocal cords. The exercise always ends up making everyone laugh. Listeners especially loved it, and they would keep talking and laughing about it for days.

Bob Gee remembers one humorous occasion that still lives with him because there was never a plan to create humour at that time.

"News and current affairs often make constant reference to the *ordinary Ghanaian*," says Bob Gee. "So, I had this idea to ask everyone, including listeners and colleagues who come to the studio, what the phrase *ordinary Ghanaian* really meant."

Bob Gee asked Kuntu Blankson when it was his turn in the studio to present his sports segment. He posed the question in the Fante language, and Kuntu spat out an answer in a dry, nonchalant way in Fante.

Bob Gee lost it on air. Kuntu Blankson's answer was so funny, made worse by the fact that he was totally casual about it.

"Ordinary Ghanaian *ye obia ne hu nnyi mfaso*," he said in Fante. It could, more bluntly, be translated as "a Ghanaian who is useless."

The tragedy in the meaning is hard to convey in the English language, but it goes something like this: "An ordinary Ghanaian is someone with no potential of any kind of success in life."

Years later, we still recall the simplicity and dry humour of Bob Gee's thoughtful question and Kuntu Blankson's not-so-thoughtful and memorably humorous response.

An Enduring Memory for Posterity

Bob Gee retains a permanent happy memory about how Skyy Power FM endeared itself to Western Region in many ways, especially through regular live outdoor broadcasts. "Skyy brought the magic of radio to the doorsteps of people in Sekondi-Takoradi," he says.

"This includes live events during which Skyy FM brought music stars from all over Ghana to converge in the twin city for various special music and entertainment festivals under the Skyy Media brand."

In the late 1990s and early 2000s, only a few privileged people were able to watch major international sporting events in Takoradi and much of Ghana, as they tended to be available only via satellite. Bob Gee recalls that Skyy broke this barrier by making it available to the people free through live commentary as well as on large screens mounted outdoors.

"The world heavyweight boxing title matches involving sensational Mike Tyson and other heavy hitters is an example," he says. "The screen was big. You found people packed way into the streets, watching from hundreds of metres away, and this created a special kind of euphoria in the city. These sorts of events happened so regularly and Skyy was constantly on the minds of people. They saw it as an institution that provided the best entertainment and cutting-edge news and information."

He looks back on the overwhelming support and acceptance of Skyy by the people and says, "for the people who have passed through Skyy Power FM, they enjoyed an unusually high level of approval, and it is the thing that they would love about having been associated with the Skyy brand, rather than any monetary compensation they had."

It is my turn to say something, as Bob Gee's recall stirs up my own memories. "There are things and facts that I have forgotten," I say. "Not just the facts, but more importantly, the feelings, and as I listen to you, I feel like you have transported me back to that time," I add, genuinely impressed with Bob Gee's systematic retelling of some long-faded memories. Rather than asking more questions, I find myself contributing a little bit more to what he says.

"When you live in the kind of bubble we were in while enjoying the internal Skyy FM relations like family and friends, it is easy to forget just how much stock people put on us. It is impossible to replicate or even fully imagine what we experienced," I say, starting to feel more personal about it than is necessary for a professional interviewer. I excuse myself, nevertheless, because I was an intrinsic part of the story.

Friends, Family and A Support System Like No Other

Bob Gee says the full positive impact of Skyy on broadcasting, entertainment, business, and society at large is incalculable and would be felt for generations to come. The one topic he keeps returning to is the friendship and warm work environment we experienced together.

"The support system across Skyy was very effective. The total teamwork is an experience at Skyy that I haven't seen anywhere else. People supported you in what it is you are doing. People just loved to be at the premises of the studio. The presenters always felt at home at the station even when it was not their turn to go on air."

The contrast he draws is sharp.

"In other places I have experienced since leaving Skyy, there always seems to be negative gossip, and not a lot of camaraderie, compared to the family that we built at Skyy Power FM. You walk into a situation, and you notice people stop talking. At Skyy, you didn't have to stop talking when somebody else walked into your conversation."

"We were very special in every way," says Bob Gee. "Presenters felt completely at home--it was more than a workplace."

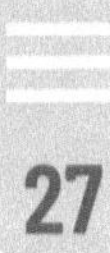

27

"Adu-Mante, You Are an Empty Coconut, But..."

"Wilson Arthur is the kind of person that will not give you fish to eat, but teach you how to fish, and 90% of our people are not ready for that."
— *Kwame Adu—Mante, the one employee at Skyy who understudied Wilson Arthur and, like him, created his own business empire*

Of the hundreds of people Wilson Arthur employed at Skyy Power FM through the decades, Kwame Adu-Mante became the one person who learned to fashion himself in the exact image of his former boss.

If Skyy Power FM were an institution that trained physicians, Kwame Adu-Mante would have graduated as the top surgeon. He spent seven years with the station, and by the time he left in 2007, he carried with him the spirit of Wilson Arthur, in addition to his own unique characteristics as a restless person with eyes wide open for infinite business opportunities.

By the time I get to interview Adu-Mante for this book, he has become a well-established entrepreneur. His own business empire is represented by the *Focus 1* Group of Companies specialising in media services, construction, and distribution of goods nationwide.

As we settle into a conversation, Adu-Mante and I feel we are literally pulling ourselves way back into the past, a past that bore very little resemblance to the present. He is on a business trip in Philadelphia in the United States, and takes time out to speak with me.

It doesn't take long for me to realise that Adu-Mante has grown from a mere boy who worked just to feed himself each day to a full-grown man who has learned how to use his mind to run successful businesses that employ many dozens of people.

He is a far cry from the boy our colleague, Ato-Kwamena Dadzie, called "an empty coconut."

The Hope of a Single Mother's Son

In January 2000, Kwame Adu-Mante arrived in Takoradi to start life as a student of Takoradi Polytechnic. "I came to study Building Technology, and being raised by a single mother, I had to learn to support myself at school," he says.

While living in Kumasi, he and his siblings and cousins were attracted to a few private radio stations that started popping out across the city, including *Luv FM* and *Kapital Radio*. "I developed a passion for radio in Kumasi. My cousins loved *Kapital Radio* and I loved *Luv FM*," recalls Adu-Mante.

His passion led him to find an opportunity on Conttato Radio, a campus radio operated by the Katanga Hall of the Kwame Nkrumah University of Science and Technology. "My sister also used to do voluntary work at Conttato Radio," he says.

He was there for just six months, but the period was long enough for him to deepen his passion for broadcasting.

Shortly after arriving in Takoradi, he decided Skyy was a station he wanted to work with. After multiple visits to the station, he met the chief executive, Wilson Arthur, and handed him his application along with smooth talk about what he was able to do. It was late in the night, and Adu-Mante's pair of piercing eyes and enthusiasm held Wilson Arthur's attention.

Wilson wasted no time and called the program manager Yaw Korankye to join them for a chat. The quick introduction immediately opened a door for Adu-Mante. Yaw Korankye, who used to work at Contatto Radio knew Adu-Mante's sister in Kumasi when she also used to volunteer there as a presenter.

The door of opportunity at Skyy opened even wider that night as Adu-Mante was taken straight to the live studio. The *Late Night Show*, a program which is a mix of music and review of the day's events, was running. Adu-Mante was made to read out a basic script with a brief comment, and that was enough to earn him a tick of approval from both Yaw Korankye and Wilson Arthur.

There was another night program called *Get Closer*, hosted by Kofi Gyetsua Ankoma (KGA) who worked part time with Skyy, combining it with his employment at Panalpina, a freight forwarding company with operations in Takoradi and Tema.

"Just around the time I came to Skyy, KGA was transferred to Tema for his work with Panalpina, so I was made to host his program, *Get Closer*," recalls Adu-Mante.

It was his biggest break in radio up to that point, but the transition was anything but smooth.

The First Show was a Flop!

Get Closer was a weekly program designed for those in love to exchange messages publicly on radio and request music for their partners. "I had a good voice for radio at that time, and so I was a perfect replacement for KGA. I had a whole week to prepare for the show, but my first show was a blunder; it was a mess," recalls Adu-Mante.

"At the time, we were using the Soundmaster console, and it had about twenty-four faders, and each time you needed to move them in pairs. The campus radio I was used to had a much smaller console, so it was easy to use. But here, I was sitting in front of this much more complex console along with a Mini Disc player that I was not familiar with. Apart from that, there were all these advanced professional CD players and I had to juggle all these with the microphone and two separate lines for phone calls."

Adu-Mante remembers it all as a confusing experience. "I could not pick up calls, I could not play the right music at the right volume, and I couldn't get my voice right. Wilson Arthur, to his credit, still had faith in me because of the passion I had for radio," says Adu-Mante, still feeling sorry for his younger self from decades ago.

Another colleague, Nana Kwame, whom we called *Master Planner*, along with Sammy Arthur were asked to help Adu-Mante with production and assistance in the studio. Sammy Arthur and Nana Kwame were very skilled in operating all the equipment in the studio and were helpful to all the presenters who had challenges handling the machines. Once Adu-Mante could work all by himself, he was given a night radio slot from midnight to 4 am, and as he says, "that is when I perfected my skills on radio. I think I played night radio for a whole year, and that is when I started moving into different areas of on-air operations."

The Most Efficient Election Reporter

Kwame Adu-Mante continued studying building technology at the Takoradi Polytechnic (now Takoradi Technical University). He also started feeling completely at home with Skyy Power FM and developed a strong interest in journalism. He assisted in producing news and current affairs and sought help to report the news. Adu-Mante's most memorable contribution to the newsroom occurred during Ghana's general election at the end of the year 2000.

To ensure Skyy covered the election as much as possible, we enlisted and provided basic training for many of our colleagues at the station. Adu-Mante was right at the top of the pile, and Ato-Kwamena Dadzie took a particular interest in him.

Ato, a brilliant and most reliable colleague in the newsroom, is a person fully at peace with being both blunt and effective on the job.

"Adu-Mante, I know you are an empty coconut, but you can do this," he told Adu-Mante and assigned him to report from the Shama constituency which lies at the outskirts of the metropolis. It was considered one of the hot seats with a highly anticipated outcome, and Adu-Mante took his assignment seriously.

"I didn't know Shama that well, so I devised my own means to gauge the voters' preferences and who they were likely to vote for," recalls Adu-Mante.

"I went to the Shama public transport station in Takoradi where hundreds of passengers were traveling from and to Shama every hour, and I asked for their opinion."

It was by no means a scientific study, but Adu-Mante had a clear sense of the outcome by the time he finished talking to people. "I used common sense, and based on my analysis and numbers, I made projections that the election was going to go in a particular direction."

When the official results were declared, Adu-Mante's forecast proved to be accurate. His certainty and confidence in the projections he made stood out so clearly that he attracted enough attention to be invited on the *Jolly Breakfast Show* live on air to help discuss the result and his own analysis.

"Our morning show was of such high quality that people like me were not allowed to get anywhere close to the production team when the program was on air, but somehow, I was allowed to be a guest on it. In fact, I could not sleep when I was told the night before that I should join the morning show and help the team with on-air analysis."

As a group of journalists at the Skyy newsroom, we collaborated extensively with Joy FM in Accra. We relied on Joy FM for some news stories from Accra, and Joy FM relied on us for developments around Western and Central Regions. For many years, I personally worked for Joy FM as their Western Regional Correspondent. It was not a surprise that when Joy FM reached out to us for election-related news from Sekondi-Takoradi, we put Adu-Mante forward for it, and he did not disappoint.

Adu-Mante brought excitement to the newsroom during that election, and his efficient delivery together with impressive analysis made us all begin to believe that there was more to him than just a boy with an "empty coconut" head. His profile rose astronomically immediately after the 2000 election, but as future events unfolded, it became clear that Adu-Mante had only started a warm-up exercise to achieve dreams beyond everyone's imagination. He wanted to be financially free, and his whole being was primed and alert to finding the opportunity.

"A Commission is What You Receive When You Bring Adverts"

"One day I was at the reception and someone came in, and Esi Gyan of blessed memory gave him a substantial amount of money."

Esi Gyan was our colleague who passed away in 2014. She worked as our Administrative Manager and also handled payroll duties.

Esi Gyan counted the money and handed it out to the gentleman called Mark, a sales officer for Skyy. Adu-Mante heard the amount, which was equal to his monthly wage at Skyy, and that made him curious, so he turned to Esi Gyan to find out more.

"What is that money for, and who is that guy?" he asked.

"Oh, he is a sales guy, and the money is his commission," answered Esi Gyan.

Adu-Mante was baffled.

"What is a commission, what is the money for?" he asked, genuinely unaware what a commission was.

"A commission is 10% of what you are paid when you bring adverts, so you get 10% of whatever you bring," explained Esi Gyan.

An explosion occurred in Adu-Mante's mind.

"So, if I bring five million cedis, I get five hundred thousand cedis?" he asked, completely incredulous. "...and if I bring ten million, I get one million cedis?" he added, unable to believe it.

"Yes Adu-Mante," said Esi Gyan and she looked at him bemused.

"Really?" said Adu-Mante.

All he could see now was a large goldmine at Skyy.

The first vision Adu-Mante saw was that he could make more money than any other employee at Skyy.

"Who is the highest paid person here?" he asked, not bothered one bit as to whether it was an appropriate question or not.

"I can't tell you, but the top guys here are earning around..." Esi Gyan told Adu-Mante the amount, and suddenly he knew he had found the key to kicking poverty out of his life--forever. His mindset changed that very moment, and he knew he could design the trajectory of the rest of his life.

"I Want to do Sales and Marketing"

"I went to Wilson Arthur and told him I wanted to do sales and marketing, and he was not enthused. You know, Wilson is a chartered marketer, so he was not ready to put a building technology student out there for sales and marketing. He was not sure it was the right thing for me," recalls Adu-Mante.

"He discouraged me and I left. But I went back later during another conversation, and I told him again that I wanted to do sales. This time, he opened up and told me what it entails and the things I needed to do. Wilson was actually looking for someone who was cut out for this role, especially someone who understands brands in order to optimise value for clients," says Adu-Mante.

"Wilson Arthur felt that my motive and drive to enter sales and marketing was about making money rather than good results for clients. So, he wanted me to understand that I can do ten million and get one million, but I just can't get up and do that much without going through a deliberate process of creating value for clients," observes Adu-Mante.

"What I learned at that time was that Skyy was dealing with the businesses in Accra and in Takoradi. Everyone knew Wilson and they all preferred to talk to him directly."

"Being a Kumasi boy, I went back to Kumasi and checked all the radio networks. Fortunately, my brother who loved *Kapital Radio* was working there as a salesperson, and so with his help, I started picking up clients in Kumasi who had yet to come to Takoradi. Back in those days in the early 2000s, mobile phones were not common, so I called clients from phone booths and communication was a challenge. It was like shouting out information and it took a week to get a response," recalls AduMante.

Adu-Mante also discovered that there were many companies that owed Skyy money, and no one was able to chase up payment. "I became the debt collector and the sales guy at the same time," he says.

Between the sales Adu-Mante made and the debts he successfully collected, Wilson Arthur realised Adu-Mante was serious and getting results.

A special relationship developed between Wilson Arthur and Adu-Mante, which would propel him to realise the dream he now lives. Adu-Mante says he became Wilson Arthur's student, and Wilson Arthur was a capable and willing teacher. As a result, Adu-

Mante believes he learned more than a formal higher education in sales and marketing could teach him.

Around the same time that a special relationship was cemented between Adu-Mante and Wilson Arthur, Skyy Power FM's new edifice at 19/20 West Fijai was under construction. With his background in building and technology, Adu-Mante became a major point of contact on behalf of Wilson Arthur. He would discuss many ideas from the building contractors with Adu-Mante, making for a mutually beneficial relationship.

Adu-Mante's own dreams became as big as Skyy--perhaps even bigger in some ways. "I have always wanted to own a radio station, even if not permanently," he says. "I like to experience running a business and moving on to another one, just to excite myself. I get bored when I am not doing something new," he tells me.

A Business Plan Right Out of the Door

Adu-Mante's dream to run his own businesses took root before he left Skyy. He registered *Focus 1 as a business* that ran events. Before he walked out of Skyy, a few other private stations had started operating in Takoradi as competition to Skyy. One of those stations was *Radio Maxx.*

In a swift move, Adu-Mante leased *Radio Maxx* for five years and later became co-owner. The station stood up to Skyy Power FM as a worthy competitor. In 2013, Adu-Mante made another swift move: he acquired a dying radio station also in Takoradi called *Spice 91.9 FM*. The following year, he made a move on *Beach 105.5 FM* and made it his own as well and experienced the total ups and downs of running multiple businesses.

In time, the *Focus 1* group of companies owned by Adu-Mante would operate subsidiary services including:

- Focus 1 Distribution
- Focus 1 Media
- Focus 1 Construction
- Focus 1 Events

It is not a shabby achievement for a young man who arrived from Kumasi and first heard Skyy as a student of Takoradi Polytechnic.

Never Far Away From His Roots at Skyy

Almost two hours of interviewing Adu-Mante, and one of the things that stands out is that he is full of praise for Wilson Arthur and feels indebted to him and his wife Adwoa Amofah. "I learned so many useful things from Wilson Arthur and his wife Adwoa Amofah. They gave me a lot of opportunities to make a difference," he says.

"It felt like they took me through four or five MBA classes. All the mistakes I made under Wilson were corrected by him. I was not at the helm of affairs, so I could afford to make mistakes and he corrected them. That is why I feel he took me through a whole marketing course. He exposed me to marketing directors and brand managers who understood the craft and I just had the privilege of learning so much. By the time I went out on my own, I made only a few mistakes," says Adu-Mante.

About 200 metres from Skyy Power FM's mighty 19/20 West Fijai office and studios is a fresh edifice Kwame Adu-Mante himself erected as the headquarters of the *Focus 1* group of companies. Across the top of the building is the name *"aduMANTE"* written in beautiful blue letters. The address of that five-storey building is *20/21 West Fijai* in Takoradi.

On days when he is not too occupied with multiple business meetings, he walks up to the balcony at the top of the building and, occasionally, he sees Wilson Arthur or his wife Adwoa Amofah. Something magical always happens at that moment: Wilson or Adwoa Amofah exchange special greetings with Adu-Mante in the form of a hearty wave of hands. That greeting always holds a special meaning for Adu-Mante.

It takes his mind back to decades earlier when he championed the project to build Skyy Power FM's new studio. All the powers in the world at the time could not convince him that he would put up an equally huge building as headquarters of his own companies.

Adu-Mante says whenever he sees the Skyy building, he thinks of all the things Wilson Arthur taught him in sales and marketing that completely changed his life. "The tutelage actually happened in that building," he says.

Adu-Mante's own five-storey building close to Skyy is a testament that he put real meaning to the study he undertook at Takoradi Polytechnic as a building technologist. All the seven years he spent at Skyy taking in a universe of knowledge and experience resulted in something that benefits not only him, but dozens of others he has employed. Adu-Mante believes he owes much of this to Wilson Arthur, Adwoa Amofah, and Skyy Power FM.

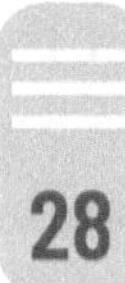

Highlife Music is Alive with Abronoma

"C. K. Mann has no substitute.

Paapa Yankson has no substitute.

A.B. Crentsil has no substitute.

So why replace them?"

— Paa Kofi Nyarko on why Ghanaian Highlife music must have its proper place.

Paa Kofi Nyarko's biggest break in radio occurred in 1998. His friend Kwete Quaynor, who was already working at Skyy Power FM, recommended him to Wilson Arthur, the Chief Executive.

The highlight of his career is marked by the complex tapestry of relationships he built with the most talented and the most celebrated music makers across Ghana. Over a period of more than two decades, he systematically formed an extraordinarily close relationship with these artistes at a deeply personal level.

Starting from Sekondi-Takoradi, the home of the great singer-songwriters of Ghana, Paa Kofi used Skyy Power FM as a tool to elevate the legends to the dizzying heights they deserved.

His routine was simple: he played music made by these outstanding composers; afterwards, he went out to have lunch with them, followed by conversations, the sort that only the closest of friends would have.

Two of his legendary friends died in the last few years: Paapa Yankson in 2017, and C. K. Mann in 2018. For Paa Kofi, the passing of these men was more than the loss of national music icons. He fought back volumes of tears over them, men he loved and admired so much.

"I lost my friends. They were both like fathers to me because they opened themselves to me. They entrusted me with their whole life story. I miss Paapa Yankson and C. K. Mann everyday," he says.

There are a few other older friends of Paa Kofi who also stand out, not just because of their age, but because they are living music legends: Gyedu-Blay Ambolley, Pat Thomas, and A. B. Crentsil. They are all in their seventies.

"I am finding new ways to treasure these remaining (older) friends and I want to absorb their musical sense as much as possible," he reflects.

A Welcome with Standing Ovation

Papa Tony Ashun-Codjiw now lives in Calgary, Canada. He and Paa Kofi were students at the University of Cape Coast, and he was the first to recommend Paa Kofi for employment at Skyy Power FM. Papa Tony, a Takoradi boy, observed Paa Kofi on Atlantic Radio (ATL), the campus radio where he was presenting programs in Fante. He spoke to Adwoa Amofah, who is one of the three owners of Skyy. Shortly after, Paa Kofi himself reached out to Kwete Quaynor, who was also his school mate at the University and both of them used to volunteer as presenters on ATL campus radio.

Kwete Quaynor believed in Paa Kofi's abilities, and Paa Kofi believed in himself even more.

"After Kwete's recommendation, I met with Wilson Arthur who asked me what I could do with the Fante language on air," recalls Paa Kofi.

"I came at a time when Skyy needed another Fante presenter, because Uncle Opia was on leave and Aba Moses was the only one presenting Fante programs--and she was having difficulty juggling all the responsibilities."

"Naa Adoley Thompson had just finished reading the news in English when Wilson and I finished the short chat," says Paa Kofi.

"He immediately had me translate the news into Fante, and the next thing I knew, I was asked to read the news in Fante, live on radio and that was easy for me," continues Paa Kofi.

"When I walked out of the studio, I was given a standing ovation by Wilson and all the other presenters that were there." Paa Kofi's desire to join Skyy was complete by mid-morning.

"Because I was used to being in the studio hosting Fante programs on campus, moving into Skyy to do a similar thing was very easy for me. What I really wanted was to build my own personal brand, grow and mature as a broadcaster, and I knew Skyy Power FM was an excellent place to achieve this dream," he says.

The "Abrrrrrrronoma" Phenomenon

The top Fante program called "*Odem Sokoo*" was hosted by Uncle Opia. As Opia was on leave, Paa Kofi was asked to host the show.

The review afterwards was impressive. Only Paa Kofi himself was unhappy with an aspect of the program.

"When I opened the phone lines, listeners started calling me *little Uncle Opia*. Even though this was very complimentary, I actually wanted recognition of my own personal brand, rather than just a version of the already popular Uncle Opia," explains Paa Kofi.

To circumvent the challenge, he came up with an ingenious solution through the way he introduced himself on air. He would mention his full name, "Paa Kofi Nyarko," followed by a deliberate, and almost annoying but attention-grabbing, pronunciation of the word "Abronoma."

He pronounced it by elongating the letter "r" for as long as possible. The word "Abronoma" takes exactly one second to pronounce, but Paa Kofi will use anything from five to ten seconds or more to pronounce it.

You have to try pronouncing it yourself to see how striking it is. The word itself doesn't mean much, except that it is a traditional Fante language appellation or epithet for anyone who has his rather common family name, "Nyarko." Some traditional names have such appellations, but they tend not to be used often.

Paa Kofi wanted to be known as "Abronoma" on air, and so it was that listeners called him as such, permanently differentiating him, exactly the way he wanted.

A Clash of Tastes in Music

The love of authentic Ghanaian Highlife music is universally shared in Ghana. The passion for it never faulted, but with the advent of new forms of musical expressions, including Hiplife and the adoption of other rhythms into Ghanaian compositions, Highlife started losing some lustre and was no longer always a first choice.

Paa Kofi set out to change that, even at the risk of clashing with the genius Wilson Arthur, the man who owns Skyy Power FM and is himself an authority on music.

Wilson's love of music was so alive and expansive that he was arguably the one person in Ghana who owned the biggest collection of music across the country.

One of the pillars on which he stood to build Skyy was his experience in selling music in Accra and at the same time renting music on CD to Joy FM and Vibe FM, music that only he alone owned.

Wilson also believed that every song played on Skyy on any program must reflect a certain classic trait based on who played it, when it played, how it was played, as well as the preceding music and the one that follows.

Wilson attracted and trained many Skyy Power FM employees to develop sophisticated tastes in music. Some of the outstanding employees with refined taste and knowledge of music include Joe Enuson, Nana Otu Gyandoh, JM Caesar, Maame Esi Mark-Hansen, Sammy Arthur, and Ato Parry.

Wilson expected and promoted a high level of euphonic "flow" of music on Skyy FM--24 hours a day, seven days a week.

He was also hands-on in choosing music for all presenters and programs. Between him and Paa Kofi, however, an uncomfortable silent game started.

Wilson would carefully make a list of tracks for Paa Kofi to play, but during the program, Wilson would notice some of his selections didn't make it on air. Instead, Paa Kofi would insert his own secret selections.

Wilson was not impressed, and he told Paa Kofi. Paa Kofi in turn was not impressed and ignored Wilson. Employer and employee continued playing the game for a few weeks, unable to declare a ceasefire.

Eventually, Wilson gave up. He realised he had become the only one feeling uncomfortable about Paa Kofi's apparent one-way choice of music.

"I learned a lot from Wilson and admire his taste in music, but I also believe in my own sense of music, especially Highlife," says a defiant Paa Kofi.

Giving a New Life to Authentic Highlife Music

Ever the smart reader of people, the environment, and how it benefits the broadcast enterprise, Wilson realised his "recalcitrant" employee was becoming immensely popular with listeners around Sekondi-Takoradi.

Paa Kofi's secret sauce was that he kept playing the authentic Ghanaian Highlife, mostly made in Sekondi-Takoradi by national icons Paapa Yankson, Jewel Ackaah, C.K. Mann, A. B. Crentsil, and Gyedu-Blay Ambolley--all musicians who call Sekondi-Takoradi and Western Region their home.

Paa Kofi's style and focus on the indigenous music woke up the near-dormant love for Highlife again, bringing back a new appreciation for the talent manifested in the evergreen music made by legends who continued to walk around the Sekondi-Takoradi community.

It was only later that it became clear Paa Kofi was doing far more than playing the music of local heroes. He was honouring their talents, passion, and devotion in serving their community with music they produced for posterity.

In the process, Paa Kofi became the go-to person for these musicians when they wanted a friend to just chat with, someone who understood them, beyond dancing to their music. The closeness of the bonds he formed became unbreakable.

Paa Kofi believes he fought hard to play as much Highlife music as he wanted, while resisting what he felt was tantamount to censorship. In his interview for this book, Paa Kofi reflects deeply on this with an even greater passion for the cherished Highlife music, especially for those made in Sekondi-Takoradi.

He says, "C. K. Mann has no substitute. Paapa Yankson has no substitute. A.B. Crentsil has no substitute. So why would you attempt to replace them?"

At Takoradi's Planters Lodge hotel in March 2000, Paa Kofi was elated when Skyy Power FM singled out C.K. Mann for a special lifetime award to recognise his service to Highlife music.

It was as if all his dreams for keeping Highlife music in its rightful place were coming true; with Wilson Arthur and Skyy Power FM as the dream makers.

Thinking Big, Deep, and Wide

Paa Kofi's love for music started when, as a child, he became a chorister at the Methodist Church in Salt Pond. He discovered that he had an aptitude for appreciating good music. His uncle, Jos Acquah (also called Superbad), a researcher at the University of Cape Coast, also introduced him to other kinds of music, leading him to pay particular attention to all the different elements that come together to make good music. It was a harbinger of how his life as a music lover and radio presenter would turn out.

"I used to listen to Wilson Pickett (an American soul music singer and songwriter), and others, and then I switched to Ghanaian traditional music and Highlife, including music by Koo Nimo and other great Ghanaian music makers," says Paa Kofi.

His happiest moments are when he gets a chance to speak to musicians, on and off-record. With his background, he can regale music makers with simple but piercing questions that make them feel like Paa Kofi understood their curiosity, impulses, and creativity. He interacts with them while indirectly recognising them as special individuals who think big, deep, and wide. In the process, he endears himself to these artistes and connects with them at a deep level.

An example of this occurred while he was interviewing Kojo Antwi, one of Ghana's music heavyweights. More than an interview, it was like a conversation between two insightful men with a passion for music.

Paa Kofi asked specific questions of Kojo Antwi about his many and varied performances, his appearance at the first or second Pan-African Festival in Cape Coast, as well the circumstances that made Kojo Antwi arrive on stage on a white horse for one of his famed end-of-year performances.

After Kojo Antwi laboured to remember details for the answers, Paa Kofi told him how he started appreciating music from childhood.

"As a kid," he said, "I listened to albums, then I took the LP, turned it around to check who played the trombone, who played the guitar, the horns, etc., and it helped me appreciate music. I started getting the sense of music back then. I used to listen carefully to Carl Agyeman Bannerman..."

Suddenly, Kojo Antwi interrupted Paa Kofi, apologised for doing so, and started commending him.

"I am glad you are the person behind the microphone. We have too many people with microphones these days. They request an interview, but they don't do research on your background, or they don't know where you are coming from or how far you've come. And the interviews become boring and monotonous with a question like, 'so what should the fans expect?' It doesn't allow me to give out my best, so I am glad you are talking about Carl Agyeman Bannerman," said Kojo Antwi, acknowledging Paa Kofi's background, knowledge and insight.

Similarly in another interaction, Paa Kofi asked Paapa Yankson how he and his bandsmen achieved a distinctive baseline in one of his songs. Impressed at his perception, Paapa Yankson said, "...you have followed music for long--not all of your people know what a baseline is in music."

In the same interview, he got Paapa Yankson to explain that there were three types of Highlife: Slow Highlife, Mid-tempo Highlife and Fast Highlife.

Paapa Yankson concluded that there was a fourth type of Highlife called Funky Highlife which he invented together with C.K. Mann.

The highly conversational and meditative way Paa Kofi interacts with artistes keeps the unbreakable bonds he forged, starting from his time at Skyy Power FM. He certainly started in Cape Coast and blossomed in Takoradi. Later, he took his craft to the national capital, Accra.

Bonds Unbound and Unbroken

Paa Kofi Nyarko was living in Accra when Highlife music giant Paapa Yankson died at 73.

It broke his heart.

With many fond memories and appreciation for his contribution to music, Paa Kofi accepted the privilege of being the Master of Ceremonies at the funeral which took place at the forecourt of the State House in Accra.

At 81 years old, C. K. Mann followed the live broadcast of the funeral in Takoradi. During a short recess at the event, one of C.K. Mann's sons who attended the funeral in Accra handed his phone to Paa Kofi.

"My father wants to speak to you," he told Paa Kofi.

C.K. Mann had a short request. "Listen, Paa Kofi," C. K. Mann said. "When I die, I want you to be the Master of Ceremony at my funeral, the same way you are doing for Paapa Yankson right now. That's all I want from you."

Tears welled up in Paa Kofi's eyes, hidden by the dark glasses he was wearing.

He felt his heart breaking again.

The heavy and emotional request was made within fifteen seconds on the phone.

Eight months after that conversation, C. K. Mann died at age 82 in Takoradi.

Paa Kofi's heart broke once more when he heard the news.

Part of C. K. Mann's funeral was held at C. K. Mann Park, a public park located at the Anaji suburb of Takoradi, which was named after him.

Other events forming part of the funeral took place at Jubilee Park and at the Takoradi Sports Club. Paa Kofi fulfilled the wishes of his old friend and served as Master of Ceremony at his memorial.

One poster celebrating his life simply read, "C. K. Mann, King of Highlife."

"I miss my friends, and my commitment to keep Highlife music alive on and off-radio has only just started," he says in reflection.

Not once did Paa Kofi ever imagine his love for music and radio would bring him to Takoradi and Skyy Power FM, a place where he would form unbreakable bonds with many musicians, including the King of Highlife, C. K. Mann.

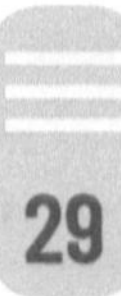

Humour Unlimited with Kwame Dzokoto

There ought to be a written rule in broadcasting as follows:

Under no circumstance must a funeral announcement be delivered with any kind of humour.

There is no such rule.

Even if there was, the man called Kwame Dzokoto would not only contort the rule, he would snap it repeatedly with glee.

Dzokoto deliberately broke the unwritten rule in the mining town of Tarkwa when he made a live, on-air funeral announcement. The radio station was Dynamite FM, a non-commercial campus radio operated by students at the University of Mines and Technology in Tarkwa.

Because Dynamite FM was designed primarily for the benefit of students, they had been broadcasting only in English. The townsfolk, however, wanted to be part of it and started requesting announcements, mostly for funerals. They also started requesting that the announcements be read in the Fante language.

Dynamite FM agreed.

In the meantime, Kwame Dzokoto had become well known as a humorous and enchanting Master of Ceremonies available for various social events.

A Life Changing Discovery

Seeing the increasing interest for announcements in Fante, the Station Manager at Dynamite FM, Ralph Menz, decided to recruit some locals to run the station when student volunteer presenters were on holiday. Then he discovered Dzokoto after observing him moderate a social event in Tarkwa. Ralph was convinced that he had found the right person to read funeral announcements in Fante.

Dzokoto, after some basic training and instruction, received his first assignment; then everything went south.

In presenting one of the first funeral announcements, Dzokoto managed to insert a deeply emotional humour that no one had ever heard. Staff at the station, including Ralph, monitored Dzokoto's most unusual presentation. Curiously though, the extremely humorous but bizarre presentation of a funeral announcement didn't sound disturbing or even objectionable.

Staff at the station didn't feel he had done the best job of the delivery; neither did they think Dzokoto needed any correction or admonition.

A Bereaved Man Walks into a Studio

Shortly after the comical announcement went on air, a man dressed in a mournful attire arrived at the station and demanded to know who read the humourised funeral announcement.

He didn't look particularly happy, so the staff he met at the station suspected he was a family member of the deceased who was understandably upset by the announcement that apparently trivialised a traumatic loss of life.

None of the guys wanted to disclose that Dzokoto made the announcement, even as the unhappy-looking man kept repeating that he wanted to see the person who read the funeral announcement.

So they asked their boss, Ralph, to make a decision on whether to reveal Dzokoto as the culprit.

Ralph walked in with Dzokoto by his side to meet the bereaved man who promptly repeated his request, still seemingly distressed.

Pointing to Dzokoto and fully expecting an angry reaction, Ralph said, "the announcement was made by him."

The man readjusted his large black funeral cloth, putting his hand into the deep fold close to his body.

Time seemed to stop for a moment as everyone watched the man. The uncertainty felt heavy. The man may very well be reaching for a hidden gun or dagger, in which case Ralph and Dzokoto as well as the other onlookers at the station were ready to sprint.

During the heart-stopping moment, the man pulled out his whole arm. There was no hidden dagger or gun in his hand.

Instead, the man brought out a loaf of bread.

Looking at Dzokoto, he said, "you did a very good job with the announcement. Now, everybody knows we have lost our loved one. This announcement has been made in English so many times, but people didn't even pay attention, but the way you announced it in Fante was so good. Take this loaf of bread as a thank you!"

Ralph let out a huge sigh of relief.

This confirmed to Ralph that Kwame Dzokoto was an unusually talented person, and it was time to hold him closer.

"We need to talk," he told him. "I will cancel my lecture for tomorrow morning. Let's meet for a serious chat."

Ralph Menz was going to make sure Kwame Dzokoto remained the property of Dynamite FM. Ralph didn't know it then, but his plan was not going to withstand the searching eyes and ears of Skyy Power FM Chief Executive Wilson Arthur.

The Meeting of Ralph and Dzokoto

The gift of bread, in recognition of Kwame Dzokoto's unconventional, but effective communication on radio, was the first event that indicated he was going to end up at Skyy Power FM.

For Dzokoto, the memory of how it all started is clear.

"I was at this wedding, and the MC was very late. My friends and the people at the wedding believed I could step in," recalls Dzokoto.

He felt comfortable and happy running the show for the bride and the bridegroom. As Ralph Menz watched, he could not believe how comfortable Dzokoto felt in his own skin as an entertainer as well as the effective way he held everyone's attention at the wedding.

Ralph was convinced Dzokoto may have had some specialised training in communication or even broadcasting. "Wow, have you worked on radio before?" asked Ralph as he shook Dzokoto's hand to congratulate him after the event. He introduced himself and then made a proposal.

"Come and work with us at Dynamite FM; you can do it," said Ralph. Dzokoto didn't hesitate to say "yes." He could work at Dynamite FM as well as spend the rest of his time at his mother's stationery store where he could continue interacting with hundreds of customers. He couldn't think of a better combination for a fulfilling life. He believed he was fortunate to be noticed by Ralph Menz.

A Boy Between Tarkwa and Sekondi-Takoradi

Even though Kwame Dzokoto was born in Tarkwa, he spent a lot of his formative years at his family home in Sekondi. Employment and business activities in Sekondi centered around fishing as well as commercial activities at the Takoradi port.

As a tradition, the fishermen and women in Sekondi do not work on Tuesdays. The men, especially, will spend a lot of time mending their nets in groups and playing games afterwards, talking and singing among themselves.

There was always a place for young ones among these folks, and Dzokoto always found the fishermen's Tuesday holiday experience most refreshing. It offered him a lot of exciting interaction.

"I spent a lot of time with the fishermen while they worked and played draughts. I heard and learned the way they spoke and the many ways they joked every day," recalls Dzokoto.

Even without high-level academic qualifications, many members of his extended family became seafarers. It was the family's wish that he would graduate from Nautical College in Accra and perhaps end up as a ship captain. While waiting for that dream, Dzokoto learned the unique language, expressions, and the entire culture of Sekondi-Takoradi.

He also attended Cape Coast Polytechnic where he studied mechanical engineering. Then he proceeded to the Nautical College in Accra, now called Maritime University, but he dropped out like the way a container sometimes slides off a ship in the middle of the ocean.

"During one of the vacations, I came home to Tarkwa and told my mother I will not be going back to school," says Dzokoto. His mother did not try to persuade him otherwise, most probably because the two had a very close relationship and tended to understand each other's feelings.

So Dzokoto never became a seafarer or a ship captain. He returned to Tarkwa with the invisible treasure of a genuine culture he absorbed in the twin city.

He spent time working at his mother's shop, where he interacted with hundreds of customers every day to satisfy his innate desire to constantly and joyously connect with people. The experience of observing, listening, and talking with the fishermen and women in Sekondi enabled him to communicate freely and heartily with all sorts of people, including crowds at social gatherings where he volunteered regularly as Master of Ceremony for events around Tarkwa.

That is how the door to Dynamite FM opened for him. That is how he got a free loaf of bread from a bereaved family member who was moved by the unique way he introduced humour into a funeral announcement, managing to keep it both effective and inoffensive.

It was a fine triangular life: working with his mother at their shop, getting busy every weekend with MC gigs around town, and being a little star in the Tarkwa community by working at Dynamite FM as an announcer and comedian, telling jokes in between playing music.

Dzokoto was also, at heart, a learner with an insatiable appetite for knowledge and self-development.

As he would soon find out, there was nobody in all of Western and Central Regions of Ghana he could find as a better teacher than Wilson Arthur.

The young Chief Executive of Skyy Power FM in Takoradi became Kwame Dzokoto's teacher and employer, rolled into one.

When The Student Is Ready, The Teacher Appears

To expand the market for Skyy, Wilson Arthur drove up to Tarkwa to study the environment and colonise it for his station as well.

Kwame Dzokoto didn't know this until he met Wilson at the Dynamite FM studio.

"I heard of Skyy, but I didn't know Wilson Arthur, I had not met him before," recalls Dzokoto.

Wilson Arthur arrived in the mining town of Tarkwa in his old KIA Sportage. He drove the 85-kilometre distance with a couple of staff from the marketing department.

The car at the time was unbranded and, therefore, helpful for the reconnaissance mission. He was familiar with the commercially inconsequential Dynamite campus radio in Tarkwa. He wasn't sure of the frequency, so he kept playing with the dial while driving around the town until he settled on 88.9 FM. He immediately felt the energy from the voice that came from the car stereo.

The man on air was speaking a style of Fante that is unmistakably identified with Sekondi-Takoradi. Wilson wanted to undertake some market research by speaking with small business owners at various shops. But as he continued listening to the voice, the only person he was now keen to speak with was the man at Dynamite FM whose voice was being carried straight into Wilson's car.

He had a full command of the Sekondi-Takoradi lingo, his jokes made the tummy hurt from laughter, and he sounded like he was completely enjoying himself in the studio.

"To be frank," says Dzokoto about Dynamite years later, "I was very happy at Dynamite FM and never thought of going anywhere else."

Wilson Arthur kept driving around town, but by now he was not sure where he was going.

"This is the language Sekondi-Takoradi wants to hear," he whispered to himself, in reference to the way Kwame Dzokoto kept talking and cracking jokes.

"This is the language Sekondi-Takoradi wants to hear," he repeated.

Wilson kept repeating the phrase to himself unconsciously, and all the while, becoming convinced that Kwame Dzokoto could become a celebrity on Sekondi-Takoradi's Skyy Power FM. In an instant, he decided to drive straight to the studio to meet the campus radio presenter whose name he still didn't know.

The man of Wilson's dream at Dynamite FM was still on air when he arrived at the studio. Wilson waited with anticipation, asking only to see "the person presenting the program in the Fante language."

The Fante-speaking presenter, of course, was Kwame Dzokoto.

Wilson didn't want any of the other people around the studio to know that he is the owner of Skyy FM, scouting in Tarkwa with a desire to poach the campus radio's most valuable presenter.

In a deliberately quiet tone, Wilson introduced himself to Dzokoto and then asked for his name.

"My name is Seth Kwame Dzokoto," he said.

Wilson nearly froze.

"But Dzokoto is an Ewe name, so how come you speak Fante so well?" he queried, both as an observation and a question.

Perhaps under the pressure of trying to poach Dzokoto, he was groping for the right words to say now that he was face-to-face with the man. He was completely taken aback in his own mind about how the language Dzokoto spoke did not match his name.

The Poaching is Complete

"Wilson was so sweet, and he managed to convince me to join Skyy, so I accepted," says Dzokoto. Once he settled into Skyy, Dzokoto found out that he didn't fit in.

"Eighty percent of programs were in English, and every presenter is highly rated with a lot of popularity. The standards were very high, so he decided to let me start playing night radio from midnight."

When Dzokoto got ready to play night radio, he got bumped, so he played between 1 am and 3 am, when most listeners were asleep.

After a few weeks, some of the people who were listening called in to demand that Dzokoto was so good and entertaining that he should be moved to primetime.

But Wilson was not in a rush.

Says Dzokoto, "after I play overnight with the desire to sleep because of tiredness, Wilson will call me early in the morning and spend the whole day with me, teaching me a lot about the dynamics of radio and how to succeed. He taught me like a son, and he became like my father."

He adds, "he started developing me. He made me understand what radio is, why I am doing radio and to understand who I am speaking to on radio. He knew I had talent, but I was raw and inexperienced, so he decided to transform me."

Teaching and Learning Intensified

"One day, without warning, Wilson decided to give me the prime midmorning slot, relegating another presenter who was a huge star. It was a big risk, but he had a plan to ensure I really succeeded. He spent every morning with me, reviewing the entire program. He would even review the jokes I would be telling. He would let me tell him the jokes and then help me refine it. This put a lot of pressure on me to perform," recalls Dzokoto.

"He encouraged me to learn every day from everywhere. I would go to the Newsroom to get a full briefing on all the current affairs and try to incorporate it into my program in a way that is humorous."

Wilson Arthur was so hands-on with Dzokoto that he would often drive around the city to monitor people's reaction to his presentation. He would then return to the studio, give him a thumbs up and say, "check it, everyone in the city is listening to you."

Dzokoto says the best training Wilson gave him was how to sell effectively on radio through advertising and live presenter mentions.

Dzokoto remembers how Wilson helped him to sell a particular brand of mattress on-air by engaging listeners through a short but effective story, with a strong call to action.

"Tell your listeners," said Wilson "if you don't wake up early, you can spoil your day, and that is why you have to sleep well," adding, "that is why you need this mattress. It helps you have a good day everyday by helping you sleep well. Don't pay money for a bad sleep followed by an even worse day. Make your day easy by buying the right mattress."

Dzokoto was an astute student who took in everything Wilson taught him.

When The Teacher is Done, The Student Departs

Because Dzokoto was fundamentally a comedian, he eventually threw away the radio rule book, replacing it with a skilled presentation that was fully his own.

"With the full support of Wilson, I institutionalised my style of being able to do anything on radio, and the more I kept my authentic style, the more people loved it."

He began to appear in many Ghanaian films, exhibiting a rare ability to remain authentic in imaginary situations. His euphonic Fante language caught the attention of businesses who wanted their message delivered with effective humour.

Like a highly skilled football player, Skyy as a team could no longer hold onto him. Another team was coming for Dzokoto with a bazooka load of cash and incentives.

Happy Days With Mercedes Benz

In Kumasi, the owner of *Hello FM*, Osei Kwame Despite, realised Dzokoto had become a gold mine for radio. He contacted Kwame Dzokoto, offering him a new and expensive Mercedes Benz if he agreed to join the Kumasi-based station. That was apart from an offer to pay him far more than Skyy was paying, along with the equivalent of five-star accommodation.

Wilson Arthur lost a student and a quality human resource in radio. But he had actually just given the industry a gift that would keep on giving.

That gift was, and still is, Kwame Dzokoto.

The gift is just one of many dozens, which according to Philip Osei-Bonsu, makes Wilson Arthur "the one person who has done more for the development of radio in Ghana than any other individual."

About twenty years after being taught and trained by Wilson, Dzokoto still drips with gratitude. He says, "I am grateful to Wilson Arthur, and I will forever be grateful to him. I wish that every radio presenter would work with him, because if you are ready to learn, respect the system and follow advice, it will take you to places."

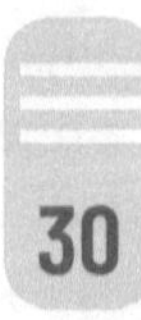

30

"I would Have to Kill Myself for Skyy"

"I told Wilson Arthur to give me a chance and I will not disappoint him. When He gave me the chance, I was overjoyed and I told myself I would have to kill myself for Skyy."

— Michael Gawu, award—winning DJ looking back on the opportunity he had to work with Skyy Power FM for more than two decades.

On Saturday, 21 November 2021, Michael Gawu, popularly known as Premier Gawu, received a Lifetime Achievement Award, conferred on him by the Board of Deepest Western Awards in an event that took place in Takoradi.

The award was in recognition of more than two decades in which Michael Gawu exhibited a rare and unique talent of bringing music to life on and off radio, using his skills as a DJ. Michael Gawu's longevity at Skyy is in keeping with a private commitment he made to himself that he would remain with the station for as long as possible.

Michael Gawu's employment at Skyy nearly didn't happen. When he was interviewed to join Skyy Power FM, the first few words that came out of his mouth almost cost him the job. Somehow, his interviewer, Wilson Arthur, noticed something in him that was far more valuable than his words.

He is, First of all, A Teacher

Michael Gawu was born in the cultural hub of Sekondi. "My late father loved music too and had a lot of collections on old vinyl which he always played. My mother says I always responded enthusiastically to music even as a toddler," he says.

"There was always live music everywhere in Sekondi when I was growing up. There was live band music, night clubs and open-air music everywhere, including traditional music. All my pocket money went into buying music gadgets and cassettes," he says.

Beyond the musical environment, Michael Gawu, propelled by pure talent and passion, learned to become a DJ when he was a young teenager. When his mother set up and operated a pub in Sekondi, he helped to run the entertainment portion of the operation. After secondary school, he continued to Enchi College of Education where he qualified as a professional teacher.

Michael Gawu's talent and capability were quickly recognised at the Enchi College of Education where he was elected as the entertainment prefect after a fierce contest between him and Frankie Taylor, a close friend of his from Sekondi with similar talents.

When Michael Gawu and Frankie Taylor completed Enchi College of Education, Frankie went straight into broadcasting and has worked with Fox FM in Kumasi for more than 20 years. Michael on the other hand moved to Cape Coast and started teaching at Adisadel Basic School, also called St. Nicholas Primary School.

It was during this time that Michael Gawu discovered Atlantic FM (ATL FM), a small campus station operated by students of the University of Cape Coast. "I heard them playing music, and after listening to it for a while, I said to myself, I can do this paaaa, I can do it better," recalls Michael Gawu.

"I can do this paaaa" is a Ghanaian expression, where the word "paaa" is a local parlance that emphasises a person's belief that he can do something to a very large degree.

"I am a music man, I love music," says Michael Gawu as he recalled the events leading him into broadcasting.

"I Can Do This Paaaa"

Fully convinced he could do a better job of playing music on radio better than what he was hearing on University of Cape Coast's ATL

FM, Michael Gawu walked up to the station manager and asked to be given a chance. "The manager at the time was a man called Aikins. Aikins asked me whether I have been on radio before, and I said no, but I can do it. I know the studio craft, I play at nightclubs and events, so I can do it," Michael Gawu assured Aikins. Within a few weeks after he started playing on ATL FM, Michael Gawu was noticed and acknowledged for his ability and style. He continued teaching in Cape Coast while delighting his listeners.

He also became close friends with other presenters at the student-operated station, including Eric Ahianyo and Paa Kofi Nyarko, both of whom later worked for Skyy. "Skyy was so big and influential that I dreamed for a long time to work there, but I had no idea how I could make the approach," says Michael Gawu.

One day, he heard Paa Kofi Nyarko on Skyy, then he decided to call him and find out how he could also work for Skyy. After their chat, Paa Kofi agreed to introduce Michael Gawu to Wilson Arthur, the owner and chief executive of Skyy.

Face to Face with Wilson Arthur

Michael Gawu finally came face to face with Wilson Arthur for a job interview. He was shocked by the first question.

"Do you know what a CD is?" Wilson asked.

Wilson Arthur's question was against the background that around Ghana, the use of Compact Disc (CD) for music in the mid-1990s was uncommon. It was still a relatively new technology right up to the time Wilson Arthur established Skyy Power FM in 1997 and into the year 2000. Before Michael Gawu met Wilson Arthur, he had not seen or used a CD.

"I have heard about it, but I have not seen it before. I know it is used to play music," he told Wilson. Just by the way Wilson looked at him, Michael Gawu suspected he would not win Wilson Arthur's approval to join Skyy Power FM. He thought the interview was over with the first question, so he was surprised when Wilson posed another question.

"We use CDs at Skyy. If you are a DJ and still don't use CDs, then how do you play your music?" asked Wilson. "I know the songs I play very well," replied Michael Gawu. In saying that, he mirrored the singer Bob Dylan who, in "A Hard Rain Is Gonna Fall," sang, "I'll know my song well before I start singing."

"I know all the beats and how to merge one song into another," continued Gawu. "So what I do is, I play cassette A, and when it is about to end, I cue cassette B. I time it carefully and release it on time, so the two tracks merge. I make sure the merging is so smooth that you don't always notice the old song fade into the new one. When you do this very well, people on the dance floor love it, and when you do it on radio, listeners enjoy it and stay glued to the station."

Michael Gawu is a naturally humble person, very competent at what he does but not very good at exhibiting a strong "can-do attitude." Only his actual work speaks for him. As a result, he is easily underestimated in the short term. Wilson Arthur realised this after Michael Gawu explained how he gets results as a DJ. Without any more words, Wilson gave him a chance to play night radio. He was asked to understudy Eddy F, a DJ who was already working for Skyy.

Michael Gawu has vivid memories of his transition to Skyy.

"I told Wilson Arthur to give me a chance and I will not disappoint him," he recalls in my interview with him. "When Wilson gave me the chance, I was overjoyed and I told myself I would have to kill myself for Skyy. I knew I could now prove my worth and I promised never to disappoint and I have kept my promise until now."

The strong emotions with which Michael Gawu expressed appreciation for the opportunity he got with Skyy left me speechless.

Becoming "Premier Gawu"

To the west of Ghana is the French-speaking country called Ivory Coast (Republic of Côte d'Ivoire). The main border town on Ghana's side to the southwest is Elubo which is less than 140 kilometres from Takoradi. Close ties between the two countries are assured, not just by geography, but also historical, cultural and ethnic links, with the various shades of the Akan people concentrated across the border. Popular music from Ivory Coast tends to cross the border into Ghana at the speed of sound. Those sounds of music often quickly become well-known hits in Ghana. One of those hits was called "Premier

Gaou," performed by Magic System, a group of four university students in the mid-1990s.

It was Magic System's "Premier Gaou" hit that left a permanent mark on Michael Gawu. He single-handedly made the Premier Gaou song very popular, playing the rhythmic composition over and over again.

One day, as he was playing it live on air, one of the presenters, Kofi Gyetsua Ankoma entered the studio, looked straight at Michael and said "so you are the one that has been playing this music repeatedly. Why don't you drop your first name and simply call yourself Premier Gaou? It rhymes with your surname."

Michael Gawu smiled. With the big overhead earphone on his head, he nodded, and moments later, he announced to Sekondi-Takoradi that his name was now "Premier Gawu," a name now synonymous with the skills of a man who plays good music on and off radio.

Fulfilling a Promise, Decades On

The online news headline by Accra-based Citi News said: "Takoradi Radio presenter donates to nursing mothers at Effia-Nkwanta hospital."

The opening words of the news item said, "about fifty nursing mothers at the Effia-Nkwanta Regional Hospital Children's Ward in Sekondi have received support from Michael Gawu, a Takoradi-based Radio Presenter."

The donation made by Michael Gawu was his way of celebrating 25 years in radio as a DJ since he started with ATL FM in Cape Coast.

He was quoted as saying, "I could have had a party with some of my colleagues as suggested by some… but I said no, people need help. You don't have to be rich or a billionaire before you give…" Michael Gawu's gesture was welcomed by the Medical Director of Effia Nkwanta Regional Hospital, Dr. Joseph Kojo Tambil.

Apart from wanting to give to the less privileged, Michael Gawu said his other motivation comes from Wilson Arthur. "He gave me the opportunity to work at Skyy Media Group, and I have benefited so much."

"I feel humbled when I consider my long and eventful journey with Skyy Power FM over many decades," observes Michael Gawu. "My breakthrough with Skyy came soon after I was employed. I had the chance to play solo on air so I went to the CD library and found many old songs that I knew well. When I started playing them, Wilson Arthur walked into the studio and asked how I knew all those songs. Wilson knows music very well, so he saw it for himself that I also knew music. Ever since, he and his wife Adwoa Amofah have given me the opportunity to grow at Skyy," he says. Michael Gawu is referring to his various high-profile roles on Skyy, apart from the regular on air-duties.

"I was given the chance to become Events Manager for the station and later, Programs Manager. I even went on to study Marketing at the Takoradi Technical University. I graduated with high competence because Wilson Arthur trained me very well in all these areas."

Premier Gawu's status as a superstar in Sekondi-Takoradi is indisputable. As he said decades ago, he is committed to "killing himself," metaphorically, for Skyy. "I am still here because I love the exciting life in Sekondi-Takoradi," he says.

His decades-long experience turned him into a bundle of loyalty and satisfaction. "Skyy has made me who I am," says Michael Gawu.

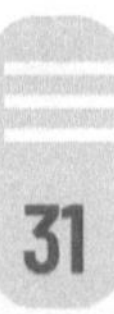

31

You'll Never Walk Alone

"One of the things that was so outstanding about Skyy is that the owner himself, Wilson Arthur, was a young man. What I saw was an organisation that wanted to give young people an opportunity to express themselves."
— *His Lordship, Justice Kweku Ackaah—Boafo, remembering Skyy when he used to be a sports analyst.*

By virtue of the professional work he does these days, Kweku Ackaah-Boafo has earned a judicial title that he will keep for life. As a judge of the High Court of the Republic of Ghana, most forms of communication referencing his name, whether written or verbal, are preceded by either "His Lordship," or "Justice." In real life dramatic court scenes, he is most respectfully addressed as "My Lord."

Years before his elevation to the High Court, though, the young lawyer Ackaah-Boafo was just one of us boys who passed through Skyy Power FM in Takoradi.

Then and now, the first thing you are likely to notice about him is that he is a short man. He is possibly the shortest man I have ever sat across from in the Skyy studio. I am a short person myself, but Ackaah-Boafo is shorter.

The otherwise insignificant matter of height comes up quite often in our conversations, and we talk about it with lots of laughter. It is always a reminder of how a thousand other experiences we shared can quickly put us on a slippery slope of laughter with many fond memories.

I can still remember Ackaah-Boafo sitting comfortably in the studio chair, and, at times, it seemed as if he would disappear in the relatively large leather chair. But once he opened his mouth to answer questions about law from listeners, his words opened up a whole new vista of a truly brilliant lawyer, familiar with making cogent arguments within the law.

The program on which he served as my panelist is called *Legal Issues*. It is designed to educate listeners in a budding democracy about the fine points of the law. Ackaah-Boafo also became a dynamic host of the same program on Skyy, working with the late lawyer Bordza-Lumor.

The statement, "the law is an ass" is made popular in Charles Dickens' novel, *Oliver Twist*. Far more often than not, though, Ackaah-Boafo demonstrated that every successful community is stabilised only by a meaningful operation of the law. "Rule of law is the cornerstone of a well-organised society," he would say.

His life is now dominated by presiding over complex civil and criminal cases followed by endless hours of research and deliberation to deliver judgment with real world consequences for plaintiffs and defendants. It is a painfully lonely work that leaves Justice Ackaah-Boafo with very little time to spare.

Thanks to enormous goodwill from decades ago, the honourable judge gave me a full hour of interview as proof of his cooperation to make this book possible.

Passion for Sports Brings a New Lawyer to Skyy

Ackaah-Boafo's passion for football is split equally between the English Football Club, Liverpool, and everything else the world-famous sport can offer.

When he lived in England for the whole of 1997, he spent a considerable fortune on football paraphernalia, including high-quality football magazines containing the most exhaustive information on numerous football clubs and players across Europe and the world. His collection was a virtual gold mine he brought back to Ghana.

Ackaah-Boafo qualified as a lawyer in 1996, exactly a year before Skyy was launched. But he had no idea about the station until he returned to Ghana in February 1998. This was during the Africa Cup of Nations football tournament in Burkina Faso, a French speaking country north of Ghana.

Feverish football commentary from Burkina Faso's host cities, Bobo Dioulasso and Ouagadoougou, was all over the airwaves. At Skyy FM, the delectable commentary was being broadcast as the commentators watched the live match on large television screens.

"That football tournament is what drew my attention to Skyy," says Ackaah-Boafo.

"Before I left for the United Kingdom, there was only the Ghana Broadcasting Corporation radio, but now there was a new radio station, and they were making all the jingles and all the news in town."

"I was walking home from the office when I heard a lively football commentary on radio. It attracted me because I was like 'who is this person giving the commentary,' because it was so good!"

"The commentator happened to be Kojo Frempong. His language was apt, it was precise, and the fluency with which this young man was speaking was so impressive." With his own passion for football, Ackaah-Boafo at once fell in love with Skyy and Kojo Frempong's expertise in football commentary.

"When I got home," he says, "I turned on the radio to finish listening to him."

"The next day," recalls Ackaah-Boafo, "I decided to check out who the commentator was, so after court, I went to Skyy. I wanted to see the owner of Skyy and the commentator. I was introduced to Wilson Arthur and Kojo Frempong. I shook Kojo Frempong's hand and I was amazed because he was so young."

"Is that you?" asked Ackaah-Boafo, looking intently at Kojo Frempong. Even though his voice was a little bit croaky from hours of commentary, it was instantly recognisable.

"Yes, I am Kojo Frempong," the young Skyy FM employee responded.

"Young man," said Ackaah-Boafo, "you have a wonderful future. Please keep it up!"

Joining the Team as "The Summariser"

Ackaah-Boafo had a flourishing career as a lawyer and didn't need a job at Skyy Power FM, but he wanted to do some of the sports analysis at the station on a voluntary basis.

Any opportunity he would get to be on Skyy Power FM would not be his first experience in broadcasting. "I used to participate in a sports quiz program on GBC TV hosted by Karl Tufuoh," recalls Ackaah-Boafo.

Facing the Chief Executive of Skyy Power FM, he knew he had the best opportunity to put his foot in the door. "Mr. Arthur," said Ackaah-Boafo addressing Wilson, "I have a keen interest in sports and would be interested in contributing to your programs on air."

It was a perfect pitch that landed well.

"Oh good, boss," said Kojo Frempong, also looking Wilson Arthur straight in the face. "Let's bring Mr. Ackaah-Boafo on as a summariser."

The summariser is the person on the sports panel who would lead a discussion to summarise the outcome of a game.

Like the front page of a newspaper, Wilson quickly read Ackaah-Boafo and was convinced he would be an asset. So, just like that, Ackaah-Boafo got his name written in the Skyy register of regular panelists and contributors.

For Ackaah-Boafo, becoming part of Skyy in his beloved Takoradi was nearly as sweet as the law degree he spent years to acquire.

Quick, smart, and productive decision-making exemplified in bringing Ackaah-Boafo on board within minutes is one of the experiences Kojo Frempong later referred to when he says, "we had no inhibitions at Skyy about making decisions or taking risks. If we believed in something, we just did it. Good decisions are made on the spot, and we move quickly to implement it."

More than a Summariser-in-Chief

Ackaah-Boafo played his *summariser* role perfectly. More than that, he quickly became an integral part of the sports team that covered the African Cup of Nations as well as the 1998 FIFA World Cup hosted by France.

The football magazines he brought from England, including *World Soccer* magazine, became valuable as they contained wide-ranging information on many top players. The famous Uncle Opia provided commentary in the Fante language while Kojo Frempong and Ackaah-Boafo tackled it in English. Another presenter, Kuntu Blankson, who joined Skyy around the same time, assisted Uncle Opia.

"Those days, we didn't have the kind of Internet that allowed you to find certain facts easily," says Ackaah-Boafo.

"I had the names of these football players, their dates of birth, places of birth in the magazine and I would throw in this sort of information to the amazement of all. Kojo Frempong and I dramatised this. He would ask about a lesser-known Brazilian player, for example, and I would tell him, 'this player was born on 12 January 1974 in Sao Paolo, and he plays for this club or that club.' Listeners would be fascinated, and they would call in from everywhere including Cape Coast and Tarkwa to try to find out how I knew the facts about all the players and their circumstances."

Ackaah-Boafo is breathless as he recalls this, as if it happened yesterday.

Radio Lawyer and Legal Issues

While sports remained Ackaah-Boafo's passion, his everyday job and profession as a lawyer became increasingly useful for Skyy Power FM. Kwesi Bediako Quayson, who we called Jazzy B for his love of jazz music, also hosted *Legal Issues* with regular radio lawyer Bordza-Lumor. Over time, Jazzy B made way for Ackaah-Boafo to become the new host of *Legal Issues*. Ackaah-Boafo played a more dynamic role by being a panelist himself, allowing him the opportunity to educate the public on legal matters.

"Ghana at the time was a young democracy, and the idea of people clinging to military rule mentality was pervasive," recalls Ackaah-Boafo.

"Because of that, we informed and educated people using the new democratic constitution and considered various human rights provisions. We took on issues embedded in the law that people were not aware of. For example, we considered the rights of the individual to take on the local council for failing to live up to their duties under the district assembly rules," says Ackaah-Boafo.

Despite the seriousness of the *Legal Issues* program, Ackaah-Boafo could not leave his humorous and jovial nature out. In true Takoradi-fashion, he would end every program with a joke that listeners came to love.

"On one or two occasions that I didn't offer a joke, people would call into the studio after the program to complain, saying the program cannot end without a joke," recalls Ackaah-Boafo.

Looking Back With Fondness

"One of the things that was so outstanding about Skyy is that the owner himself, Wilson Arthur, was a young man. What I saw was an organisation that wanted to give young people an opportunity to express themselves. Apart from the late Uncle Opia and a few others, most of us were young, in our 20s," says the judge.

As much as the work and the people at the time were full of many happy memories, Ackaah-Boafo says having our words broadcast everyday was a very responsible thing, especially when some of our programs raised a few eyebrows.

"I remember for example," he says, "when there was an issue with the then-sports minister, E. T. Mensah, who made a particular decision which we criticised, and Wilson Arthur was forced to request that we tone it down. Personally, being a lawyer was very helpful in that respect, as it was easier to recognise the parameters within which we could operate while taking into consideration the needs of the business. Through it all, we never failed to educate, inform, and entertain responsibly."

He says, "even for my practice, it did help indirectly. But at some point, some senior lawyers ganged up and said I should be stopped from appearing on Skyy because under the Ghanaian code, lawyers cannot advertise. Some of them felt I was advertising myself by being on Skyy. But of course, I never once announced on my own that I was a lawyer. They found that I was becoming popular, and indeed I was. I recall one day I was at the High Court arguing an application.

Afterwards, someone approached me and said, 'Are you the one who speaks on Skyy?'"

You'll Never Walk Alone

After his time at Skyy, Lawyer Kweku Ackaah-Boafo moved to Canada where he operated his own law firm in Toronto for more than ten years, practicing mainly as a criminal defence lawyer. "I really missed Skyy Power FM when I left Ghana. I really missed Skyy," he says, looking back at the experience over a quarter of a century.

"The idea of being a judge was never part of my plan when I became a lawyer. There is a belief that when you become a judge, you live a life of solitude, and you know me: I am the sort of person who likes to go around cracking jokes to make people laugh. In my mind, being a judge and a fun-loving person could not co-exist, and it is not something I envisaged," says Ackaah-Boafo.

"As I hit my 40s," he continues, "I faced the question about whether I could retire in Canada. My decision to become a judge was influenced by a now-retired Supreme Court Judge, Justice Julius Ansah, who happened to know me as a young lawyer in Sekondi-Takoradi. The other person was a Court of Appeals Judge, Justice Philip Bright Mensah who was my mate at Law School," says the former lawyer and judge.

After thinking it through, Ackaah-Boafo chose to be patriotic and traveled to Ghana to accept an appointment as High Court judge. Then he went back to Canada to go through the long process of closing his Toronto-based private practice.

More than anyone else, Ackaah-Boafo knows the judgments he renders in his work will outlive him in the permanent records of the *Ghana Law Report*. The thought exerts considerable weight on the judgments he renders in each case, while fully aware of the awesome judicial power vested in him.

In his 2019 book *Doing Justice*, Preet Bharara, the former United States Attorney for the Southern District of New York, made a sublime statement about judges as follows: "Everyone is a human being, judges included." Ackaah-Boafo remains human, always taking his job seriously, himself less so.

The memories he made at Skyy are still precious to him and are among the things that bring him much laughter and pride, along with his love for Liverpool Football Club.

One of the finest days of Liverpool's long history came while this book was being prepared. It was 24 October 2021 during a match with dreaded opponents, Manchester United, playing at Old Trafford. The final score was Liverpool 5, Manchester United 0.

Like lightning, Egyptian star Mohammed Salah scored the fourth goal. I was watching the match on the Optus Sports network in Perth, Australia, and the commentator moaned, "for United, it gets no worse than this, given the context, given the meaning of the game."

Then in the forty-ninth minute of the game, Mohammed Salah was on target again for a gleaming and twinkling hat-trick. "The man is extraordinary. The match is extraordinary. The scoreline is extraordinary. That picture would be framed and kept forever by Liverpool fans all over the world," the commentator howled and predicted.

Kweku Ackaah-Boafo the lawyer, and now judge watched that match too. He still absolutely loves Liverpool Football Club, even more than he did when he made his first appearance at Skyy Power FM in Takoradi a quarter of a century ago.

I spoke to him after the brightest day in Liverpool's history against Manchester United.

He confirms that on this day, he sang the club's famous song including the words, "you'll never walk alone."

It is a song he usually sings whenever the solitude that goes with his work gets too much.

On 24 October 2021 though, he sang it, with memories of his time as a sports analyst as Skyy, together with all the friends he made at that radio station.

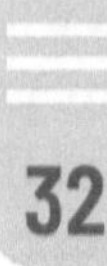

32

Kuntu Blankson: From Errand Boy to Sports Paragon

"Any presenter in Western and Central Regions that had a celebrated status was someone who worked for Skyy, so joining the winning team was something that was bound to happen for me."

— *Celebrated sports presenter, Kuntu Blankson on why ending up at Skyy was a certainty.*

The day Spain beat Switzerland in the Euro 2020 football tournament was the day Kuntu Blankson agreed to be interviewed for this book. When I call through, he had just finished watching the match and was making notes of relevant statistics to include in his sports presentation on Skyy Power FM and its affiliate station, West Gold.

"I will be staying up late to compile the story for presentation and discussion, so we can talk for now," said Kuntu Blankson after I explained my purpose in requesting an interview.

It was clear to me that Kuntu Blankson's life-long commitment to get the most informative and interesting sports stories out to millions of people was still intact.

A Solid Reputation

Across Ghana's Western and Central Regions, Kuntu Blankson is regarded as a paragon of information on sports, particularly football. He has been to every sports venue in Ghana as well as travelled the world to bring the freshest report in a way that is completely unique to him.

His towering achievement with Skyy Power FM started with Ghana Broadcasting Corporation's (GBC) Twin City Radio in Takoradi. There, Kuntu Blankson was nothing but a simple errand boy in 1994 when *Twin City Radio* was still in its first year of operation.

Before Twin City Radio arrived, Kuntu Blankson's life was completely defined by his passion for football. He knew all about the game, being inspired by exploits of local football clubs, Sekondi Eleven Wise and Hasaacas Football Club. He had infinite knowledge about all the players and management. He cultivated close relationships with all the key personalities in the game, and his contacts quickly expanded to include players from other teams around Ghana who visited Sekondi Gyandu Park every week.

The only thing bigger than his contacts was his memory. He seemed to remember every detail about every player, and acquired historic knowledge of dozens of matches along with heroic stories that defined various periods.

A Hole to Fill

When *Twin City Radio* was established, Kuntu believed it needed to become a mouthpiece for football. But *Twin City Radio* did not include sports in its programming for a long time. During that period, Kuntu Blankson cultivated deep friendships with all the presenters at *Twin City Radio*, including senior employees who worked in management. It did not get him far though, as he was used only as a reliable errand boy for the station.

His enthusiasm in being used for errands, however, deepened his relationship with all the employees at the station. He was a cheap and readily available labour that everyone used and loved.

But then change came for Kuntu Blankson.

The Proposal

Like Kuntu Blankson, John Nyankumah who was then the Regional Director of GBC started to think that it was time to include sports information on Twin City Radio's programming.

But there was a snag.

None of the presenters at the station was eager to be a sports presenter. The presenters at the time included Morris Bissue, Kwame Insaidoo, Eric Sampson, Benji Kumassah, Jojo Graves-Woode and Nana Ofori. Their collective appetite for sports was nearly non-existent. That is when Kuntu Blankson, powered by nothing but sheer passion, put up his hand for the pioneering role. In the ears of most of the presenters, his suggestion was the exact equivalent of a bad joke.

But Kuntu was unperturbed.

He made a daring proposal to produce and present the sports program. His proposal was dismissed instantly. Still, Kuntu Blankson did not give up. He continued to offer his service freely as an errand boy.

One day John Nyankumah heard him pleading once more to be given a chance.

Mr. Nyankumah actually liked Kuntu because of his humility and his willingness to serve. Still, he ignored the request. Then he sent Kuntu Blankson to buy him his favourite brand of cigarette. He lit up one of the cigarettes afterwards and inhaled the smoke. With his lung full of nicotine, John Nyankumah looked at Kuntu Blankson and said, "Kuntu, I will give you the chance to prove yourself."

"I could not believe it; and I was so happy," recalls Kuntu Blankson.

"Mr. Nyankumah said he would give me five minutes on air to present the sports so everyone can listen, after which he would make a final decision. He asked me to prepare the synopsis to show him."

On any ambitious journey from nothing to something, there is often someone who exhibits belief in one's dreams. For Kuntu Blankson, that person was Kwame Insaidoo, who now works at GBC's Uniiq FM in Accra.

"Kwame Insaidoo and Eric Sampson helped me to develop the synopsis," says Kuntu Blankson. The synopsis was approved and he spent a few sleepless nights putting together what he believed to be an irresistible program.

But soon, he would learn that progress and success almost never occurs in a straight line.

The Disappointment

Kuntu Blankson had never spoken on radio before. He had never engaged in public speaking, and he had never learned the art of presenting on air. But he was now just minutes from having his voice heard by the entire city.

The plan was for the person on air at the prescribed time to welcome Kuntu into the studio and then it would be up to him to impress Mr. John Nyankumah or make a fool of himself. The appointed time came and Kuntu Blankson made his grand appearance in the studio with a script for the show that would give him an up or down vote.

Sitting comfortably behind the console was the most hostile presenter Kuntu Blankson has ever seen. Not only did the presenter refuse to allow him to present the show, but he dismissed Kuntu Blankson with a few words of contempt. "The presenter called me "Bodamfo," recalls Kuntu Blankson. *"Bodamfo,"* is a Fante word meaning *a clown, mad or despicable person.*

The scorn and insult echoed through the room as Kuntu Blankson walked out of the studio like a sickly chicken caught in a storm. The use of the word "bodamfo" also suggests that the presenter in question believed Kuntu Blankson will never amount to anything.

The Second Chance

The plan to get Kuntu Blankson to go on air was faulty and incomplete. The presenter who ordered Kuntu out of the studio with his sports script was actually unaware that he was approved to go on air.

When Kuntu tried to explain that Director John Nyankumah had given the green light, the nameless presenter was even more enraged, because as the presenter put it, "only in your dreams will the GBC Regional Director think of a scheme like that."

The dream was reconstituted with John Nyankumah's intervention, and this time, the presenter who was going to be on duty was duly informed.

That friendly presenter, according to Kuntu Blankson, was a lady called Nana Ama Andrews. "Nana Ama Andrews was very kind," said Kuntu Blankson. "She went out of her way to promote my segment, promising that I would, for the first time, present sports news on radio." The promotion really worked, and by the time Kuntu presented his first sports program, all the presenters were listening, and paying more than the usual attention.

Kuntu came alive during his presentation, feeling like he had been born into a completely new world he had always dreamt of. At the end of it all, there was no meeting to review what Kuntu Blankson had accomplished and whether or not he could have other opportunities in the future as a sports presenter.

"Everything happened so fast after I came out of the studio," recalls Kuntu Blankson. "It seems like everyone at the station was waiting at the entrance of the studio, and when I came out, they lifted me up, shouting and rejoicing. They congratulated me over and over again for doing a good job."

That is how Kuntu Blankson earned his place in history as a sports presenter. His presentation skills and passion increased. The quality content he produced also kept getting better and better until Skyy Power FM's Wilson Arthur noticed.

Wilson Arthur Hunts for Kuntu Blankson

Regular chatter in sports circles about a certain Kuntu Blankson on *Twin City Radio* made Wilson tune into the station to listen to him. Kuntu Blankson presented only in Fante. At the time, more than 80% of Skyy Power FM's broadcast was in English.

Within a short time after hearing him, Wilson decided his station's sports program needed to be revamped to include a greater amount of Fante, with Kuntu Blankson as lead sports presenter in Fante. It was the beginning of January 1998, and Wilson was counting down to February when the biggest African sports event, the African Cup of Nations in Burkina Faso, would start. He wanted the strongest possible team for the commentary and analysis in both English and Fante. He ramped up the pressure on Kuntu Blankson and by the beginning of February, the presenter from *Twin City Radio* buckled down, gave up his resistance and became part of Skyy Power FM.

Giving up and giving in to Skyy Power FM actually meant Kuntu Blankson had moved up in rank and relevance as a presenter. "Going to Skyy was a good move for me at the time and up to now," says Kuntu. "Any presenter in Western and Central Regions that had a celebrated status was someone who worked for Skyy, so joining the winning team was something that was bound to happen for me."

Altercation with Victor Thompson

Kuntu Blankson's high standard in getting only the best in sports news increased even more as he settled into Skyy. "I found Skyy to be an environment that fully supported a sports presenter's will to get the best stories, including exclusives, so I went many extra miles to get the very best," recalls Kuntu.

That commitment to get nothing but the best resulted in a clash with a fellow sports presenter, Victor Thompson. In those early days, phone calls tended to be expensive, and so apart from the main newsroom, the only other phone with a direct dialing capability was the phone in Chief Executive Wilson Arthur's office.

Whenever the phone in the newsroom was busy, the sports team would go into Wilson's office to make their calls.

On one occasion, Kuntu had to make an emergency call with less than ten minutes before going on air with breaking news. He rushed into Wilson's office only to find Victor Thompson on the phone.

He immediately urged him to get off the phone so he could make the urgent call. Victor, who appeared to be in the middle of a conversation did not take kindly to the forceful request. Kuntu repeated the request with more urgency, his voice rising, but Victor did not oblige. And then, like lightning, Victor felt a fast moving hand across his face, and by the time he could process what was going on, Kuntu was on the phone asking questions in quick succession.

Kuntu Blankson had slapped Victor Thompsom.

Reconciliation Effort Blows Up

Kuntu Blankson was summoned to Wilson Arthur's office as soon as he finished presenting his breaking news on air. "A two-man committee, Wilson Arthur and Bob Gardiner, decided to hear the matter and arrive at some sort of reconciliation after Victor Thompson lodged a complaint," says Kuntu Blankson.

Victor Thompson repeated his story during the informal hearing. Kuntu Blankson, still highly irritated by Victor Thompson's presence, was asked to explain what happened. Instead of telling his own story, Kuntu simply said if Victor Thompson blocked him from making an emergency call again, he would get another slap.

Shocked at hearing this, Wilson said "Kuntu, you can't do that," and Kuntu's reply was, "boss even if it were you who behaved that way by blocking access to the phone, I would have slapped you."

He delivered the shocking warning in Fante, and it sounded more outrageous than in English. In that instant, Wilson Arthur realised he had built a machine that is not fully controllable with talented and passionate people like Kuntu Blankson.

Still surprised, Wilson Arthur spoke in Twi, asking Kuntu with incredulity, "will you really slap me?" Kuntu, in a fairly angry response said, "yes boss, I will."

At that point, the focus shifted completely from Victor Thompson's ordeal to an effort to convince Kuntu not to entertain the thought of making a habit of slapping people on the job. The reconciliation effort was a failure, and by the time the short inquiry ended, there was only one feeble message: an indirect admonition to Victor Thompson not to stand in Kuntu's way.

Decades after the fact, Victor Thompson in a separate interview confirmed the substance of the event but says the altercation did not result in an actual slap across the face.

"He actually used his hand, not to slap, but to strike my cheek," he said. "Initially I was furious, because I wasn't expecting him to do that." Victor's hearty laughter during the interview when I pointedly asked him was proof that time rendered the incident as a flash in the pan, and Kuntu Blankson and Victor Thompson are still good friends, who would occasionally laugh at the memory of that incident.

Kuntu Blankson is a man whose passion to get results could get him clashing easily with a colleague, and if possible with his boss.

Through those years, his mostly gentle and caring nature emerged, leading him to train Paa Kwesi Simpson, a fellow presenter from New Takoradi. Together, the two became the winning team from New Takoradi.

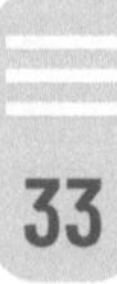

33

A Winning Team from New Takoradi

"There was an award being organised for radio personalities in Sekondi-Takoradi to recognise the best presenter. I found out that my name was in the same category as Kuntu Blankson. I called the organisers and told them that if Kuntu Blankson is in the same category with me, then I am withdrawing. I respect Kuntu. He taught me so much that I would never be better than him."

– Paa Kwesi Simpson on how he feels about Kuntu Blankson at Skyy

"I should say you like talking and you are incapable of shutting up."

That is what I tell Paa Kwesi Simpson while interviewing him.

He is gracious in speaking enthusiastically, recalling decades-old memories and stories with accuracy.

But within moments, I fall into the old habit from Skyy FM where, as friends and colleagues, we liked to banter.

Of course, he takes no offence, but rather gets caught in an endless bout of laughter. Paa Kwesi has inexhaustible energy for talking, and wherever there is some form of talking, Paa Kwesi is drawn to it.

That is how he became a frequent caller on Kuntu Blankson's sports program on the public broadcaster's *Twin City Radio* in the mid-1990s. His contribution to the program was good enough that Kuntu sought to know more about him. The two struck up a friendship, as they both lived in the exciting suburb called New Takoradi.

By the time Kuntu Blankson moved to Skyy Power FM, Paa Kwesi Simpson resolved that he had what it took to be on radio himself. He had developed a high degree of expertise in Fante language, both in reading and writing. And he was already the best talking head from New Takoradi.

Making A Case With Fante Language Skills

With Skyy FM now featuring more Fante programs, he believed he deserved to be considered for employment.

He carefully wrote his application letter and walked all the way to 37 Windy Ridge to hand it over to Wilson Arthur after which he was told to go back home and hope to be called someday.

As he left Skyy premises about a hundred metres away, a passenger in an approaching taxi waved at him frantically. The taxi stopped, and the passenger wanted to know what Paa Kwesi had come to do at Skyy.

The passenger was Kuntu Blankson.

He was arriving at Skyy to host his weekly program *Sports World*. Paa Kwesi told him that he came to hand his application to Wilson Arthur. "Come to the studio with me for the program," Kuntu Blankson told Paa Kwesi.

At the Skyy premises, Kuntu briefed Paa Kwesi on the content of that day's *Sports World* program. For the first time, Paa Kwesi was going to be present live in the studio--and be part of the most popular sports program.

Based on Paa Kwesi's phone-in contributions over the years, Kuntu was sure Paa Kwesi was going to be a good panelist on the program.

"You know enough about sports, so I will let you talk throughout the program," Kuntu Blankson told Paa Kwesi.

Paa Kwesi reflected on what had just happened over the past twenty minutes at Skyy. He handed his application to Chief Executive Wilson Arthur and was told to go back home. One hundred metres from the studio, a fellow New Takoradi resident and the most popular sports presenter brought him back to the station and in a short time, his voice was heard across the metropolis live from the studio.

Kuntu Blankson had just put Paa Kwesi live on air, because he had the authority to feature whomever he wanted on his *Sports World* program.

"Can getting on live radio from the studio be as simple as being a friend to a fellow New Takoradi resident--even if it were Kuntu Blankson?" Paa Kwesi asked himself.

Kuntu's confidence in Paa Kwesi was huge and it was not misplaced. Paa Kwesi was now in the studio with Kuntu. He could feel and hear the pounding of his own heart out of fear and trepidation. But he knew he could not afford to disappoint Kuntu or himself.

The energy from the sports signature tune was blasting around the studio as Kuntu introduced the program. He mentioned that he had a guest called Paa Kwesi Simpson who would be assisting him throughout the two-hour program.

Something Like a Nightmare

When he heard his name from Kuntu's lips, he also knew he was about to wake up from his midnight dream and say to himself, "I was right, this couldn't happen in real life."

He was wrong.

The dream was real, and it was happening for real on a Saturday afternoon from 37 Windy Ridge on 93.5 FM, the frequency to which more than 90% of the population always tunes into.

Other guests and panelists joined them in the studio. Paa Kwesi had a persistent feeling that he was sitting at the wrong place with the most knowledgeable people in sports; people who knew how to speak live on radio.

He told himself this was a do-or-die affair and ignored his fears. Soon, it was his turn to speak. That was the first time Paa Kwesi realised his inability to keep his mouth shut was an asset. His mouth worked like the staccato of a machine gun, complimented by well-reasoned arguments mixed with passion and conviction. His Fante was faultless, and if a camera were in the studio, it would have shown his eyes brightening up to show his love of radio was complete.

Outside the studio, Wilson Arthur and Uncle Opia were doing their usual monitoring of the program. *Sports World* made the mark once more to everyone's satisfaction. No one noticed that Paa Kwesi was speaking on-air live from the studio for the first time. That was more than a big win.

After debriefing at the end of the program, Kuntu Blankson told Paa Kwesi Simpson that he had earned a place on the program for the foreseeable future.

Kuntu took time to train Paa Kwesi properly, giving him all the trade secrets of being a good presenter who constantly earned the trust, approval, and admiration of listeners.

Uncle Opia, the broadcast heavyweight, noticed Paa Kwesi's contribution and was pleased. Around the same time, the growing Fante language broadcast needed more hands to assist.

Realising this, Uncle Opia approached Wilson Arthur and strongly urged him to do two things: employ Paa Kwesi Simpson immediately and move him from the sports program into mainstream Fante program.

Wilson, who had also noticed Paa Kwesi's excellence, agreed. But there was more than a little problem to making this work, especially moving Paa Kwesi from working directly with Kuntu Blankson.

As far as Kuntu was concerned, Paa Kwesi Simpson was his baby, and no one, under any circumstance, had the right to change the way he should be used in the Skyy establishment. Together with Uncle Opia, Wilson sought a meeting with Kuntu and put forward a proposal.

"No," said Kuntu Blankson, as soon as he understood that Paa Kwesi was going to be taken off the sports program and used in a different capacity. He emphasised that he was not open to any negotiation on the matter.

At that point, Kuntu's name could have easily been changed to "Dr No", because when he says no, he really means it, especially when he perceived that someone is trying to break up the winning team from New Takoradi he had formed with Paa Kwesi Simpson for his sports program.

So, for Wilson and Uncle Opia, it had become a case of finding an effective strategy that could get "Dr No" to say "Yes."

The Circle Around Kuntu Blankson

The strategy Wilson and Uncle Opia adopted worked.

They broke up the link between Paa Kwesi Simpson and Kuntu Blankson.

Taking Paa Kwesi aside, they explained that he had a brighter future in radio as a formal full-time employee with a specified salary, rather than just remaining an exclusive teammate of Kuntu Blankson doing sports.

He was going to be used fully as a leading presenter in Fante, including reading the news and hosting other programs. It worked, especially because Kuntu actually wanted Paa Kwesi to succeed.

In Kuntu Blankson's days on Twin City Radio, Uncle Opia was one of his teachers. Kuntu taught Paa Kwesi Simpson what he learned in broadcasting from Opia. Now, Paa Kwesi had a chance to be taught directly by Uncle Opia as he came to work directly with him.

More than just specialising in sports, Paa Kwesi understudied the great Uncle Opia with keen interest. By the time Opia died in 2006, Paa Kwesi Simpson became the man who inherited most of his broadcasting capital, keeping alive the memory of Uncle Opia, one of the most memorable names Sekondi-Takoradi has ever known.

In Paa Kwesi Simpson's life, the only thing that got sharper than his mouth was his appreciation for those who made him come alive in radio.

Even though many years have passed, Paa Kwesi Simpson's loyalty and appreciation for the help he received from Kuntu Blankson is enormous.

"A few years ago, there was an award being organised for radio personalities in Sekondi-Takoradi to recognise the best presenter. I found out that my name was in the same category as Kuntu Blankson," says Paa Kwesi.

You would think that was a development that should make him happy. Not Paa Kwesi. His loyalty and appreciation stood in the way.

"I personally called the organisers and told them that if Kuntu Blankson is in the same category with me, then I am withdrawing;

give the award to Kuntu because I respect him so much and he taught me so much that I would never be better than him."

That is how deep Paa Kwesi's loyalty runs.

Five years after moving on from Skyy to Connect FM, also in Takoradi, he says many still associate him almost exclusively with Skyy Power FM. Even though he now works for an organisation that competes with Skyy in Takoradi, he never shies away from crediting Skyy Power FM for all that he learned in radio with the help of Kuntu Blankson and the late Uncle Opia.

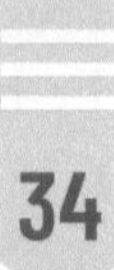

34

Akavani's Breakthrough To Skyy

> *"I think, with the kind of training Wilson gave us, I seem to have a problem wherever I go, because I want everything to be done very well."*
> — *Andrews Akavani on his memories with Skyy and the valuable training he received as a sports reporter*

In Sekondi-Takoradi, there are two football teams that the residents support: Sekondi Eleven Wise and Hassacas. Each team has an evocative nickname: Hasaacas is the "Giant of the West" while Eleven Wise is called the "Western Show Boys."

A clash between the two sides in a derby is a match that always sends the city into a frenzy.

A match involving any of the two teams against either Asante Kokoto or Acca Hearts of Oak also generates similar excitement.

In the 2003/2004 league season, a less fancied team, Heart of Lions from Kpando had been causing havoc by beating league contenders, Asante Kotoko.

As much as they threatened all the strong teams, their might and recent exploits seemed like a fluke that was easily dismissed.

Kpando Heart of Lions vrs Hasaacas

It was the turn of Sekondi-Takoradi's own Hasaacas to face this relatively unknown and underrated enemy all the way to the lion's den in Kpando. It was a match that will attract the interest and sympathy of the people of the twin city. Somehow, Skyy Power FM, the powerful and highly influential private radio station in the city seemed to have forgotten about the match.

Andrews Akavani, the unassuming head of sports at the lightweight Twin City Radio and his team made a crucial calculation that the clash between Hasaacas and Kpando Heart of Lions was going to be a big match that most sports pundits were ignoring.

Akavani learned that even Ghana Broadcasting Corporation, GBC, in Accra declined to send reporters there for live commentary.

If GBC's sports gurus in Accra had arranged for a live commentary, Twin City Radio would have tuned in to carry the match live.

They declined.

This meant the outcome of the match would be known in Sekondi-Takoradi only through a relatively dull Ghana News Agency report to be filed by a lone reporter after the event.

"They didn't see the game as we saw it," says Akavani, recalling his conviction that it was a mistake not to carry live commentary for the match.

He explains, "for low-key games, we don't send out our own reporter. We just find someone else to summarise the outcome for us."

But Akavani and his small team at Twin City Radio prioritised this particular game and decided to do whatever it took to get a live commentary for the benefit of football fans in Sekondi-Takoradi.

Taking on The Big Risk

Casting aside his usual humble demeanor, Akavani set out on the long journey to report the match live on the the less fancied Twin City Radio. "We had to break long-standing GBC protocols to do this, because with GBC, who dare you, every decision has to come from Accra, because someone like Nii Lante Vanderpuye is the one who runs full commentary for us," says Akavani.

He also found out that Skyy Power FM made no plans for a live coverage of the match. "The match didn't get much attention from the start, but we carried the commentary live for the full 90 minutes. During the commentary, I was getting lots of messages back from Takoradi, telling me that they were enjoying the match," says Akavani.

"I think they enjoyed hearing a Takoradi boy giving commentary involving Hasaacas and a team in Kpando, a team that was starting to make a dent in the league. They preferred the live commentary to a five minute summary at the end of the match by somebody they don't know."

The match ended with a goal each for Hasaacas and Heart of Lions. Those precious 90 minutes was one of the rare occasions Twin City Radio pulled a chunk of sports fans away from Skyy FM.

An Even Greater Approval

Positive feedback on Akavani's adventurous and creative coverage of the match also came from an unexpected source: the management of Twin City Radio.

"My bosses were like, waaoo, we didn't know you could do this. You took over the place; the whole city listened to your commentary," recalled Akavani. He was always on a temporary contract with Twin City Radio, but now, as he says, "the probability of being offered a permanent and secure job with GBC was now almost 100%."

"It was a breakthrough for me," he says, adding, "later Victor Thompson and Paa Kwesi Simpson at Skyy said that exclusive 90 minute football commentary was a breakthrough."

Emergency Sports Desk Meeting at Skyy

At Skyy Power FM, a mini crisis meeting was convened to find out why the sports team failed to organise resources to bring a live commentary of the clash between Kpando Heart of Lions and Hasaacas.

It was a short but heated meeting in which the shame of being beaten by Twin City Radio, even for a few hours, was declared unacceptable.

It led to a steely resolve that it would be the last time Skyy would cede a scoop to Twin City Radio.

Wilson Arthur came up with a plan endorsed by Kuntu Blankson.

The plan involved cutting off the services of Akavani. The young man, they decided, had grown into a live wire that Skyy Power FM must now use for good.

Kuntu Blankson volunteered to initiate the communication that will deny Twin City Radio the services of Akavani.

Cutting off Some Oxygen

When Akavani returned to Takoradi the next day, he received a message from Kuntu Blankson that Skyy Chief Executive, Wilson Arthur would like to meet with him. Akavani was petrified, and his mind went into a wild spin.

He didn't think he was worthy to be invited by Wilson Arthur for a chat.

"I have seen Wilson before at different events, but I have never spoken to him," he said. "I was surprised, and I thought, what is all this about, that Wilson wants to talk to me." He didn't have to wait too long to find out. "I have been listening to you for a while. You have the potential to make it with Skyy, so I want to bring you in," Wilson told Akavani.

The Skyy boss fixed his gaze on the young man, an assuring smile breaking through his trademark gap teeth.

Akavani was downright flattered and speechless.

Not once had he dreamt that he had the qualities to match the high standards Skyy portrays every day on and off air.

"Those days," he says in reflection, "Elloeny Amande, Kuntu Blankson, JM Caesar, Kojo Frempong, where would I possibly fit? To complicate matters, the time Wilson spoke to me was also the time Ghana Broadcasting Corporation was about to make me a permanent staff of Twin City Radio"

Akavani is a humble person to the core, with an easy manner that always projects a modest estimation of himself. His attitude remained the same even after he became head of Sports at Twin City Radio - long before the prospect of becoming a permanent staff member was discussed.

An Embrace with Skyy

"I really admired Skyy Power FM. Skyy was Western Region, and Western Region was Skyy, so even though I was not sure how I was going to fit in, I decided to go to Skyy because Wilson himself asked me. It was a difficult decision for me," recalls Akavani.

Even after being ushered into his dream job at Skyy as a sports reporter, Akavani lived with fear that he would soon be declared unfit to work for Skyy. Assurances from Wilson Arthur didn't help.

"Not long after I started working for Skyy, I overheard Uncle Opia making a comment about my performance, saying, who is that new boy on air? When I heard it, I said to myself, 'I am finished,'" Akavani says, laughing at the memory of it all.

Akavani also held a peculiar belief that Wilson didn't hold the ultimate power to make the most consequential and final decision on staffing at Skyy. "I heard that even though Wilson is the boss, if his wife Adwoa Amofah is not impressed with your performance, then you are out," reveals Akavani.

The problem for Akavani was that when he was taken on at Skyy, Adwoa Amofah had travelled to London, so in his mind, unless Adwoa Amofah returned and approved his employment, he would never feel secure.

So he waited with bated breath for the assessment of his performance by Adwoa Amofah, a Skyy Power FM executive he barely knew. **Mother-in-Chief**

Adwoa Amaofah is a full bundle of soft-power, wrapped in diplomacy. She knows how to exert a calming influence on her environment, especially at Skyy. Adwoah Amofah, more than anyone else, had the exquisite awareness that the business of radio broadcasting is a deeply human-centred enterprise. Skyy Power FM employees from the start were mostly young men and women who were inspired to do some of their lives' best work.

Knowing that, Adwoah Amofah transformed herself into a mother figure, exerting a calming influence on many of the presenters, the way a mother would in a family.

Everyone calls her either "Sister Adwoa" or "Auntie Adwoa." The use of "sister" or "auntie" as a title denotes unconditional respect and affection. The reference is also a Ghanaian and African cultural manifestation in which most people grow up unaccustomed to calling an older person, or someone in authority simply by their first name.

"Until Auntie Adwoa Amofah came, my happiness was incomplete," confessed Akavani. Akavani himself is a young man that was very easy to read. His work ethic was unquestionable, with a constant hunger to learn. Like the rest of the employees at the sports desk, he loved his work at Skyy.

Within days of her return from London, Adwoa Amofah read him like a child's book and was well pleased with his attitude.

"And you know, later, Auntie Adwoa became my main person. She liked me so much! I don't really know what I did, but she liked me a lot. It was Auntie Adwoa Amofah who even recommended a pay rise for me, I remember very well," recalls Akavani, his voice revealing his gratitude.

After his years of work at Skyy Power FM and Sekondi-Takoradi, Akavani traveled to Europe during the 2006 Football World Cup in Germany and later worked in a few different countries.

Everywhere he went, his experience and memories of Skyy was never far away from him.

"I have gone to Europe, I have worked with Television and Radio stations, but the experience I had at Skyy, I don't think I have had it anywhere else," he said, in deep reflection.

"I still remember very well how we went about our work and how Wilson would want us to do the job with passion to get results... I think, with the kind of training Wilson gave us, I seem to have a problem wherever I go, because I want everything to be done very well. We don't joke with our work. I think I was lucky to work for Skyy."

Asked to talk about his personal legacy, he said "I also left my mark at Skyy." In his usual humble way though, he adds, "but my mark won't be as significant as those left by earlier Skyy presenters I admired such as Yaw Korankye, Kojo Frempong and Elloeny Amande."

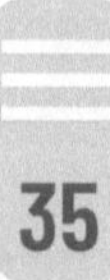

A Gemstone Appears at Skyy Power FM

Abena Bondah was a young girl living in Takoradi when Skyy Power FM started broadcasting. She was stylish with a sophisticated taste for fashion, quality lipsticks, and high heels. When she spoke, her good diction and grammar were immediately evident. Before she turned six years old, her family and friends called her "Lady Abena."

Abena's family and friends, especially her late uncle Samuel Moore, thought she was destined for something special, so when Skyy Power FM started, he encouraged her to apply for a job with the station. She did not listen, and the more she didn't, the more her uncle kept urging her to approach Skyy.

"You have the voice of a radio presenter, and you are an intelligent girl as well," her uncle would say, repeatedly. "My uncle actually used to call me 'Miss Skyy' all the time, and he never stopped asking me to go to Skyy for a job," says Abena.

Making a Debut on Air

When Abena did speak into a live radio microphone for the first time, it was not with Skyy. She was on ATL FM, a campus radio station at the University of Cape Coast. Her aptitude for radio was discovered shortly after she entered university as a teenager.

Joe Anim, a veteran in Ghanaian private radio production, spotted Abena's talent and convinced Wilson Arthur to employ her.

By the time Abena joined Skyy Power FM in early 2000, she had listened and observed Skyy from a distance. She liked and admired Skyy.

"When my uncle heard I had been given an opportunity at Skyy, he said to me, 'you see, I always said you belonged at Skyy,'" says Abena. "He was very happy and proud of me, and once I started working there, he never called me by my name. He always called me 'Skyy,'" recalls Abena.

"Why didn't you make any effort to be employed at Skyy, given all the encouragement you received from your uncle?" I ask Abena.

"Interesting question, no one has ever asked me," she says.

"I was concerned about nepotism and, also, I was really young, just a teenager at that time. I knew I had a great voice and I could do the job, but the deterrent factor for me was that I felt I couldn't get a job unless I knew someone there. I just didn't feel drawn to go and interview or audition, but somehow, I knew I would end up at Skyy one day; I just didn't know how," says Abena, her confidence still intact, with a firm belief that she was a gem that was simply waiting to be discovered.

Introducing Lady Abena to Skyy

Joe Anim, the man who found Abena and recommended her for employment at Skyy, agrees that she was special. "Wilson Arthur trusted my judgment and experience so much that he wouldn't question my recommendations. When I recommend someone for employment, he doesn't bother doing any extensive interview before taking the person on," says Joe Anim.

I know Eric Ahianyo who worked in the Skyy newsroom was one of those who received a gentle treatment from Wilson Arthur because he was recommended by Joe Anim.

Abena confirms that she had something close to a royal treatment by Wilson Arthur.

"There was no audition or formal interview. Wilson just took me straight to start hosting *Skyy Spicy Lunch*, and then I was made to assist Joe Enuson on the *Drive Jam* and learn. Paa Kofi Nyarko also helped to pick songs for me. In a short time, I was on *Get Closer* and *Coast-to-Coast* programs on Skyy," she recalls. "I did *Skyy Kiddie Time* as well, which is the children's show on Saturday afternoons. I read the news, too, and at some point, I felt like I was in the studio every day."

As our conversation gathers steam, Lady Abena is excited to look back on the decades that have passed since she made her own dent at Skyy as a young lady.

"Skyy was that thing that everyone talked about, that thing that everyone wanted to be a part of. One of the things I loved about you guys was that you had powerful voices. You guys really pioneered the whole private radio broadcast business in Ghana," she says.

Remembering the Helping Hands at Skyy

It is refreshing to hear this particular perspective from a lady who was first an outsider listening to our broadcast and then later joined us. "We were one of the pioneers," she adds, clarifying her perspective by including herself.

"When I joined," Abena continues, "I realised that Skyy was like a family. It seems everyone was there just to help you. It was a lovely, nice family and you were all very kind and generous towards me."

"The cutest thing was that everybody loved their job. There was no one there who didn't love what they did," says Abena. "Joe Enuson used to pick and arrange music for me. He did my compilation for *Skyy Spicy Lunch*, the lunchtime show I hosted. JM Caesar would also come in to help. Wilson Arthur himself would always check which music was playing on the various programs, and I remember he often chose some of the music, including those we played on the children's program."

The details of Abena's vivid memories seem to surprise even herself. As if she is doubting her own recollections, Abena says, "I didn't see the in-fighting that is sometimes common in life. Maybe I just lived in a bubble and couldn't see it or maybe I was not looking hard enough."

"It was one big family," she adds. "They liked each other, they yelled at each other, laughed at each other, and teased each other while goofing around all the time. Sometimes, people would goof and act crazy on purpose just to create annoyance."

This is true.

Working in the newsroom, I personally observed the constant goofing among all of us. Many times, I described Skyy jokingly as "a house of insanity." That everyone agreed this was true provided only a little comfort. Also, just about everyone accepted that we were all "belle," a strictly jovial term in Sekondi-Takoradi that means a person is being an *idiot*. Kofi Kinaata, a musician who explains the unique Fante culture of the city in many of his songs explained in one interview that calling anyone "belle" is generally acceptable, but repeating the word in relation to someone, such as "belle-belle," constitutes an instant declaration of war.

A Place for Everyone in Her Heart

At various turns during the interview, Abena recalls individual colleagues at Skyy, and says something to indicate how special she felt about each person.

"Oh, yeah, Ato-Kwamena Dadzie was there… Ato was really crazy, funny and always making people laugh," she notes of our colleague journalist who is famous for being totally irreverent, especially when he discusses politicians and public figures.

"Oh, Bob Gee, I can't forget Bob Gee!" says Abena, recalling how kind Bob Gee was to her.

Next, it is the memory of Elloeny Amande, and Abena says, "we used to enjoy panel debates on topics that Joe or Kwete Quaynor would bring up on the *Drive Jam*."

When she talks about Kwame Dzokoto, she gets excited about the easy way Dzokoto, as a comedian, would make anyone laugh. "Oh, Kwame Dzokoto, he is on a whole different level of crazy," she says.

It was her way of saying if "crazy" were a disease, Dzokoto's level was incurable.

Close to the end of the interview, Abena remembers Root Eye and says, "the problem with Root Eye is that he has a very cool demeanor, but he says the craziest things. You look at him and you'll never think he would say the things he says," recalls Abena.

Her observation leaves me laughing, as her words open a stream of memories.

I understand Abena's frequent excitement because I saw similar traits with dozens of other colleagues I interviewed for this book. The collective memories we share keep gushing out, often with humorous episodes in our professional and personal lives that are no longer remembered very often.

Most importantly, Abena remains appreciative of all the assistance she received from all the other presenters when she joined Skyy.

"I was great at talking and presenting on air, but I didn't know the songs and how to play them with the right flow. All these guys at Skyy were very willing to help me pick the right music for the show."

The passing of time has given Abena a deeper insight into life. She looks back with greater clarity about her life in broadcasting two decades ago.

"Radio gives you access to people in power, and men in power do not always have a good moral compass," she says. "Because radio gives you a lot of access, and especially as a girl, you can go crazy. I was so young, but well treated and protected. JM Caesar and others would tease me that I was Wilson Arthur's baby and daughter, and Wilson was always protective of me. He was careful that I was shielded and protected for the most part and I am grateful for that."

What Abena Learned About Music at Skyy

"Given the serious attention music received at Skyy, how much did you learn about it?" I ask Abena.

"I was surrounded by music all the time. Whatever I am not very good at, I make it my business to be sure I become the best at it. So, while Joe Enuson, Paa Kofi, JM Caesar, and Bob Gee were helping me, I started learning the flow, the rhythm, and how to intelligently transition between one track and another. The actual DJs did it best. They let the music rhyme into another by picking the right tempo and rhythms. I learned the different genres of music, such as Hiplife, Country, RnB, Hip Hop, Highlife, etc."

"That is why I know you don't go from playing traditional *Osode* music to a random genre. You could, if the tempo is the same, but you cared enough to make sure your transition is smooth from one track to another."

"Working with Skyy helped me to get to know a broad range of music, artistes, song titles and even the complex history and culture of the industry," says Abena.

She continued: "Skyy became a beacon for the Western Region. It brought flair, changed minds, powered economic life, and modernised our environment through high quality broadcasting. It was a great training ground for all of us and I am personally grateful to have been part of it."

Looking Back at the Trajectory

Lady Abena Bondah left Ghana for the United States shortly after she completed University of Cape Coast. Now living in the Washington, DC, area, she works as the Managing Principal Consultant for a hospitality, sales and marketing business. The business entity, Gemstone Marketing and Business Consulting, was established by Abena herself.

"When you own a business, you work day and night," says Abena.

She settled into the entrepreneurial life after her experience in senior management roles at some of the largest hotel chains in America.

While keeping busy with life as a businesswoman, Abena volunteered enough of her time and effort to win the US Presidential Gold Award for service to the United Nations Children's Fund (UNICEF).

Regarding her volunteer work, she says, "Ghana is my home, so is the United States, and I like to give back by volunteering. My ultimate legacy is to help women and children, especially in Ghana."

"I am no longer in the media, but I find that everything I do in my life is strongly influenced by the many things I learned in broadcasting."

"What I cherish most is the group of people I worked with, that is why 25 years later, we are still talking, and our friendships remain fresh and strong. It is something we cannot let go of."

While keeping the old bonds strong, Abena believes she is also permanently attached to radio and broadcasting.

"I worked with people who were not looking forward to payday; they were looking forward to being on air and that was inspiring. Everybody had to make a living, but the passion and the work came before anything else," recalls Abena.

"Broadcasting is the one job I will do at any time for free; you don't even have to pay me. Radio is still at the core of my heart," says Lady Abena, her voice laced with conviction.

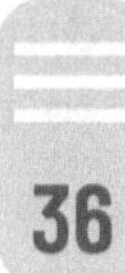

Becoming a Quality Human Resource

> *"I was not prepared for the enormous practical work that came with TV production at Skyy. I had to learn really fast... Those days were tough, because I would sometimes leave home around 3 am for work and not return until 11 pm."*
>
> — *Ewurama Shirley Smith who started her career in the media with Skyy Power FM*

Before the year 2000, Ghana had only three major universities, all run by the state: University of Cape Coast, University of Ghana (also called Legon) and the Kwame Nkrumah University of Science and Technology in Kumasi. Annual admission to these universities was always very competitive with no assurance of placement.

It was 1998 and young Ewurama Shirley Smith was confident she would get a place.

She was wrong.

"My whole world collapsed when I didn't get admission to the University of Ghana. I was so deeply hurt that the feeling was close to depression and my mother was very worried about my wellbeing," she says.

Finding Purpose at Skyy

Describing her deep disappointment after more than twenty years, Ewurama says, "the experience was all the more painful because I actually had good grades and still didn't get the chance. Most of my friends and schoolmates got admission and I was facing a whole year of just being at home after senior high school."

The dreadful episode crushed her enthusiasm and drive, but, somehow, it also led Ewurama to the doorstep of Skyy FM.

"My Mum helped me to redirect my energy. She advised me to find a job to take my mind off the disappointment, so I bought a bundle of envelopes and a writing pad. I wrote numerous application letters to hotels, shops, schools, and other businesses," says Ewurama.

"Someone else suggested that I should write to Skyy Power FM as well, so I did and took the letter there myself."

Ewurama met Wilson Arthur at the station, and he promptly read her letter along with copies of her school transcript.

"After Wilson read my letter, he was impressed and said, 'you have good grades, why didn't you go to the university?'"

A Whole Year Without University

Before Wilson Arthur asked her, Ewurama knew why she did not obtain admission to the university.

"My school mates applied to all the three major universities knowing if they didn't get admission in one, they could get it in another. I preferred the University of Ghana and only applied to go there without realising I narrowed my opportunity considerably," she tells me.

Because of limited opportunities in Ghana across the three universities serving a population of twenty million at the time, many young people were unable to enter the university--at least for a period--not because they did not have satisfactory grades.

Ewurama explained this to Wilson who immediately empanelled Samuel Ansah, Maame Esi Mark-Hansen, and Adwoa Amofah to interview her for a job.

"I was taken to the studio and made to read a script. I mispronounced a word, but the panel were still impressed with my performance and recommended that I be employed."

On that very day, Ewurama was offered a position as a receptionist, and that was all she needed to feel a sense of reassurance from deep despair. She made up her mind that she was going to shine as brightly as possible in her work. Wilson Arthur and the rest of the crew at Skyy expected nothing less.

As one of our colleagues, Yuki Ampofo, observes in a separate interview, "whether you were the driver, security man or the administration officer, you were trained and empowered to sell whatever we had on offer, and that includes taking announcements and explaining the cost of airtime to clients."

Opportunities to develop personal capabilities at Skyy went beyond those necessary for making sales or competent representation of the organisation as a brand.

Even in her craziest dreams, Ewurama never thought she would rise through the ranks at Skyy and become a news editor who managed current affairs across both radio and later Skyy TV, while also fulfilling other managerial roles.

"My life in the media was bound to happen because I was always fascinated by the work of radio presenters since I was a young girl," she says. "I loved reading and whenever my father brought home newspapers, I pretended to read like Barbara Sam, the famous public radio newsreader at Ghana Broadcasting Corporation. I remember trying to sound exactly like her."

Finding herself in a supportive and collaborative environment with a strong desire to learn, it took Ewurama just a few years to become a capable newsreader--and more.

While working as a receptionist, an opportunity came for her to learn how to read the news. "I had a lot of assistance from Samuel Ansah who was one of the news editors at Skyy at the time," she recalls.

Samuel Ansah, a man who loved appropriate use of the English language with immaculate diction, went on to become a lawyer, and later, a judge at the Circuit Courts in Ghana. As one of our colleagues, I interviewed him for this book. While writing this chapter in December 2021, I received the sad news that Samuel Ansah passed away in Ghana.

Becoming A News Reader

"My service as a newsreader was needed for the late afternoon news. Esi Gyan, who was also our administrative manager, and I often presented the news together," says Ewurama.

Esi Gyan was another beloved colleague whom we lost to cancer in March 2014, and as Ewurama recalls working with Esi Gyan, her voice carries the pain that comes with losing someone whose passing still feels unreal. "I was just a newsreader at the time, and I didn't know much about journalism or how the news is produced," she says.

As a newsroom, we were occasionally desperate for extra hands, and I remember the excitement when we made the decision to let Ewurama read the news. We saw her potential, and it was a relief to have another member of staff who could present the news, especially in late afternoons when some of us may be out on assignment.

A little over a year after Ewurama joined Skyy, she earned a permanent place in the newsroom. "I remember the first news item I wrote which Sylvia Odonkor edited. The two of us had gone on assignment and afterwards, I wrote a script that turned out to be meaningless. Looking back, I can't even see the head or tail of that story," recalls Ewurama, her voice tinged with humour.

Life in the newsroom was never a straight line. Sometimes, it seemed to be worse than the rough and tumble of a full-contact sport. Despite that, there was always a high dose of fun, laughter, and constant drama. The environment was maddening, but Ewurama had the appetite, the determination, and grit to succeed.

Ewurama presented herself as the quintessential Takoradi girl-- intelligent, capable, smart, fun-loving, and effortlessly sophisticated.

Twelve months after missing out on being admitted to the University of Ghana, she clinched a place at the same university.

During holidays, she would return to the newsroom in Takoradi. When she completed school, she became one of those who had a job on hand at Skyy on the day she graduated.

The Newsroom—a Total Mixed Bag

Ewurama Smith took up her place in the newsroom around the same time that Ato-Kwamena Dadzie, a graduate from Ghana Institute of Journalism, joined Skyy.

With his particular sense of humour and high intelligence, Ato quickly became an integral part of the Skyy newsroom. Other characters in the newsroom made the place feel like a dysfunctional entity that somehow still got extremely good results on all metrics.

Kezia Morgan, Enoch Yeboah, Eric Ahianyo, Joycelyn Sey, Kweku Temeng, Angela Oppong, and Anny Osabutey were among those in the newsroom during that period. Even though he was fresh out of journalism school, Ato-Kwamena Dadzie demonstrated high level skill in journalism that made you think he was a veteran in the profession.

The real veteran, though, was the late Kwesi Mould, who was already in his 60s before joining Skyy with valuable experience in journalism gained through decades of practice. He taught us many aspects of journalism on the job that involved the use of good judgment and taste.

Ewurama remembers both Ato-Kwamena Dadzie and Mr. Mould not just for their skills in journalism but also for their sense of humour and seriousness. Some of the stories Ewurama recalled were simple and funny but left a strong imprint on our collective memory.

"Once, Ato was writing a news story on the computer and I leaned over his shoulder. A mobile phone I was holding at the time rested on him," recalls Ewurama. "Just then I had a call which caused the phone to vibrate quite violently. Ato was so startled that he jumped up and started shouting deliriously saying, 'hey, Ewurama, you are vibrating, you are vibrating.'"

"Mobile phones were still new at the time. Ato didn't have one and didn't know they could vibrate when a call came through, so he sincerely believed the vibration occurred directly on my skin."

The Joys of the Newsroom

Once, Ewurama Smith presented a news bulletin that we deemed a disaster. Quite a few of her pronunciations were awful. She knew she let herself down and it showed in her voice. As was the usual practice, we held a brief meeting to review what went wrong and how to prevent it in the future. The news editor Mr. Mould was out in the city when this happened, so we did the review without him. Sadly, he monitored the news in real time and was naturally unimpressed.

Old Mr. Mould returned to the office like a raging bull. As his deputy, I rushed to protect Ewurama from his anger, telling him that we had resolved the matter and knew what went wrong. To our relief, he calmed down. Shortly afterwards, Kennedy Arthur, one of the owners of Skyy, arrived from Cape Coast. We all called Kennedy Arthur "Big Bro." He had heard the poor presentation on air and came into the newsroom to enquire about what went wrong.

Well, Mr. Mould flew into a rage once more after hearing Big Bro's concern. "Ewurama, the news you read was so bad that even Big Bro heard it all the way in Cape Coast," shouted Mr. Mould.

In his renewed rage, it was as if Mr. Mould now wanted the proverbial pound of flesh from Ewurama, so once again, I found myself interceding.

"Mr. Mould," I said, "I think you should leave Ewurama alone because the nature of our broadcast is such that it is heard everywhere, including Cape Coast, with or without mistakes." My comment caused a bit of laughter, and Mr. Mould's demeanour changed instantly, as I added, "Old Mr. Mould, always trying to be bold."

The phrase was part of a playful poem we composed and used to tease Mr. Mould. He was a man who would almost intentionally get angry on the job just to shake things up, but at his core, he was a delightful character who loved us, and whom we all loved dearly. He made us laugh in the newsroom everyday as he regaled us with many stories from before we were born.

In later years, Ewurama became closer to Mr. Mould more than all of us. During the period leading to Mr. Mould's death in 2019, Ewurama was one of those who rendered assistance that could only be motivated by a mixture of love, respect, and affection.

Growing Up With Skyy

Being a predominantly young workforce, we all grew up with Skyy Power FM and barely noticed the speed with which the station's operations expanded.

Our old studio at 37 Windy Ridge became too small to contain our activities and the growing ambitions of the business. In early 2002, about five years after Skyy started, we moved to *Skyy House*, a new palatial two-storey building put up by Skyy. This was followed by the establishment of Skyy TV, a groundbreaking digital multi-channel television service.

Staff in the newsroom had no option but to become multiskilled in radio and TV news production. With a growing business empire, Wilson Arthur was always motivating employees to find more of their creativity and talent.

The result was that many of the employees found they could become part of the locally produced television shows. Content for the TV included locally produced drama that had a strong appeal to viewers.

"At the University of Ghana, I studied Linguistics and Theater Arts which included some stage work for the screen, but I was not prepared for the enormous practical work and the long hours that came with TV production at Skyy," says Ewurama.

The Grind Gets Harder with TV

Ewurama remembers the challenge at Skyy during this period with considerable clarity. "The late Kwesi Turkson, a longtime videographer in Takoradi, became the Director of Photography along with many other technicians that were brought onboard," she says.

"They were mostly professionals who produced Ghanaian movies and had to adapt their skills to live TV work, including news production. I had to learn really fast and get to know terminologies like *white-balancing, bird's eye view, close-ups* and *long shots*. Those days were tough because I would sometimes leave home around 3 am for work and not return until 11 pm," recalls Ewurama.

Ewurama became so indispensable that after some of us left, she became the Head of News and Current Affairs for both radio and TV. Along with those responsibilities, she also played pivotal roles in the entire operations at Skyy. Unwilling to limit her ambitions, she also enrolled at nearby University of Cape Coast for a Master of Arts degree in Communication Studies.

Looking back, she says, "I learned a great deal on the job and gained a lot of experience because Wilson Arthur offered me extensive opportunities. He moved me through numerous departments where at various times, I was managing events, operations, as well as news and current affairs."

"For some time, I moved from Skyy and joined Media General in Accra. Because of the training and experience I had at Skyy, I did not struggle at all and became an asset to the organisation. Media General was moving to a model that combined radio and TV news at the time. People with the required skills were in short supply, but my background from Skyy made it easy for me to excel and even train others," she recalls.

After missing Ewurama Smith's services at Skyy for a few years, Wilson Arthur brought her back, where she once again made outstanding contributions. Her skills and experience remained extremely attractive, and it was only a matter of time before Media General returned to take her back into its fold.

She continues working as the Western and Central Regional Bureau Editor for Media General with an office at Connect FM in Takoradi.

Fred Chidi, a veteran broadcaster who also worked for Media General and knew her, says, "Ewurama Smith is a hard-working journalist who likes to get results."

Like dozens of our colleagues, Ewurama remembers our collective professional journey at Skyy with much fondness. "Wilson Arthur's attitude was great because he did not come across like a boss," she says of our Chief Executive. "We didn't have any bureaucracy. Each of us could walk into his office at any time and tell him what we felt. If he believed he was right, he would present his argument, but if he felt there was a better option, he would give in. We held meetings anytime and anywhere, and within minutes, decisions were implemented," she recalls.

For the rest of the crew, Ewurama says, "We were always playful but serious with our responsibilities. And we were also so close as friends that we spent time in each other's homes even after work. We were a great team, a real family of friends. I remember the likes of Ato-Kwamena Dadzie, Elloeny Amande, Abena Bondah, Naa Adoley Thompson, Kojo Frempong, Root Eye, Sylvia Odonkor, and Eric Ahianyo. Every one of us went on to achieve a lot in life after learning so much at Skyy," she says, with a sense of nostalgia.

Reflecting on the legacy of the business, she says, "I believe a major legacy of Skyy Power FM is that it produced quality human resources for the entire broadcast media industry in Ghana."

37

Blakk Rasta: A Lion Is Not a Peacock

> *"Skyy was so big. In my opinion, it was legendary back then. Quality radio, quality sound, and for me to have the opportunity on Skyy, it was so big. For me to even walk around and tell one or two people I was on Skyy, that alone was significant for me."*
>
> — *Musician and Radio presenter, Blakk Rasta on the relevance of Skyy Power FM*

In early February 2007, then-junior United States Senator from Illinois, Barack Obama, braved icy weather in Springfield to announce his candidacy for the presidency of the United States. About ten thousand kilometres away in Ghana, a radio presenter called Blakk Rasta watched the news, thoroughly amazed that a relatively young black man found the guts to announce his intention to wage a battle to capture the most powerful political office on earth.

Blakk Rasta's real name is Ahmed Abubakar. He was curious that Barack Obama carried a middle name, Hussein, very likely indicating an Islamic heritage, something he felt did not portend well for someone seeking to lead from the White House.

That notwithstanding, Blakk Rasta felt that Obama had a shot at an improbable victory. On his radio program, he talked about his hopes for the young man far away in America. The name Barack Obama didn't mean much then, so no one paid attention. Many thought the reggae music presenter just needed to fill airtime with some talking.

A Song for Barack Obama

Apart from hosting a radio program, Blakk Rasta was also a musician. He was so fixated on the little-known Barack Obama that he wrote a song for the man he believed was a promising global politician.

As if he had run out of creativity, Blakk Rasta named the song "Barack Obama."

Shortly after, Blakk Rasta met Zapp Mallet, one of Ghana's greatest music producers. Zapp Mallet was well versed in American politics, including the version in Chicago where Barack Obama learned to become a community organiser and, later, politician.

"Zapp Mallet and I discussed Obama, and like me, Zapp Mallet believed Obama was going to be a great leader," says Blakk Rasta.

After their scintillating discussion about politics in America, Zapp Mallet and Blakk Rasta recorded the song "Barack Obama" long before most of the world got to know who Obama was and who he became.

Somehow, the song caught the attention of Barack Obama and his high-stakes campaign team, and it was eventually used during the campaign for the election Obama won to become the first black man elected as President of the United States Amercia.

Long before his faith in Obama's future was rewarded, Blakk Rasta was just one of the many radio presenters who passed through Skyy Power FM in Takoradi.

Coming to Takoradi

Regarding his association with Skyy Power FM, Blakk Rasta says,

"it all started with Joe Enuson when we were students in Kumasi."

"It was my dream to live in Takoradi because I just love the Fante language, and the Fante friends I met in school inspired me to come to Takoradi."

Joe Enuson was one of those Fante friends.

Joe himself joined Skyy after he completed studies at Kwame Nkrumah University of Science and Technology in Kumasi. He and

Blakk Rasta were mates. More significantly though, they were also both volunteer presenters on the University campus radio, Contatto.

With Takoradi on his mind, Blakk Rasta chose to undertake his national service in the Twin City. His friend Joe Enuson, who was already an employee of Skyy Power FM, hosted him for a short time to help him transition into Takoradi.

"I told Joe Enuson how much I wanted to be on professional radio, and he already knew what I could do because of our experience on Contatto student radio in Kumasi."

At the time, Joe Enuson was the program manager at Skyy, so he sought Wilson Arthur's permission to put Blakk Rasta on Skyy as a presenter.

The experience of being on Skyy through Joe Enuson meant so much to Blakk Rasta. So much so that he speaks of it with much passion and deep reflection.

"That was my first experience of being on radio in Takoradi," he says. "It was a beautiful experience, considering the fact that Skyy Power was the only private radio station in Takoradi at that time; it was beautiful and very prestigious," he adds.

That was 2001.

Getting Tossed Out of Skyy

In reality, though, Blakk Rasta's association with Skyy was like hiring an old lion to act like a peacock in a zoo. It simply didn't work, and the resulting snafu came swiftly.

What he still describes as "a beautiful and prestigious adventure" lasted for only seven days.

Blakk Rasta explains, "it lasted only one week because the CEO, Wilson Arthur, believed that the kind of reggae I played, roots reggae, was not something he wanted for his radio. He wanted me to do some Lovers Rock, softer reggae, you know, and I was more interested in the roots reggae, roots as in traditional reggae, conscious reggae, what they call cultural reggae; the one that will afford me the opportunity to speak *patois* and talk about issues relating to the development of our country and beyond, to criticise and be criticised, you know..."

Referring to Wilson Arthur, whom he calls Uncle Willie, he says, "he was not interested in that. He tried me on Lover's Rock, which I did, but it certainly wasn't my mainstay. He told me he was not satisfied with my lover's rock and he did not intend doing roots reggae," at least, the kind that Blakk Rasta set his heart on.

"So that is how my stint with Skyy ended," recalls Blakk Rasta.

Not Made To Be Tamed

Consistent with his vision and continuous insistence on a certain style for Skyy, Wilson urged Blakk Rasta to tone down his revolutionary language and ways. But Blakk Rasta is the first to admit that he is not easily tamed.

To use another analogy from the animal kingdom, Blakk Rasta was like a beautiful zebra resembling a prized thoroughbred, except Zebras cannot be tamed and no one can ride it.

Blakk Rasta is a fighter--he believes he was born as such, totally unafraid to speak his mind, no matter how uncomfortable people feel about it.

"My father told me that you don't get what you want by sleeping, you need to fight. If you sleep, you will wake up and everything is gone. I always have this in my mind," says Blakk Rasta.

The courage of his convictions comes to him easily, and whether it is an unpopular opinion, harsh criticism, or the occasional insult, he doles it out generously. In March 2021, a fiery national dialogue erupted after the prestigious Achimota School in Accra refused to admit two Rastafarian students with dreadlocks unless they cut their hair.

The school said their long hair did not conform to the institution's rules and threatened conformity and discipline. The controversial decision attracted Blakk Rasta, who is himself a Rastafarian. So, he lobbed a few words over to the school's headmistress.

"The headmistress at Achimota school refusing admission to Rastas is herself wearing fake, Peruvian hair," he wrote on his Facebook page.

New Beginning

Blakk Rasta and his radio story didn't end when Skyy Power FM kissed him goodbye. He hung around his favourite city Takoradi for a whole year--for a new beginning, while Skyy, the station he loved, continued broadcasting.

Then he received some good news.

A new radio station, a second private radio station in Takoradi called Goodnews, started, and he was given a chance to live out his character on that station.

The name "Goodnews" sounded pretty harmless for a radio station. By Skyy Power FM standards, however, it carried no funkiness at all.

Along with its new crop of presenters, the unspoken understanding at Skyy was that Goodnews FM was a B-class station with B-class presenters. Skyy was still the A-class station with A-class presenters.

When Blakk Rasta eventually went on air on Goodnews FM, though, the lone Blakk Rasta didn't fit into A or B class. What you saw and heard was simply a *Blakk-Rasta-class!* He created a brand of his own, attracting a large listenership that Skyy did not anticipate. It became more than a mild cause for concern.

"I was giving Skyy Power a run for their money," says Blakk Rasta, adding, "that was when Wilson Arthur realised he had lost a gem."

According to Blakk Rasta, some effort was made to bring him back to Skyy, but the long, drawn-out process didn't work.

Even though Blakk Rasta was deeply disappointed by his rejection by Skyy, he still easily acknowledges the significance of the station and the historic role it played in the Ghanaian broadcast industry.

"Skyy was so big. In my opinion, it was legendary back then. Quality radio, quality sound, and for me to have the opportunity on Skyy, it was so big and so nice. For me to even walk around and tell one or two people I was on Skyy, that alone was significant for me."

Blakk Rasta takes pride in his personal honesty and integrity. That quality is at the root of his readiness to speak so charitably of Skyy, despite being thrown out of the station.

Responding to the question about Skyy Power FM's legacy, Blakk Rasta applies the benefit first to himself.

"Without Skyy, I would have taken a lot of things for granted. Because when I got that rejection from Skyy, it gave me the energy to prove my worth," he says.

"Sometimes, you need to get rejected for you to have reality come down on you, so you realise that you need to prove something."

"When I left Skyy," he continues, "my mindset was that Skyy is big; strive to be a good presenter to that level and even beyond. So Skyy was like a yardstick for me…and that helped me."

Blakk Rasta also feels proud of his strong character and intuition. That is what led him to Sekondi-Takoradi and into the first private radio in that part of Ghana.

His intuition led him to compose a song about a little-known politician who eventually occupied the most powerful office in the world.

Blakk Rasta has seen the reward for his strong character. The biggest of those rewards came from former US President Barack Obama.

When Obama visited Ghana in 2009, he specifically requested to meet Blakk Rasta. He stood face to face with Obama and shook his hand while cameras flashed.

Blakk Rasta tells me that the occasion is a monumental memory he reflects on every day.

The other thing he keeps in mind every day is the power of radio as a means of reaching millions with inspiration that he desires to share in his own way.

And he shares it regularly to prove that he would always be a lion, rather than a peacock.

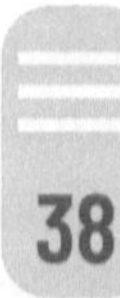

38

The Uncompromising Eric Ahianyo

"At Skyy, we were like a family living in an apartment. Each individual was like a gatekeeper who ensured we were doing only our very best at all times. Everyone at the station also knew that there was never any room for flimsy excuses."

— Eric Ahianyo, recalling the start of his journalism career at Skyy Power FM

If there was a prize for the most uncompromising individual at Skyy FM, Eric Ahianyo would easily wear the crown. First, he is a gentleman, good looking and thoughtful. You will only ever see him smartly dressed with the broadest smile. When he speaks, he chooses words dripping with seriousness.

"I try to be as frank as possible," Eric tells me when I interview him for this book. His voice is deliberate.

Even the few words he says to confirm his steadiness reminds me of our days at Skyy when we all quickly learned to take his words and views seriously.

It is almost a matter of contradiction that Eric is also exceedingly friendly. It is easy to be drawn to his loud and genuinely infectious laughter and jokes. When he is focused on his job as a journalist, however, this same man turns into a relentless professional hunter for the best version of news stories, with no room for compromise or gentleness.

His devotion and readiness to sacrifice to achieve high professional standards was evident even while he was at the University of Cape Coast and volunteered as a presenter on ATL FM, the rookie campus radio station for students. "We were working for fun, we were not being paid," recalls Eric.

A Passion to Learn and Work

Eric lived at the SSNIT flats at the nearby historic town of Elmina. It is fair to describe it as nearby, but not when you have to walk the ten-kilometre distance. As a student, he was broke most of the time, with no money even for public transport. Eric says, "sometimes, I work at ATL FM as late as 10pm, and I would walk the ten-kilometre stretch from the campus back home."

"That is one and a half hours of walking in the middle of the night," I interject, marvelling at his commitment and resilience in continuing in an activity for which he was not paid.

"I had the passion and I loved what I did," he says. "I was doing current affairs programs including newspaper review and the morning show. Skyy Power FM was the only private radio station in the Western and Central Regions at the time, and sometimes we picked up the signals. I admired the professionalism I heard on air, and I had the ambition that someday, I would work there," says Eric.

After university, Eric was posted to Sekondi-Takoradi metropolis for his mandatory National Service. He was now physically close to Skyy Power FM, the radio station of his dreams.

Paa Kofi Nyarko, another presenter on Skyy from Cape Coast, was known to Eric when they were both at the university, so Eric asked if he could be introduced to Wilson Arthur for a job.

Before this, Joe Anim, a veteran radio producer whom Eric knew from Komenda and Cape Coast, heard Eric on ATL FM. He sensed that he had not just the talent but a good work ethic. Because he was close to Skyy's Chief Executive Wilson Arthur, Joe Anim recommended that Wilson consider employing Eric. When Paa Kofi Nyarko introduced Eric to the Skyy Chief Executive, he was surprised by the warm welcome he got.

"I heard a lot about you from Joe Anim. I had been planning to look for you, so I am excited to meet you," Wilson told Eric.

"Joe Anim had a professional relationship with Wilson Arthur, so his recommendation for my employment made my move to the Skyy FM family a smooth ride," says Eric. "Wilson Arthur not only employed me, but he provided accommodation for me. It was a comfortable two-room flat, and that was very motivating for me, especially as I came fresh from school."

Meeting "Old Mr. Mould"

One of the memorable figures that worked in the Skyy Power newsroom was Kwesi Mould, a man who was long past sixty years of age before joining the station. The wrinkles and depth of seriousness in the old man's face revealed that he had lived a life many of us would never know. He was also a beloved father figure who regaled us with stories of his younger days as a newspaper journalist in Nigeria. He worked tirelessly and it seemed the older he got, the more tireless he became.

Sadly, our beloved Mr. Mould passed away in 2019 at the age of 80. Described as an "exceptionally brilliant man" in his funeral brochure, Mr. Mould remains a man we remember with fondness.

After speaking with Eric, Wilson Arthur directed him to speak to Mr. Mould to chart his course as a prospective Skyy employee.

"I initially thought I would come to Skyy to be a DJ and play music, but after Mr. Mould spoke to me, I was convinced I would make a better impact on the community in the area of current affairs," recalls Eric.

So, old Kwesi Mould, as we used to call him, and the rest of us welcomed Eric Ahianyo into the newsroom. He arrived like a blank canvas on which old Mr. Mould and the rest of us in the newsroom painted an artwork of journalism.

Learning and Growing in the Newsroom

Sylvia Odonkor, Ato-Kwamena Dadzie, Kezia Morgan, and I were some of the journalists in the newsroom at that time. There was also Enoch Yeboah and Kweku Temeng.

Mr. Mould, with a lifetime of experience, was effectively our teacher. The rest of us, particularly Ato and I, were far more skilled in the creation of broadcast news with the use of mini disc technology that allowed us to record and edit voice-overs.

Over time, Eric Ahianyo mastered both the technology and skill to write compelling news stories after covering events and carrying out exclusive interviews. Before that, Eric had to go through a period of pain and adjustment in learning.

"I adopted a culture towards work which I learned from home. I was also mentored by people who were well grounded, including well known figures like Kwamena Duncan, a lecturer and politician, Mustapha Hamid, also politician and Eric Nyarko-Sampson, Vice Chancellor of University of Environment and Sustainable Development. Given all the goodwill I had, including Joe Anim's recommendation, I knew I could not disappoint," says Eric.

Despite Eric's preparedness and willingness to excel, he found the newsroom most challenging and even competitive in the way news stories are produced, edited, and presented on-air.

"I came to the newsroom with no idea about story writing. In fact, I was blank, and I had to learn from scratch, and it was difficult," he recalls.

Eric ramped up his diligence, hard work, and dedication, but that did not always make it easier for him.

"One day, Ato-Kwame Dadzie challenged me in the newsroom," says Eric. "You have been to the university. I am only a student from Ghana Institute of Journalism, and yet look at the useless script you have written." That was Ato, ripping into Eric and whatever ego he had left at that point. Ato makes the most efficient use of words without much regard for diplomacy and as soon as Eric told me what Ato said, I remembered it.

Being Tough as a Nail

I remembered the way we communicated in reviewing scripts for presentation as news. I personally remember reading only half of a paragraph before angrily rejecting a news story by derisively asking, "where is the story in this sentence?" and then demanding it to be rewritten to reflect logic and sanity.

Looking back, there was some unintended brutality in the way we assessed the quality of writing, except it was never personal and always done under pressure. Perhaps a measure of maturity was also missing, with the oversized presence of our youthful vigour.

Kweku Temeng, Keziah Morgan, and Enoch Yeboah bore the brunt of our professional rage against anything we perceived as poor writing and presentation. All these colleagues, however, went on to distinguish themselves in journalism. Kweku Temeng became a star anchor on Skyy, both on radio and TV, and later on Accra-based TV3.

"When I sat down and thought about Ato's criticism, I decided to put my university degree aside," says Eric. "I believed I was intelligent enough to function in the newsroom, but I had to prove it through practical work."

"There was a crop of people who were naturally committed to making sure the operations of Skyy would succeed. You had people like Elloeny Amande, Joe Enuson, Kwesi Fletcher, Maame Esi Mark-Hansen. You watched these people and you know they knew their job and did it very well. Wilson Arthur himself was inspiring. He was always around us like one of us, working with us and reprimanding us occasionally to stamp his authority without over-reaching," says Eric.

"The only way anyone qualified to continue working at Skyy was to perform at a high level, and I found myself rising to the occasion after observing all of you in the newsroom. I was trained to adjust to any situation, so I grew up in the newsroom as a learner," says Eric.

Becoming Productive, Reliable, and Dependable

Eric became a most dependable and reliable hand in the newsroom even before the departure of Ato-Kwamena Dadzie and Mr. Mould and right up to the time Skyy launched its television service. The two of us especially worked closely together in running the newsroom to produce current affairs programs including *News Review* and *Big Issues*. Eric describes *News Review* as "the must-not-miss program" in the Western and Central Regions.

I was the main anchor for news and current affairs programs, but I was just the figurehead, the one whose voice was most recognised as the tip of the spear. Eric Ahianyo and all the colleagues in the newsroom were really the powerhouse behind the production that came alive on air.

When I referred to some of those memorable times of close cooperation, Eric started laughing and reminded me of the regular runs we both took to the studio from the newsroom at the top of the hour for the major bulletin in the morning and afternoons.

"You always run to the studio with me following you at the heel," he says, adding, "about the last five metres before the studio, you developed this habit of sliding on the smooth floor, right up to the entrance of the studio without falling," he notes, causing me to laugh with him as we both relive the dramatic scene from decades ago.

I conducted many high-profile interviews, most of which were possible only with close involvement of Eric. Many times, Eric would be present in the studio, and he would write questions and give helpful directions that made my newsworthy live interactions more fruitful. This is apart from the effective technical production value he always offered.

I remember one interview with former President John Atta Mills in which Eric could see I was running out of steam, and he knew what to do: he wrote me a quick note and gave me signals that fired me up to come up with a new line of questions that startled the learned professor.

It was an unwritten rule in our news and current affairs practice that an interview is not robust enough unless you asked questions that caused the interviewee to feel uncomfortable--or even occasionally revealed some hidden incompetence in whoever we were interviewing. We also believed that those whom we interviewed give off their best only when we have done enough digging and research to pose the most challenging questions.

Once I was reading the news live in the studio only to realise to my horror that the next page was not with me. Somehow, I managed to recite the rest of the script from memory while looking intently into Eric's eyes. Eric understood that I was almost making it up without

a script. Because the original script had a soundbite at the end, Eric
signaled to me that he understood and was ready to play it when I
signaled him. I introduced the soundbite as if reading the script, and
right on cue, Eric played it. It was a smooth transition and no one
except the two of us knew we worked as a team to avert a disaster.

No Room for Flimsy Excuses

"The environment at Skyy was such that only the laziest person
would fail to perform, because everyone was self-motivated. Skyy
was an enormous success story because of that, and it was a matter
of pride to be associated with it," says Eric, feeling proud of his own
contribution through the years.

"You guys in the newsroom were hard to deal with, but you had
such a high standard," recalls Elloeny Amande, a colleague whom I
interviewed for this book as well.

Engaging in fiery arguments was a daily routine for us in the
newsroom. Eric was robust and strong in his arguments. The same
can be said of the rest of us, especially Ato-Kwamena Dadzie, Mr.
Mould, and me.

The things we argued about were strictly journalism and broadcast-
related, and they ranged from the mundane to life-or-death. We don't
back down, and we raise our voices to the highest decibels our vocal
cords would allow. When we argued, no one outside the newsroom
was allowed to come in; not even Wilson Arthur, the owner of the
station. The rule, though unwritten, was clear: "don't cross our paths
or we will eat you up, flesh, bones, and all."

Over time, Wilson developed the habit of entering the newsroom
with extreme care because if he came at the wrong time, we were
crazy enough to ask him to walk out. Other members of staff also
learned quickly not to interfere with the high-voltage operations of
the newsroom.

"It is crazy how you guys in the newsroom would argue before
every news bulletin, but when it is all over, you behave as if you were
the best of friends," our colleagues at Skyy would tell us over and
over again.

Recalling the past, Eric says, "I could openly tell it to your face when I am unhappy about something; not because I am better than you but because you are the face of our brand at a particular time and a certain action or inaction on your part affects us all. After a robust exchange, we go out together as friends to eat, laugh, and play."

It is true.

The end of every news bulletin was an occasion for celebration. In many ways, we were like children arguing in one moment and then playing happily together the next moment, with no trace of animosity.

"At Skyy, we were like a family living in an apartment. We saw ourselves as brothers and sisters who had a common goal of delivering quality broadcasting, and each individual was like a gatekeeper who ensured we were doing only our very best at all times," says Eric.

"Everyone at the station also knew that there was never any room for flimsy excuses."

Being Fair to the Core

Around the time Eric joined Skyy, seventeen-year-old Nelly Lomotey secured a permanent place at Skyy as a receptionist while helping to run the weekly children's program on Saturdays. Everyone was on a first-name basis across Skyy, but as she was the youngest member of staff, she never felt comfortable calling everyone by their first name. When Nelly kept calling Eric, "Mr. Ahianyo," Eric gave an ultimatum with all seriousness.

"If you don't call me by my first name, I will not respond to you," he told Nelly. I asked Eric if he remembers, and he says he doesn't. But he also says it is something he knows he would have said to young Nelly.

"Those who groomed me made me believe that you get better results from a team when as a leader, you make everyone feel comfortable around you. That is one of the elements that has helped me succeed as a person, and I will not compromise on my principles," he explains.

Eric's cherished principles and professionalism gave him a solid foundation in journalism and in his professional outlook.

His trademark diligence, hard work, and dedication continued to serve him as he moved on to other ventures. He currently leads the production and presentation of news and current affairs on Woezor TV Online. Anytime I watch and listen to him, I tell myself, "this is the Eric Ahianyo I knew and worked with all those years ago."

A Long-Lasting Legacy

The output of Skyy that Eric Ahianyo saw and participated in was near perfection. It is in some way a thing of beauty that it took a team of flawed people to achieve so much in a relatively short time in an African metropolis with a relatively low profile.

We were together, a team of winners through hard work, creativity, and commitment that required a lot of muscle with brain power.

Eric Ahianyo says the legacy of Skyy is that it was a radio station that punched way above its weight. He believes it was a symphony of outstanding people, constant comedy, a stream of trustworthy news, as well as a 24-hour, 7-day entertainment.

In a most kind way, Eric focuses attention on me as an example of Skyy FM's lasting goodwill in Sekondi-Takoradi.

"Phillip, I tell you that if you go back to Takoradi today, no matter how many years you might have been away, those who knew of your contribution would not see you as the Phillip who was a nuisance to their ears. They would see you as the Phillip who added value to radio."

I am blinded by his generous comment, but he isn't finished with me.

"Your excellence didn't start from day one," he continues. "It took the contribution of Wilson Arthur who continuously drew your attention to a few things you could do better when you started your news and current affairs program on weekends. When you eventually left Takoradi, it created a gap, and I don't think it has been filled up to today."

I am relieved when he shifts his focus from me.

"The legacy of Skyy Power FM and the contribution of Wilson Arthur goes beyond radio," says Eric. "The annual Masqueraders

Festival in Sekondi-Takoradi, which has since grown big, was initially promoted to the rest of Ghana and the world by Wilson Arthur with the full resources of Skyy FM. Every year, it grows bigger, and the credit must rightly go to Wilson Arthur and Skyy Power FM."

Touching further on the impact of Skyy, Eric says, "the long-lasting legacy of Skyy is the people who went through the institution, especially in the formative stages and became successful. They were shaped by Skyy to make a positive impact. The ultimate brain behind the opportunity we got was Wilson Arthur, and he deserves credit for it."

Recognising that the success did not rest entirely on one person, he says, "in my opinion, Wilson Arthur was lucky to have a crop of committed, intelligent and hardworking people who drove themselves hard to achieve success."

"Wilson Arthur certainly provided the leadership and training we all needed to excel. The overall impact is part of the legacy we must never forget because it is worth preserving for posterity," says Eric Ahianyo.

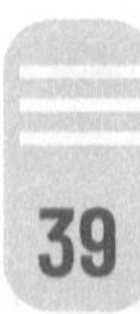

"If You Don't Call Me by My First Name..."

> *"The environment helped me to grow. Regardless of my young age, I was able to relate to everybody including staff and customers. It built my confidence and I think it has stayed with me until now."*
> — *Nelly Lomotey, reflecting on her experience with Skyy from her teenage years*

As soon as Nelly Lomotey completed secondary school, she reached for a phone and dialled the Chief Executive of Skyy Power FM, Wilson Arthur. It was 2003, and Nelly was only 17 years old. She had up to a full year before going to the university, and she needed to be occupied with something productive. So, she called Wilson Arthur with the intention to ask for a job at the radio station.

Nelly related her experience about twenty years after the fact. I tracked her down to York University in Toronto, Canada, where she was undergoing graduate training in risk management and governance. Before her arrival in Canada, she had worked in the banking and financial sector, after moving on from Skyy Power FM where she spent a chunk of her teenage years as a participant on the *Skyy Kiddie Time* children's program, and later as a host on that same program.

All I could see as she related her experience was the precocious young teenager who arrived at Skyy Power FM with an infectious attitude that seemed to say, "I can do this; I belong here."

Nelly recalls that her relationship with Skyy started when she was about thirteen years old. She was part of a group of students from the Ridge International School in Takoradi who visited Skyy

Power FM studios on an excursion. The young girl at the time was so impressive in her speech and comprehension that she was invited to become a regular participant on *Skyy Kiddie Time*, a fascinating weekly children's program at the station.

In time, Nelly progressed from being a young participant on *Skyy Kiddie Time* to becoming the actual presenter of that same program. She learned the required skills from the original hosts Naa Adoley Thompson and Yuki Ampofo. Along with that, she also reflected the endless smile and friendliness that had a permanent presence in the lives of the previous presenters.

Her professional and friendly demeanour was especially visible at the reception of Skyy House at 19/20 West Fijai. Nelly, always smartly dressed, would welcome clients with the broadest smile that instantly enhanced the organisation's image. Often, clients would recognise her voice and enquire if she was "the Nelly Lomotey" they heard on air. With an even broader smile, she would say yes, and promptly ask how she could be of help. I observed that Nelly's progress and growth was so smooth and natural that it was easier to miss than notice.

A Place Worth Returning To

When Skyy Power FM started, different schools in Sekondi-Takoradi had their turn to visit the studios, and young Nelly was full of excitement when she joined the team from her school for a visit. During the tour, she distinguished herself not only by her eloquence, but also through her curiosity and interest to know how everything worked.

When a decision was made to select some intelligent and well-spoken children to feature regularly on the program, Nelly was a clear favourite. Her selection was supported by her parents and schoolteachers.

"I always looked forward to Saturdays where I would be part of the program with the other children who were all really smart," she says.

What impressed Nelly most over time was the immense interest the Skyy FM boss, Wilson Arthur took in the children's program.

"Mr. Wilson Arthur was very friendly and open with us. He would often walk into the studio to observe and encourage us. Sometimes, he would listen from outside the studio. He would say things like, 'you guys are doing so well, and I like your conversation about this. How about you look at it from this other dimension?'"

"Even after the program, he would sit with us and talk about how the program went and ask about our plans for the following week. He took personal interest in us, and would ask how our schooling is going, so we formed the kind of relationship where we could really talk to him. He showed that he was interested in our development, so I am able to talk to him and say something like, 'I have completed basic school, and this is the grade I got,' and he would excitedly say, 'oh congratulations, keep it up.'"

Nelly Lomotey says these are some of her memories of Skyy until she finished senior high school. "After I finished senior high school, I had to wait a whole year before going to the university, and that is why I thought about working." That is when she decided Skyy Power FM was a place worth returning to, not just on Saturdays for *Skyy Kiddie Time*, but a place to work Monday to Friday.

"Do you Know Why You Are Not Working?"

With a whole year of free time ahead of her, it took Nelly a while to call Wilson Arthur at Skyy. She actually didn't even have to ask for the job on the phone. Wilson already knew she recently completed senior high school, and at seventeen years old, her most important possession was *time*.

"So, what are you doing with your time; are you working?" Wilson Arthur asked even before Nelly suggested she needed a job.

"No," answered Nelly.

"Do you know why you are not working?" asked Wilson Arthur, rather rhetorically. Nelly did not provide an answer.

"You are not working because you are not looking," said Wilson Arthur in an encouraging tone.

"Come and see me; we could have a job for you here at Skyy," he told Nelly. Nelly beamed with excitement.

"Thank you," she said.

Working at Skyy Full Time, for Real

If Nelly's meeting with Wilson Arthur was a job interview, then it was really quick. Wilson told her she was going to continue working on the children's program on Saturdays, but, more importantly, she would also juggle working at the reception and giving special attention to those who came looking specifically for the Chief Executive. Nelly was going to be a personal assistant to Wilson Arthur in interacting with his visitors.

Nelly quickly found out there was a big difference in working full time at Skyy, as opposed to coming to the station for a couple of hours every Saturday for the children's program.

"I remember the first time I came in," she says, "everybody was on a first name basis, and I felt like, err.. this is someone's dad, this is someone's wife, so why am I going to call them by their first name. But people were so open and receptive."

Wilson Arthur's wife Adwoa Amofah was the only one we called either "Sister Adwoa" or "Auntie Adwoa," "Sister" and "Auntie" being a traditional honorific title in Ghana. Adwoa Amofah was seen by all of us as a kind of "mother-in-chief."

Nelly felt out of place. She was the youngest among the employees and still technically a child. She would try addressing everyone with the titles Mr, Ms, or Madam, and each time, she was told to simply call everyone by their first name. It didn't work, and as Nelly recalls, it took Eric Ahianyo of the newsroom to change it.

"I remember Eric Ahianyo was like, 'if you don't call me by my first name, I will not respond to you.' I think that was like a breakthrough moment for me. I mustered up the courage to call him 'Eric,' and after that, I was able to relate to everyone on a first name basis."

"Eric Ahianyo would be proud when he hears this conversation later, when he is reminded that decades ago, he helped you to relax and fit into a high-level work environment by encouraging you to be assertive," I say in response. Even though the interview is over the phone, I can sense Nelly's characteristic smile breaking on her face.

Eric Ahianyo's insistence that he would respond only if young Nelly called him by his first name represents his personal values of radical and transparent fairness, especially in a work environment. It is also a reflection of the distinct egalitarian spirit of Sekondi-Takoradi.

Right in front of our very own eyes, we saw Nelly, not only grow, but flourish into a young woman with many abilities and classic professional comportment way beyond her years.

"Auntie Nelly Lomotey"

Although not a written rule, everyone who hosts *Skyy Kiddie Time* gets to be called "Auntie." Along with becoming an employee of Skyy, Nelly moved on to become host of the children's program. Apart from that, Nelly also assisted in hosting a few other programs on air, particularly, the popular *Coast-to-Coast* program which she hosted with Adwoa Amofah.

So, the girl that was simply a participant on the children's program became "Auntie Nelly Lomotey," taking full control of *Skyy Kiddie Time* with a new generation of children learning from her. She laughs as I point out how incredible it was.

"I can't believe it either," she says. "One of the things that surprised me most was just how much people paid attention to our program on air. People took us very seriously, and after the program, they would engage us and say, 'you didn't say this right, or you could have said something else better."

"Even my friends noticed, and some of them would joke that I am making them look bad, for being so articulate on air." Nelly remembers two of her close friends, Elorm and Edem, who jovially said, "don't come to our house because our dad is always saying we should listen to an intelligent young lady like Nelly who speaks on radio."

"My friends never said this out of malice," she explains. "They were just acknowledging the power of radio and how it influenced the views of people including parents."

"My years at Skyy were some of the happiest times in my life," says Nelly. When she gives an example to illustrate the happy times, it is a rather simple experience from the days when the studio was located at 37 Windy Ridge.

"Usually when we close, we would get in the Skyy minivan that took us home, but there were times we would finish and all of us would walk together. We just enjoyed the walk, from Windy Ridge all the way down to the Tractor & Equipment side before getting in a car to go home."

The "Tractor & Equipment side" is the offices of the Tractor and Equipment along the Cape Coast road between Monkey Hill and the PTC Roundabout. It is about a one-kilometre walk from the old Skyy studios at 37 Windy Ridge.

All employees of Skyy have taken this simple walk up and down the hill. The scene on this walk is punctuated by a few trees along the way, offering a refreshing shade when the tropical weather is occasionally too warm with high humidity.

Nelly is simply unable to talk about her memories of Skyy Power FM without manifesting a strong sense of gratitude. "That environment helped me to grow," she says.

"Regardless of age, I was able to relate to everybody, including staff and customers. It practically built my confidence, and I think it has stayed with me until now. I am able to go anywhere, sit back, survey, launch in, and speak to people without feeling uncomfortable or reserved."

Nelly's sentiment is shared by Emmanuel Sackey, one of the children who took part in *Skyy Kiddie Time* on Saturdays. "Emanuel and I were one of those kids who had so much fun on the program, and we remain close friends up to now," says Nelly Lomotey.

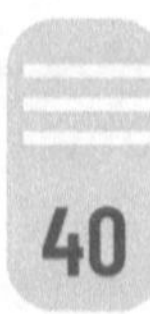

40

The Private Philosopher in Radio

"Wilson Arthur is like a tactical football coach; he works on your mind. He implants in you a certain belief that makes you perform beyond your conscious ability. He makes you feel like competition does not exist and that you are the most capable presenter or performer anywhere, anytime."

— *Nana Otu Gyandoh, former Skyy Power FM employee*

I can still remember the fiery eyes of Nana Otu Gyandoh as we both walked up the hill from Skyy Power FM's first studio at Windy Ridge. We were talking about our work and its impact in Takoradi, and how we could make it even better. The young man possessed such an intense passion for radio and broadcasting that he would spend hours talking about his own vision for it.

His intensity is also wrapped in a deep love for music and the creative energy that produces a subtle mix of lyrics, rhythms, and beats that find a permanent place in human memory. At heart, he is a private philosopher in an endless search for the fine art of communicating, entertaining, and effecting change, using radio as a medium.

As we walked, I looked across to admire a bracelet on his wrist. It was made of a mix of ancient beads and cowries. He would easily choose that bracelet over a Rolex watch. As much as he loved modern life with its electronic gadgets, Otu Gyandoh was a young man with a deep consciousness of his culture and traditional values.

His passion for radio was a long time in the making. It started when he was a student at University of Cape Coast, listening to Skyy.

The Spark from Skyy FM

Private and commercial radio in Ghana was in its infancy when Otu Gyandoh became a freshman at the University of Cape Coast. Skyy was the only private station in the Central and Western Region at that time, and Otu Gyandoh and his friends at the university listened to it around the clock.

"There was always something attractive about Skyy, and listening to that station always gave us an opportunity to imagine how commercial radio was going to be," he says.

The experience inspired him and his friends to literally create their own campus radio at the Valco Hall of the University in the late 1990s. "There was a guy who started it with just an ordinary FM microphone covering a radius of about 10 rooms, but my friends and I took it to a different level. There were about seven of us and we put money together and we built our own transmitter," recalls Otu Gyandoh.

It was a miserable seven-watt mono transmitter and belonged exclusively to the students. "We built it from scratch--from the crystal circuit to the antenna. Google was in its infancy at the time, but we were able to use it at the Internet Cafe to search for circuit diagrams, learn how to put all the components together and design everything ourselves. Because the Valco Hall was a high rise building on a hill, the signal travelled all over the campus and to some parts of Cape Coast township."

"We risked everything to build this campus radio. There were times when we skipped lectures and engaged in many experiments. I think radio was something that captured our imagination, and we were so engrossed to make sure it worked," recalls Otu Gyandoh.

The unusual venture of Otu Gyandoh and his friends was all the more remarkable because Cape Coast University already had an existing campus radio sponsored by the government, called *ATL FM*. The much smaller *Radio Valco* he and his friends built was an expression of their own independence and demonstration of their creative, adventurous, and even rebellious spirit.

Going Cold on Radio After School

After Otu Gyandoh completed University of Cape Coast, he ended up in Kumasi where he worked briefly with *Kapital Radio*. During that period, an inexplicable disillusion came over him and he says, "I lost interest in radio. I think I felt tired and lost motivation, and then I didn't want to have anything to do with radio anymore."

At that time, he came to Takoradi to visit his friend Osei Bediako, better known as JM Caesar. He knew Caesar during his days as a student in Cape Coast when he would attend a few entertainment events at which Caesar was playing as a DJ. "Caesar told Wilson Arthur about me, and they both urged me to host the *Drive Jam* afternoon program on Skyy for one day," says Otu Gyandoh.

"While I was presenting the program, Wilson Arthur came to the studio and was very pleased with my performance. He told me he wanted me to stay, even though I was visiting Takoradi for just a day. Three days later, I was still in Takoradi, hosting *Drive Jam* on Skyy. That is when I realised I had been wearing the same shirt for three days straight."

The self-confidence with which Otu Gyandoh played the *Drive Jam* totally rekindled his love for radio. He also found something deeply alluring about Sekondi-Takoradi. Wilson Arthur insisted that Otu Gyandoh should stay and host the program on a permanent basis. That is how a new and endless chapter opened in the life of Otu Gyandoh.

"Wilson Arthur Built Me"

Twenty years after rediscovering radio in Takoradi, Otu Gyandoh looks back on his journey with a lot of clarity. He confesses that he fell flat under the coaching spell of Wilson Arthur.

"I have done radio all over Ghana; in Cape Coast, Kumasi, Sekondi-Takoradi, and Accra, and I have a lot of confidence in my own ability. And when it comes to the media, nobody added onto me, except Wilson," he says.

"Wilson Arthur taught me what it takes to be on radio, how to script, as in copywriting and to produce commercials. He taught me the essence of music and its poetic value. I love the poetic essence in music, but Wilson took it much further. He got me to know the history of certain songs, how they came about, and how I could link them together on a program."

It took me a while to realise that Otu Gyandoh's generous praise for Wilson Arthur is just a warm-up act. He has more to add.

"Wilson Arthur is like a tactical football coach; he works on your mind. He implants in you a certain belief that makes you perform beyond your conscious ability. He makes you feel like competition does not exist and that you are the most capable presenter or performer anywhere, anytime. It is as if he gives you a powerful injection in your arm to make you deliver."

I am familiar with what Otu Gyandoh is describing. I have seen Wilson work his coaching skills on numerous presenters. I have seen and heard Wilson many times talk about the power of music with such tenderness and passion which he passed on to all of us at Skyy.

He made a rule for all those who played music on air: "Never talk over lyrics when the music is playing."

Otu Gyandoh took Wilson Arthur's coaching and training seriously. "Wilson is the one who taught me how to find what is called a music bed," says Otu Gyandoh.

"Finding a music bed guided me to know when to talk, what to say, how much to say and how to say it to make listening to radio a delightful experience."

Under the tutelage of Wilson, every on-air introduction, every transition, and every break was supposed to be a pure work of art. Wilson Arthur's passion for flawless radio production is something that stuck with Otu Gyandoh. As he recalls, Wilson would say, "most of all, plan, think, and talk clearly so that what you say is smooth, not jerky."

The outcome Wilson Arthur always sought was for our listeners to get hooked and stay tuned, even during commercials. It made our broadcast a totally edifying experience, again and again.

The Heartbreak After Departure from Skyy

Samuel Kojo Brace, a younger man who used to listen to Skyy, became an employee of the same station and later joined Joy FM in March 2022. He shares some vivid memories with me regarding Otu Gyandoh. "The first Vitamilk I bought was because of Otu Gyandoh's live-presenter mention, (also called LPM). He did the LPM and I felt I had to go and taste it and get all the benefits this guy was talking about," he says.

What he said sounded quite ordinary to me, but then he adds, "Otu Gyandoh on Skyy was a different guy. I didn't feel the same way again after he left Skyy. Oh my goodness, you will listen to this guy. He knew how to play music; he knew how to talk and blend everything well with the entire program. He was absolutely on a different level on Skyy. I was deeply hurt when he left Skyy. I just couldn't come to terms with it. It was a heartbreaking story for me."

Otu Gyandoh himself looks back and suggests he broke his own heart to a degree when he left Skyy. "Just about the time I should have stayed behind to solidify all that I could do and move on to bigger things in the same region and help it grow; it turned out to be the time I became more self-focused."

It was his way of admitting that there was unfinished business in his relationship with Skyy and Sekondi-Takoradi as a whole.

But long before he left Skyy, Otu Gyandoh experienced the true richness of Sekondi-Takoradi. So rich was his experience that he now feels like he was born to be a native of Sekondi in particular. It goes back to when he was still relatively new with Skyy FM.

The "Simigwa" Culture of Sekondi

Otu Gyandoh made a special discovery when Wilson Arthur engineered a promotion for Castle Milk Stout, an alcoholic drink similar to Guinness. He worked with the late Castle Milk Stout Brand Manager, Bill Quansah, to launch the product. They decided the location for the launch would be Sekondi, the centre of the unique *simigwa* culture represented by the legendary Highlife musician and Sekondi native, Gyedu-Blay Ambolley.

"*Simigwa* is a Sekondi urban parlance. It has its own dance, language, and dress. It is a whole culture," says Otu Gyandoh. The campaign for Castle Milk Stout included a competition in the *Simigwa* Culture exhibition.

"I was new in Sekondi-Takoradi, but Wilson said I should spearhead it," recalls Otu Gyandoh.

"To accomplish this successfully, I rented a place in the heart of Sekondi for a period to immerse myself in the history and culture of Sekondi. I lived there for two weeks to learn the language, behave like them, and I spoke to everyone I met, including the famous Gyedu-Blay Ambolley. I learned about public figures who used to live there, including former President Jerry Rawlings, Mike Eghan, and the filmmaker, Kwaw Ansah, and I realised the place was unique and full of history."

Otu Gyandoh's deep dive into the community, its culture and ways allowed him to run the campaign successfully. More importantly, he began to represent *Simigwa* culture on his radio program in a way that was most attractive to the people of Sekondi.

"Our broadcast rekindled the urban lifestyle they grew up with. It stirred up love, fame, and dignity because of the numerous references I made. The people, both young and old, warmed up to me, and they accepted me so much that I felt I really belonged. At some point, I was convinced that I am actually a native of Sekondi because the people adopted me and even said that I am from the Council Road portion of Sekondi," says Otu Gyandoh, with pride.

Sekondi and Takoradi are of course twin cities. Sekondi is the administrative arm with all the government offices, but Takoradi is bigger, busier, and more popular. Out of habit, people would mostly refer to both cities simply as Takoradi, but Otu Gyandoh says the subtle difference is important to him.

"Not everyone knows it, but Sekondi is quite different from Takoradi. When you are outside, you would think they are the same, but there is a difference. Takoradi has a language which is distinct from Sekondi. People of Sekondi dress differently. When the Sekondi person is dressed and walks around, you can tell there is a connection to the sea. Their dressing is exotic," affirms Otu Gyandoh.

He says, "the connection with the sea comes from the seamen who travelled all over the world and returned with their own sense of fashion. Every day between 3pm to 6pm, Sekondi changes. The people just seem to disappear from the street for an hour and come back all dressed up for the evening."

"Because of my love for Sekondi, I continue to dress like a Sekondi native even in Accra. I wear my best shorts and my best shoes together with my hat. Also, you can see my matching good quality belt on my waist."

An Extraordinary Connection with Kwame Dzokoto

One of Otu Gyandoh's enduring memories in Sekondi-Takoradi and Skyy FM is his transformation from just a presenter to a person with wide ranging ability to moderate private and public events. "Until I came to Takoradi, I didn't even know I had it in me to moderate a high-level function as master of ceremonies." He discovered this aspect of his personality in the early 2000s during a Guinness Ghana event at the Planters Lodge in Takoradi.

"There was a star-power representation led by Bolay Ray of Joy FM in Accra. Wilson Arthur wanted Kwame Dzokoto and I to feature as well, so he told us he would make sure we are on the bill. The truth is that Dzokoto and I were intimidated because Bola Ray was right at the top of his game at Joy FM at that time," says Otu Gyandoh.

From what he describes, it was a mismatch, except they had Wilson Arthur who saw the occasion as an opportunity to infuse two of his employees with confidence.

"Wilson encouraged us to go with the Sekondi-Takoradi swag. Dzokoto grew up partly in Sekondi, so we were both steeped in the powerful and attractive homegrown culture of Sekondi."

"When we got on stage, oh my goodness, then I realised we were at a place where we were not only appreciated, but the people felt we represented them. It was a resounding success and after that event, we did the first national jingle for Koala Shop in Accra. Imagine Koala Shop coming all the way from Accra to Takoradi to have their advert recorded for them. That is how Wilson set us up to succeed."

"I Miss Wilson Arthur"

At the time of preparing this book, Otu Gyandoh was working for *Asaase Radio* in Accra. As he mentions Wilson Arthur again, his voice betrays a deep emotion, and he says, "there are times that I really miss Wilson Arthur. I wish that he were part of the radio that I am working with in Accra because nobody understands this space better than him. Much of what Accra is enjoying now in terms of private broadcasting has come from Skyy and Wilson Arthur in Sekondi-Takoradi."

"You were there," he says, referring to me. "Accra had one channel TV," he continues. "We in Takoradi had four channels being beamed simultaneously from Skyy House. So, Wilson introduced and exposed us to multiple channels and content creation for various demographics and interests."

"We even ran a newspaper called *Skyy Focus* in those days. I quickly had to learn the software program called Qbase. I learned it because of Wilson. Yes, I am an artist and studied it in school as well, but to use those tools, it was because of the tutelage of Wilson and his wife Adwoa Amofah. I even had to learn how to write properly for a newspaper, all because of Wilson."

Otu Gyandoh makes reference to me and other colleagues in the newsroom, saying, "I was happy the likes of you were around. It was you, Eric Ahianyo, and also Cyrus deGraft-Johnson. We had a team of peers that helped to review and sharpen our collective production. There is something about Skyy. When you are taken on and they think you are good, you are guaranteed support from everybody, from the Librarian to a Phillip Nyakpo..."

Some Criticism, Finally

Otu Gyandoh finally has some criticism for Wilson Arthur, and it seems he is prepared to be very honest about it. "I don't know how to find the words to put it together," he says, trying to make it as constructive as possible.

Looking back on how young we all were when Wilson allocated and supervised our various creative works, Otu Gyandoh says, "the only thing Wilson Arthur didn't plan for was our successful transition from boys into men. Probably, he just saw the talent in us but could not help us transition into men. He mastered that aspect only after a bunch of us had left the scene. The remnants, or the few that stayed much longer he managed better into a safe manhood," he reflects.

"Just about the time I should have stayed behind to solidify all that I could do and move on to bigger things in the same region and help it grow, it turned out to be the time I became more self-focused. Wilson also did not appreciate and understand the fact that I was growing from a boy into a man with extra needs. He lost that transitional period and we also lost it. But I tell you what, when we meet as a group of people who used to work there, we appreciate Wilson Arthur, because we have grown, and we know the value he added to our lives."

Turning attention to himself, Otu Gyandoh says, "I was a young man who sometimes exhibited extreme emotions, but now I look back and I know I will never get back the years when Wilson cared and groomed us into professionals in broadcasting."

The thoughtfulness reflected in Otu Gyandoh's comment is exactly how I remember him. He is an even brighter version of the boy I knew and worked with; the boy who thinks deep and often speaks philosophically while embracing the deep friendship we all shared at Skyy.

A Generous Praise for Work Colleagues

My conversation with Otu Gyandoh often feels like the unveiling of his full memories of our time at Skyy. As he remembers one event after another, he starts praising all the other colleagues we knew together at Skyy.

"On radio, Paa Kofi Nyarko, [also called Abronoma] was the definition of Highlife in the whole of Ghana," he says. "Who could possibly fit into his shoes? Every musician who had something to do with Highlife would want to come around Paa Kofi. Paa Kofi had personal relationships with all the key personalities of authentic Highlife. The remnants of the famous Western Diamonds Band were all his friends: from Paapa Yankson to Ebow Cocker, the owner of the band."

"Bob Gardiner was big! He was the frontman for us in Takoradi," he says of Bob Gee, our long-time morning show host.

"Joe Enuson is the definition of urban radio and JM Caesar was the biggest R&B and Hip Hop radio super star in the whole of Ghana."

About Michael Gawu, Otu Gyandoh says, "before he joined Skyy Power FM, Michael [also called Premier Gawu] was the biggest student radio DJ in the whole of Western and Central Regions and even beyond. Gawu was huge!" he emphasises.

Regarding the legacy of the radio station that rekindled his love for radio, Nana Otu Gyandoh believes the legacy of Skyy Power FM is incalculable.

"At the time that the Takoradi Port almost collapsed along with the economy of Sekondi-Takoradi, it was Skyy Power FM that put the city back on the map of Ghana. There are many young people growing up in that city who look at life through the eyes of the great people who have come through Skyy with their talents, abilities and passion."

"I have seen so many beautiful ideas generated from Skyy. The true legacy of Skyy is that it is possible to achieve great things with local strength, determination, and passion," says Otu Gyandoh.

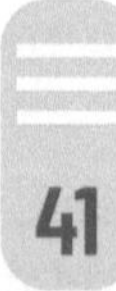

41

"I Love Wilson Arthur"

> *"The people of Takoradi took Skyy Power FM as their own. You saw a special bond between Skyy Power and the people. It was marvellous! Wilson must be commended for what he did."*
>
> — *former Skyy employee, Dr Akofa Segbefia.*

Of the more than 70 people interviewed for this book, everyone expressed some admiration for Skyy Power Chief Executive Wilson Arthur. Only Dr Akofa Segbefia said plainly, "I love Wilson Arthur."

"It was like, anything he touched turned to gold, so to speak. He was a marketing person, so he knew how to draw wealth towards his enterprises for which I admire him," confesses Dr Segbefia.

He came to Skyy as one of the few who was already fully grown, having amassed a vast experience in life. As a result, he was not hungry for Wilson Arthur's usual magical transformation. Every employee knew Wilson was unconventional and had a general disregard for dogma and traditional thinking.

Dr Segbefia "has been there and done that," and the much younger Wilson, out of consideration, felt limited in how much he could teach or inspire a much older and more experienced employee. Segbefia also quickly realised Wilson Arthur did not embrace conventional rules of business.

Insulated Idiosyncrasies

In addition to the age and experience gap, the two men operated with dramatically different philosophies. This became apparent only with time.

They were insulated from each other's idiosyncrasies by some pre-existing tolerance which was enough to keep them on a gentle course for a long while. It was impressive that they got along for so long without incident.

The harmony was also owed to the general atmosphere at Skyy. The workforce operated like a family, and people really liked, or even loved, each other. They shared a Takoradi spirit which easily ensured difficult situations quickly dissolved into plain speaking followed by humour, gentle teasing, and then laughter. Everyday tense situations often disappeared in this way, leaving little room for friction.

That is why Dr Segbefia loved his time at Skyy, but he also says it didn't feel like home. He didn't quite fit into the Skyy Power FM structure. At the same time, he did not shy away from professing admiration for Wilson, mixing it with a measure of misgivings.

"Let me confess that I wasn't too comfortable working under Wilson. Let me put it on record. I admire his industry--a young man like that having the vision to help his people, to put up a radio station to inform and entertain."

The honesty and deep nuance of Dr Segbefia's feeling is further revealed when he says "Wilson Arthur had the knack for attracting good material, but he did not have what it took to keep the good materials with him."

Seeing it All in Accra

Dr Segbefia was living in Accra and saw the birth of private radio and the excitement it generated.

His perspective and attraction to radio was shaped by his regular occupation as a media practitioner, working as deputy editor for the *Accra Mail* newspaper under managing editor Haruna Atta. *Accra Mail*, now defunct, was not a resoundingly successful newspaper.

Nevertheless, Dr Segbefia loved the paper.

He also loved the immediacy and total liveliness of radio. As a result, when he got the chance to be part of the new industry, he jumped at it. He ended up on Choice FM at the dawn of the 21st century, hosting a show called *Talk Back*.

After a while, two young men at Choice FM, Carlos Von Brazzi and Paul Adom-Otchere, advocated for a change to deal with growing competition in the broadcast industry. Dr Segbefia's continuing service did not form part of the change, and he realised this only much later.

Goodbye, Choice FM

"They [Carlos Von Brazzi and Paul Adom-Otchere] went and convinced management that they needed injection of young blood and all that," recalls Dr Segbefia.

"The director of programs at that time, George Brun just came to me and said look, we want to restructure the programs, get a good producer and then after two weeks you can come back and continue."

A week after he was gently led out of the studio, Carlos Von Brazzi and Paul Adom-Otchere started co-hosting the same program. He was never invited back to Choice FM.

After being ejected from Choice FM, Dr Segbefia's next stop was Skyy FM.

"I was looking for an opportunity, and it was Captain Sowu who introduced me to Wilson Arthur in 2002," says Dr Segbefia.

He is referring to Captain Joel Sowu, a retired army captain whose intellectual prowess surpasses what he used to do with bullets and guns.

Three years before this, Captain Sowu had established himself as a matchless panel member of the famous Skyy Power FM weekly *News Review*, a hard-hitting, deep, and lively current affairs program. He recommended Dr Segbefia as an experienced media practitioner whose fresh perspective could be an asset to Skyy newsroom.

The interview with Wilson, following Captain Sowu's recommendation, was a breeze. He was promptly offered a job as Head of News.

"I decided Takoradi is worth exploring. Being a lover of internal tourism, I decided, ok, let me give Western Region also a try," says Dr Segbefia.

A Cog in the Empire

The most important outcome of the interview with Wilson was that Dr Segbefia was going to become the editor of an entirely new venture--the establishment of a newspaper to be called *Skyy Focus*. More than just being part of the radio newsroom at Skyy, Dr Segbefia's employment was predicated on the success of *Skyy Focus*, a subsidiary business that was to generate its own income, using the existing Skyy Media infrastructure as a foundation.

Dr Segbefia became a Takoradi resident. The only thing that still tied him to Accra was a commitment he was still discharging once a fortnight as a lecturer at the Academy of Business Administration in Accra.

Around the same time that he joined Skyy, feverish preparations were underway to create Skyy TV. The means and ways to acquire a private TV license to operate in the Western Region were far from transparent.

Expenses aside, Wilson Arthur was in overdrive to satisfy the suffocating and opaque requirements for the TV license. Dr Segbefia's association with Skyy Power FM coincided with the move from the relatively small 37 Windy Ridge studios where the entire experiment started.

The whole operation was now situated at 19/20 West Fijai, a plush two-storey building, including an amphitheatre, numerous offices, and enough space for the multi-channel TV that was now Wilson's new dream. Dr Segbefia slowly came to understand that he was to become an important cog in the expanding Skyy Media.

But not everything went smoothly. The newspaper floundered with no real prospect of succeeding commercially.

"I realised that a lot of you guys in the [radio] newsroom were not interested in the newspaper at all, so the *Skyy Focus* became my baby...I had to do a lot of stories under pseudonyms; Wilson himself contributed some of the articles for the paper."

Dr Segbefia uses the phrase "a lot of you guys" to include me. This is because I was deeply involved with Skyy Power News and Current

Affairs as an editor, and I was the one interviewing him for this book, twenty years after the fact.

The Skyy Focus Newspaper generated some excitement, but it was no match for the relentless speed and zest of the radio newsroom.

The newsroom had functioned for five years before Dr Segbefia's arrival. A deep-rooted culture had been established, led mostly by youngsters who understood speed, brevity, and creativity that only the modern medium of radio allowed. Newspaper, on the other hand, was a clunky, slow-moving train that seemed to be heading for a crash. This was especially so because the existing newsroom team gave the paper only half-hearted support. Additionally, Dr Segbefia's arrival also did not cause any shake up of the newsroom, one way or the other.

The Paper is Waterlogged

Right or wrong, the blame for the washed-out condition of *Skyy Focus* rested heavily on Dr Segbefia, even as he continually contributed his quota to the general function of the newsroom, conducting research and interviews as well as working as an in-house panellist on current affairs programs.

"At a certain point in time, not that I had a lukewarm attitude towards the job; I was still interested in doing what I needed to do. He [Wilson] thought I was not in control of the newsroom. It wasn't that I wasn't in control; I wanted to give everybody the chance to prove themselves so we can work together as a team. That is what I wanted."

In the meantime, Captain Sowu kept coming to Takoradi for the weekend *News Review* program. It wasn't long before Dr Segbefia expressed his misgivings to Captain Sowu, upon which he decided it was time to say goodbye to Skyy Power FM and to Takoradi.

His departure, though, was triggered by something that happened in Accra, when John Kufour was president of Ghana. The development, which cannot be fully substantiated, was connected to Wilson Arthur's application for a TV license.

"I met someone from the office of the president and that person said to me, 'are you the one at Skyy Power FM,' and I said yes."

The unidentified person from the office of the president alleged that Dr Segbefia was an NDC man at Skyy, doing NDC's dirty job in Takoradi, and that is why Wilson Arthur's TV license application was not receiving favourable attention.

There are six letters of the alphabet--NDC and NPP--that efficiently describe politics in Ghana since democratic rule was re-introduced in 1992.

The letters represent acronyms for the two major political parties: the National Democratic Congress and the New Patriotic Party. Almost every contentious issue is viewed through this prism. Followers of the two movements find great solace in attacking or blaming each other.

Dr Segbefia says he has political sympathy towards the NDC as a result of knowing some of its leaders since his days in school. He also says his sympathy for the political movement never influenced his professional work, but he also knows his denial and explanation were not helpful.

So once he heard the allegation, Dr Segbefia said, "if because of me Wilson Arthur was not going to be given the license to operate the Television station, then the best thing for me is to leave. His enterprise was bigger than me."

He continues, "so immediately I got to Takoradi, I went to Wilson and told him this is what somebody from the office of the president had told me, and that I wanted to leave."

According to Dr Segbefia, Wilson Arthur's response was "to hell with their license."

"But I said no, your enterprise is bigger than me; let me go," explains Dr Segbefia, adding "and Wilson was stunned."

About three or four months after Dr Segbefia left Skyy, Wilson Arthur obtained his TV license.

A Generational Perspective

Dr Segbefia, who had already experienced almost a lifetime of work, joined Skyy in an environment dominated by a much younger workforce. He had enough grace to feel at home, but only for as long as he could endure the generational differences, including free-spirited ways of achieving extraordinary results in private broadcasting.

"I realised that Wilson was a nonconformist when it comes to running business," says Dr Segbefia.

The nonconformist attitude pervaded the whole operation. Whether by design or accident, Wilson built an empire that flourished to reflect his character and creativity.

As a keen observer with a lifetime of experience, Dr Segbefia was a person who not only saw the whole operation, but lived it with a big heart.

"Wilson must be commended for what he did with Skyy. When I first arrived at Skyy, I never knew he came from the Western Region. As far as I am concerned, Wilson is a genuine Ghanaian who used his knowledge, wits, and passion to create a unique media empire that opened endless opportunities for so many people in Sekondi-Takoradi and the Western Region," says Dr Segbefia.

Strength of a Woman

Regarding the impact of Skyy FM, he says, "it offered an alternative for the people to open up and speak their mind, something the state broadcaster could not do."

"The people of Takoradi took Skyy as their own; you saw a special bond between Skyy and the people...Skyy organised so many outdoor events with artists like Lord Kenya, Sydney, Daughters of Glorious Jesus, and the people responded as if they were coming to their home to enjoy. It was marvellous! Wilson must be commended for what he did."

Dr Segbefia turns his attention to the significant contribution of the one lady that has had a constant presence in the history of Skyy.

"Wilson's wife Adwoa Amofah must also be commended. I know she returned from London once and successfully chased down significant debts owed to Skyy. Adwoa Amofah will smile at you; she is a very comely woman, but you do well not to underestimate her," he reflects.

"Adwoa Amofah was an easier person to have discussions with than Wilson. Wilson had so much on his mind that whatever you were telling him, he would be listening with half attention. But Adwoa Amofah will listen to you throughout and offer whatever she has to offer, and you will feel satisfied talking to her. Wilson must thank his stars for having such a woman for a wife," he emphasises.

As Dr Segbefia offers this compliment, it brings back memories of a song credited to six men: Christopher Birch, Michael Fletcher, Orville Burrell, Ricardo Ducent, Robert Browne, and Shaun Pizzonia.

Rendered beautifully in a captivating baritone voice by Shaggy, the title is *"Strength of a Woman."*

It would be hard to hear a more beautiful poetic praise for women in one line of that song which says, "so amazing how this world was made; I wonder if God is a woman."

Wilson Arthur remains the visionary behind Skyy. And he also knows the true strength of Adwoa Amofah, the foundational force that made it all happen in Sekondi-Takoradi. According to Dr Segbefia, the success of Skyy Power FM was, in many ways, down to the strength of a woman.

"Your Voice Is Not Good for Radio at All"

"I never felt so useless in my entire life. Here I was, a responsible and full-grown man, being told to the face that I was not good for radio."

— *Thomas Dossah who left a permanent government job to join a boisterous group of presenters at Skyy Power FM*

When Thomas Dossah joined Skyy FM, he was already a responsible adult, unlike many of the other employees who were much younger and with more limited experience in life. He was working in a relatively cushy government job within the National Disaster Management Organisation. I first met him when he came to visit our old studio at 37 Windy Ridge around 2001.

I was struck by his commanding presence, self-confidence and fiery eyes that indicated he was far from being timid. Thomas also carried a modest pot belly, which in Ghana generally meant that a person had a comfortable life.

Born and raised in Sekondi-Takoradi, Thomas would later tell me that seeing the twin city being transformed by Skyy was mesmerising, and he knew he wanted to become part of the premier private station.

First Taste of Radio

Thomas had his university education at the Kwame Nkrumah University of Science and Technology in Kumasi. As a student, he served as Secretary of the Students Representative Council (SRC) in 1992.

As part of his duty, he appeared on Contatto Radio, the campus radio at Katanga Hall, where he addressed pertinent issues on student welfare. He also appeared on Continental Radio, another small station operated by the University's Unity Hall.

"I learned the joy of being on radio based on that little experience with the campus radio," says Thomas. Thomas Dossah finally had the chance to speak on Skyy as an employee.

As he got ready, Joe Enuson, one of our colleagues, sat close to one of many radio sets around the studio which we use to monitor our own output. He touched the volume control button, and turned it up a little. His ears were ready as he remained silent like a hungry lion on the prowl for prey.

Like many of the other presenters, it was his duty to evaluate the voice quality of this new employee.

The Heat Comes after Live Studio Debut

In the studio, a slightly nervous Thomas Dossah cleared his throat. Another presenter behind the console prepared to open the microphone that would carry his voice for the first time around the city.

What he did on air was simply the act of reading newspaper headlines to let listeners know the summary of the day's leading news around the country. It went on for just about five minutes. Even before he had finished, judgment had been rendered by most of us, especially Joe Enuson.

Thoroughly disgusted at what he believed was a poor performance, Joe Enuson approached Thomas Dossah, his towering and lanky figure casting a pale shadow. Thomas looked at him, unable to tell what was going to come out of Joe Enuson's mouth.

"Your voice is not good for radio at all," said Joe Enuson with unmistakable disdain. The feedback from other presenters did not mention his voice quality, but it was clear they were not impressed.

"I never felt so useless in my entire life. Here I was, a responsible and full-grown man, being told to the face that I was not good for radio," says Thomas, briefly re-living the painful memory decades later. His laughter as he recalled the memory also revealed the pain he felt at the time.

Crestfallen on Arriving Home

Totally deflated by the critical comment and observations at work, this new employee, usually quick witted, could not find a voice to offer a response or defend himself.

"When I got home that day, Phillip, I am telling you, I could not even show affection to my wife," says Thomas, echoing the pain and distress he felt. Skyy was a place where a person's ego could be quickly crushed by zealous and passionate young men and women who demanded nothing but the best.

I remember the venom with which we told people their performance on air fell below standard. We said it in a way that suggested the culprit had defiled the microphone and the entire broadcast equipment--and our Skyy Power FM brand. We were quick in dropping guests and panel members who underperformed, and there were many who came once for a program and knew they would never get another invite.

I remember the incident with Thomas very well, including the flat comment by some of us: "Thomas Dossah is not good for radio."

More than anyone else, Thomas realised that the creative environment and the expected high level of performance at Skyy was very tough and only the most skilled and determined survive and thrive.

Thomas had to go through a complete change to fit in. "I was afraid at one point that I could be fired," says Thomas. "I survived only because I learned quickly and I learned a lot."

"I learned a lot" is a phrase Thomas uses very often throughout my interview with him. He says it every few minutes and repeatedly during the interview. I am left with the impression that, despite a tough demeanor, Thomas is at heart a humble man who embraced the fierce criticisms of mostly younger colleagues and turned things around to become a notable broadcaster.

"I was fortunate, first of all, that Wilson Arthur believed in me and gave me a lot of assistance and guidance to excel," he says.

Watching History in Disbelief

Thomas Dossah had come of age in Sekondi-Takoradi and knew Wilson Arthur quite well before Skyy started. He was also a socially conscious person who would have jumped at the opportunity to join the city's first private radio station to make an impact. I was curious why he didn't join or attempt to do so when Skyy started.

"Why didn't you try to join Skyy at the beginning, and what was the environment at the time?" I ask Thomas the double-barrelled question.

"Let me tell you the truth," says Thomas. "The news about a private radio station in Sekondi-Takoradi was almost like a mirage. I was one of those who just observed without thinking anything would come out of it. All of a sudden, Wilson Arthur's radio station started for real and featured names like Kwesi Fletcher and Kingsley Boohene [also called KingB]," recalls Thomas.

"These were guys that I knew very well. I was in the same dormitory with KingB at St John's School in Sekondi. I knew Kwesi Fletcher in school as well, and we played basketball together. Wilson was my senior at St. John's School."

He continues: "Wilson was a little bit slow in some ways, but also very smart. He was that guy who could organise unexpected events. He would, for example, arrange for a bus to take some of the students to Accra on some adventures. He was always making things happen."

Looking back at the years before Wilson set up Skyy, Thomas says, "I heard Wilson had gone to the United Kingdom and returned with some ideas for business and marketing. Even at that time, it was easy to underrate him--but he always remained my friend," recalls Thomas.

Like a runaway train, Thomas saw Wilson's radio station running on full steam. Within two years, he realised Sekondi-Takoradi's first private station had become a resounding success with the promise of an even brighter future.

Sekondi-Takoradi had *Twin City Radio* operated by the state broadcaster, but by the time Skyy came with its modern style of broadcasting, the overwhelming majority of listeners tuned in.

"Skyy had that windfall, and their style was good," says Thomas. "Only a few could not switch to Skyy, including older folks and those who perhaps could not physically change their dial. The whole place was on fire as a result of Skyy," says Thomas.

Many people in Sekondi-Takoradi who fell in love with the station would, using Fanti language, say, "the sweet-smelling scent of Skyy is everywhere in the metropolis."

Thomas says, "I knew I wanted to be part of it by that time, but I was tied up working as a civil servant in a good job in the nearby Mpohor Wassa East District. I was the District Coordinator of National Disaster Management Organisation (NADMO)."

Taking the Leap of Faith with Some Help

Thomas' passion to join the movement called Skyy had grown strong, but the sacrifice required was significant. "I couldn't just leave my permanent and secure job in government. At the same time, I knew I could make a bigger social impact with Skyy," he says.

He spoke to Wilson Arthur about it. To his surprise, Wilson was willing to facilitate the transition and make it as smooth as possible. "Wilson was generous, and he enticed me," says Thomas. "He asked me how much I earned in my job at NADMO, and he doubled my salary and asked me to join the Skyy team. It was around the time Wilson Arthur was championing arrangements for the Western Regional festival, and I was committed to helping him do this," recalls Thomas.

It was only a matter of time that Thomas found out that expectations at Skyy exceeded his immediate ability to deliver. He had a short window to justify his continued inclusion at Skyy. That is why he felt crushed when Joe Enuson told him, "your voice is not good for radio at all." Rather than being just Joe Enuson's opinion, it was a sentiment shared by many at the station.

"I knew that academically, I was up there. I proved myself professionally working for the government as a civil servant. For goodness' sake, I was District Coordinator, but these small boys at Skyy will mess you up and tell you what you've done on radio is rubbish."

Thomas is laughing again as he recalls the memory. I laugh along.

"I've never met anyone at Skyy who was afraid to speak their mind. We all had very healthy egos. You were a well performing team member or you are out," I say to complement Thomas' memory.

"One day," he says, "Nana Kwame helped me to record an advert. We shared the money, after which we had to get it approved for play on air. Esi Gyan came and listened to it as part of the approval process, and then she calmly said 'this is not just bad, but very bad!' I felt crushed because I had already pocketed the money," says Thomas.

"We were our own judges at Skyy. You go on air, come out, and just about everyone at Skyy would tell you whether you have done a good or bad job. They will tell you that your program was rubbish, and you will go home, unable to sleep."

He continues, "Eric Ahianyo was magnanimous. Like me, he was married at the time and knew how it felt to go home after work with a deflated ego. He encouraged me about how I could handle it successfully."

Thomas also says, "what was really outstanding though is that if you have what it takes and you work hard enough, everyone is prepared to help you."

"I had to learn a lot, and very quickly. I learned a lot from you, Phillip," he says. "I learned a lot from Bob Gee, from Eric Ahianyo, and I learned a lot from Elloeny Amande. I learned a lot from all of you, and I learned to improve my voice quality on air. The late Uncle Opia was also very helpful to me. He took me under his wings and taught me the rudiments of quality broadcasting."

"What Do We Sell at Skyy?"

As Chief Executive, visionary, and strategist, Wilson Arthur would sometimes call special meetings during which he would help calibrate our mindset and priorities. Thomas Dossah remembers one such meeting.

"Wilson gathered us together and asked a question that we all thought was too simple or even irrelevant. He asked, 'What do we sell at Skyy?'"

"We all replied saying, 'common, Wilson, of course we sell airtime,'" recalls Thomas. He continues, "Wilson surprisingly said we don't sell airtime and proceeded to say something that I will never forget. He said, 'at Skyy, we sell attention, not airtime.'"

Thomas brings the memory of that strategy session to mind. Wilson's assertion that we sell attention and not airtime helped us to work even harder to ensure all of our programs have a ring of quality to attract the attention we sought from our listeners.

"I also remember that one day," says Thomas. "Wilson gathered us for a session and asked each of us to talk about the richness of our individual CVs or resumes. Everyone was positive about their own CV as they confidently talked about their academic achievements. I also highlighted my own, including my academic degree."

I continue listening attentively but don't realise Thomas is going to put the searchlight on me.

"When it got to your turn, Phillip, you surprised us all. Instead of talking about the content of your CV, you said, 'I have carried out this and that research and that investigation, I have interviewed political leaders, ordinary people on the street as well as international diplomats…' and Wilson commended you and told the rest of us to learn from you. I always remember that because it was the first time I realised my academic degree is not as important as the impact we make through our work."

I remember the session Thomas referenced. Yes, I highlighted my professional body of work up to that point because it was easy to talk about my activities as a journalist and media practitioner. Also, Wilson was a strong influence on me, and I knew the answers he wanted from us.

"You are rewarded not for your effort, but for your results," he would often say. Something else Wilson often said is, "you are only as good as your last work."

Returning to the old theme, Thomas says, "I learned a lot. I am serious, I learned a lot from you and from Skyy."

A Permanent Place in a First Class Team

When Thomas learned all he could, he became an essential part of Skyy, distinguishing himself as a broadcaster through his curiosity and persistent desire to make a positive impact in the community. He often identified himself as the Public Servant on air, or *Amansuon Akowa* in the Fante language.

"I started by doing simple things, such as reading letters from listeners, presenting newspaper headlines, and eventually hosting my own programs," says Thomas. "The first full program I produced and hosted was the *Golden Age* program which unearthed people who lived impactful lives in our community."

"I came to the newsroom and there I observed and learned how interviews are conducted, recorded, and edited with the Mini Disc player," he says.

Finding his feet at Skyy also gave Thomas the confidence to champion many initiatives, including lobbying successfully for Skyy to present more programs in the Fante language. He believed, and rightly so, that a large population of the city would appreciate more programs in their native language, rather than the heavy concentration on English.

Thomas made so much progress and impact that Wilson Arthur later decided to appoint him as Events Manager. "I didn't know anything about events management, but Wilson again believed in me. I am no longer an employee of Skyy FM but a lot of what I do for myself and for work revolves around events management. Many of the things I now do are things I learned from Skyy over many years," says Thomas.

"I have so many fond memories," he says. "For example, when we moved from our old studios at Windy Ridge, you and I created the address of the new property. We settled on 19/20 West Fijai."

When Thomas says this, it brings back the memories. The land was undeveloped, and the authorities were never quick in creating a sustainable address system at the time, so between us, we chose 19/20 West Fijai. Wilson Arthur approved it and the authorities accepted it.

After listening to Thomas, I am left with the impression that he tells his stories like a collection of memories of war or battles in which he was glad to have lived to tell.

"We were a first-class team at Skyy", says Thomas. "No radio station could put together such a team the first-time round," he says.

His words were a thumbs up to the entire team at Skyy. It was also a recognition of Wilson Arthur's talent in the way he led a restless group of talented men and women to make history in that part of Ghana.

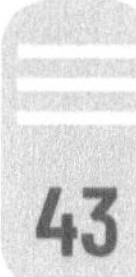

43

From Skyy Power FM to "Ekosiisen"

By the time Philip Osei Bonsu reflects on his career as part of his interview for this book, he had picked up two prestigious awards: the Chartered Institute of Marketing Ghana (CIMG) Radio Program of the year and Radio Political Programme of the year award.

It is a mark of triumph for the man popularly known as OB (from the acronym of his last two names). He is about the only one in this book whom I interview but never met in person. He joined Skyy Power FM in Takoradi long after I left Ghana.

Edwin Phillips, a businessman and longtime resident of Takoradi first mentioned him to me. Edwin Phillips, who once served as presiding member of the Sekondi-Takoradi Metropolitan Assembly, was for many years a panelist on *News Review*, a current affairs program that I hosted at Skyy for many years.

"I don't think you met Philip Osei Bonsu; you left Skyy before he came," says Edwin Philips when I tell him I am writing this book. "You should talk to him," he implores. "OB is now hosting one of the biggest talk show programs in Accra."

The next person I interview is Aba Moses, a colleague from Skyy who was among the pioneers of the station.

Aba Moses later moved to Spark Radio in Dunkwa-on-Offin, taking up a role as Head of Programs. She met Philip Osei Bonsu at that station. Osei Bonsu was undertaking his national service after obtaining a degree in Linguistics and Theatre Arts from the University of Ghana.

"The first day I heard his voice on air, I called him, sat him down, and encouraged him to pursue a career in radio. He is intelligent with a good radio voice, full of confidence," says Aba Moses

She continues, "I told him he is radio material, the kind of presenter Wilson Arthur needed at Skyy Power FM."

Aba Moses tells me she wrote a letter to Wilson Arthur, urging him to employ Osei Bonsu, the boy who would go on to achieve glory in radio.

During the three years he spent at Skyy, Osei Bonsu says he was completely retooled by Wilson Arthur.

"The relationship I had, and continue to have, with Wilson Arthur can be described as that of a son and a father," he tells me with a sense of loyalty and gratitude.

His days at Skyy are well behind him as he now works for Multimedia Group's Asempa FM, the same company that owns Joy FM in Accra. He is the host and captain of *Ekosiisen*, a popular late afternoon talk show. *Ekosiisen* is a word in the Akan language that literally means, "how did it go?" or "how did it end?"

A Place to Learn and Grow

Philip Osei Bonsu made an entrance to Skyy ten years after the station started. "I have always loved radio and I knew a lot about Skyy when I was a student of St John's School in Sekondi. I feel I was destined to work there," he says.

His path into Skyy opened only after Wilson Arthur received the introduction letter from Aba Moses with a glowing recommendation that Osei Bonsu was good material for Skyy.

"Wilson knows how to identify talent and hone it to become something extraordinary," says OB, as he reflects on the first conversation he had with Wilson for his employment at Skyy.

Wilson himself is an old student of St John's School, just like Osei Bonsu. He believes in the quality of graduates from St John's School, having already worked with other former students, including Ato-

Kwamena Dadzie, KingB, Thomas Dossah, and Kojo Frempong. It was like a little club of old Saints from Sekondi who never disappoint. Beyond that, Wilson Arthur could easily see Osei Bonsu's potential as spelt out by Aba Moses in her letter of recommendation.

"It was during the period of the African Cup of Nations in 2008, when I started with Skyy originally as a sports reporter," recalls Osei Bonsu. "I met professionals who had been in the job for a long time, especially Kuntu Blankson, Toni Nkrumah-Boateng, and Osei Bediako. Skyy was huge, about ten times bigger than what I knew."

"Later, I moved into the newsroom. When I first entered the Skyy Newsroom, they were having an editorial meeting and it was quite a crowd of reporters and journalists. The station had both radio and TV, and I met people like Cyrus deGraft-Johnson, Kweku Temeng, Christian Baidoo, Francis Abban, and Ewurama Smith. I told myself this was a place with abundant opportunities to learn and work with professionals," says OB.

"Being employed at Skyy was a dream come true. If you worked in radio in the Central and Western Regions at that time, the ultimate for you was to join Skyy Power FM, everybody wanted to be there. That is why I purposed in my heart to take advantage of every opportunity at Skyy. It turned out very well for me. That is why I got to work with folks from the BBC, including Farayi Mungazi and Martin Davies during the 2008 Africa Cup of Nations tournament."

Osei Bonsu's hard work and willingness to learn was rewarded when he was given the chance to host the highly rated *Jolly Breakfast Show*. "Kofi Bentum was the regular host at the time, and when he went on leave, I was asked to host the show," he recalls.

What was supposed to be a stint on the morning show became a permanent role. As a result, Osei Bonsu joined a long line of presenters who hosted the Jolly Breakfast Show, starting with Nana Fynnba Derby and followed by Kwesi Fletcher. Other names who occupied the spot include Kwete Quaynor and Bob Gardiner, and later, Winston Amoah and Samuel Kojo Brace.

I personally hosted the *Jolly Breakfast Show* for a few weeks in the early days when Bob Gardiner was on leave. However, the top-ranking current affairs program *News Review* on Sundays was a place where I was most comfortable over many years. Cyrus deGraft-Johnson and others stepped into the role after I left Skyy for the United Kingdom in early 2005.

"I also started hosting *News Review*," says OB, to my delight. I didn't know this. Even though I have never met Osei Bonsu, I feel, not for the first time, that he is a kindred spirit.

"I remember Wilson telling us that if you work at Skyy, you have an intellectual stake in Skyy, and that is why he has a philosophy that he would welcome all former staff members with open arms. If you go away and you feel like you want to come back, Wilson will welcome you," says Osei Bonsu.

He adds that he saw Wilson's philosophy in action.

"During my time at Skyy, I saw a lot of former staff coming back to work. I remember Joe Enuson coming back; I remember Paa Kofi Nyarko (Abronoma) coming back. I remember Ewurama Smith when she left Skyy and then returned to Skyy. I remember Kuntu Blankson leaving and coming back to work at Skyy," says Osei Bonsu.

"That idea of always creating a community of staff, creating a family among the staff, motivates us all to continue to cooperate and collaborate. Anytime I visit Takoradi, I happily go back to Skyy and feel at home, and occasionally, I even go on air and host a program on the spot."

A Place Where He Flourished

While Osei Bonsu was working at Skyy, he also served as the Head of Public Relations for the Electricity Company of Ghana in the Western Region. The speed with which he learned and continued flourishing also made Wilson Arthur appoint him as the Brand Manager for Skyy Media Group. The time arrived when he had to step out of Skyy FM to obtain a master's degree in Corporate Communication and Public Affairs from the Robert Gordon University in Aberdeen, Scotland.

His departure became a beautiful spectacle.

"When I had the opportunity for further studies in the UK, Wilson organised a huge farewell party for me, and besides, he gave me one thousand US dollars as a gift."

"When I returned to Skyy after my studies, there was a welcome-back party for me. That is how Wilson cherishes talent, when he believes you have something to offer," says OB.

As much as he appreciates the benefit he realised from his association with Wilson and Skyy, Osei Bonsu says his former boss and mentor did far more than that.

"In terms of the production of radio and television talent, Skyy has given a lot. If you take the major morning shows and leading talk shows on TV and Radio around Ghana, many of the top presenters are products of Skyy. Winston Amoah, Francis Abban, Daniel Dadzie, and Mamavi Owusu-Aboagye are all products of Skyy. If we look at past presenters of Skyy from the first generation and the impact they all made, the picture becomes even more impressive," says OB.

Regarding his former boss, he says, "Wilson Arthur has done more for the development of private broadcasting than any other individual in Ghana. The legacy of Skyy is that it became a huge source of talent for the broadcast media industry in Ghana," reflects Philip Osei Bonsu.

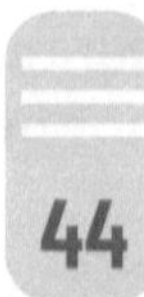

Through The Eyes of an Englishman

> *"Takoradi itself could benefit through the development of the Ankobra River as an inland water transport system to move the bulk of manganese and bauxite all of the way to the Atlantic Coast, avoiding the roads and congestion."*
>
> — Martin Hiles, Transport and Logistics expert and relentless advocate for inland water transport for Ghana.

At 70 years plus, Martin Hiles still considers himself a "Takoradi boy." A full Englishman, born and bred in England, he first arrived in Takoradi in early 1994, three years before Skyy Power FM was established.

During his nearly three decades in Ghana, Martin witnessed the transformation of Sekondi-Takoradi through the revitalisation of the Takoradi Port, the introduction of mobile phones, and the Internet.

What he also witnessed was the impact of Skyy Power FM as the first commercial radio station in that part of Ghana.

Martin, a transport and logistics expert, arrived in the Twin City to lead a project for Alhaji Asoma Banda's Antrak company. At that time, Antrak was involved only in the clearing business under its Roll-on-Roll-off (RORO) shipping operations in Takoradi.

The Son of Farmers

Martin Hiles grew up on a farm in England with his parents in the 1950s. Still vivid in his memory is their large farm on which his parents owned and operated an iconic single-engine, four-seater *Miles Messenger* airplane.

On completing school as a restless and inquisitive young man, he worked his way around New Zealand and Western Australia, reared cattle in Wales, and co-led two overland expeditions to southern Africa in the early 1970s.

When he settled into professional life, he chose logistics and transport and became a founding member of the UK Chartered Institute of Logistics and Transport in the south of England.

"I undertook voluntary service in the British Territorial Army, which is equal to the United States National Guard, and that is where I was extensively trained in logistics and transport strategic thinking," he recalls.

With that experience, Martin accepted an opportunity to work in Ghana, and settled in Takoradi.

Takoradi, a city on the Atlantic coast of south-west Ghana, had a thriving port and railways industry. It also had a base for the Ghana Airforce with a small airport used as a training ground for military pilots.

Not far from Takoradi, mushrooming gold mines and traditional industries of cocoa, rubber, coconuts and timber that were going through the Takoradi Port helped the city's economy to thrive.

The bustling little metropolis became well known for its vibrant music and entertainment, including the famous Western Diamonds. With a history dating back to the 1920's, the port produced a culture influenced by seafarers who often patronised the live band music scene.

The locals loved it and soon declared that the best of everything in Ghana came from the Western Region. "The best comes from the West," became a popular expression across Ghana.

By the time Martin Hiles arrived in Takoradi however, the economy was in sharp decline and Takoradi was starting to lose its lustre. Fresh from England, Martin says he remembers how some members of the expatriate community in the national capital, Accra, used to call it *the wild west of Ghana.*

"All my colleagues in the company were in Accra, and I was the only one in what was considered an outpost, because my role was the start of a new project."

Memories of Saddle Club

"I stand to be corrected," says Martin, "but at that time, there were no cable networks or satellite TV broadcasts. There was only GBC TV, the state-controlled television service operated by the Ghana Broadcasting Corporation. I recall only one swimming pool in Takoradi at that time, and it was at the Saddle Club."

Saddle Club earned its name because in the past, the stables were used by military officers in Takoradi to keep their horses.

"It was the people of Sekondi-Takoradi, who made it liveable for me, and it was absolutely cosmopolitan and culturally educational," says Martin.

"The Takoradi Saddle Club also had a well-run creche for children. At the end of the day when families went to collect their children from school, they would meet and have a drink, swim and relax. Children and adults could ride the few ponies left."

"It seemed to be the only place in town where you had that sort of community and meeting opportunity. All nationalities, all races, all colours, all creeds, all religions would go there. It was such a mixed bag, and you met people who were probably your competitors during the day, but you were friends and their children were friends of your children."

Martin's memories of Takoradi are vivid, and his recall is free-flowing.

"We had about ten days of Christmas, because some nationalities like the Scandinavians celebrated Christmas before the 'usual' day and then we had the traditional Ghanaian-British Christmas and boxing day. That is followed by other celebrations into the new year. It was a lovely time, and you got to learn every nationality and religion's approach to life."

"I was fortunate enough to be asked by Sam Barnes to join the Rotary Club, and that was probably one of the best things I have ever done in my life."

Sam Barnes, a native of Takoradi, was well known for his community service as a member of Rotary International and also as the Managing Director of Ghana Railways Corporation at the time.

"The friends in the Rotary Club really helped me to become a Takoradi boy to live successfully outside my comfort zone. Until that point, my knowledge of Takoradi was limited while my work took me to other African countries like Mali and Burkina Faso."

"As a result of assistance from Sam Barnes and other friends, I got to know Takoradi more intimately including many of the deprived villages just a few miles outside Takoradi."

"The experience," says Martin, "changed me, especially as I considered the deprivations in villages not far from Takoradi, where I was living a comfortable life."

Meeting Mr. Hiles

When Martin Hiles first came to Skyy Power FM on my invitation, he stood out clearly. He is tall, respectable, a gentle giant and very knowledgeable.

I was with Skyy Chief Executive, Wilson Arthur, during a public forum on Corporate Social Responsibility when I first met Martin. It was around the year 2000. His contribution during that forum was both thoughtful and impressive. Wilson Arthur told me Martin was a good resource person to use for some of our current affairs programs.

I agreed and started inviting him to our studio.

Martin became one of the reliable contacts I maintained within the British community in Ghana during my work as a journalist. When Dr. Rod Pullen took up a post as the UK's new High Commissioner to Ghana, Martin was instrumental in helping me convince him to grant me an interview live at Skyy FM studio around 2003.

Martin was also my contact in reaching Craig Murray, the famous Deputy High Commissioner to Ghana a few years earlier. Craig Murray left a mark in Ghana as a diplomat who would go rogue and speak plainly to defend the freedom of the media in Ghana - even in undiplomatic terms.

I had a lot of respect for Martin and we became good friends after which I introduced him to the paramount chief of Essikado Traditional Area, Nana Kobina Nketia V.

"I learned a lot from that Englishman, Martin Hiles," said the paramount chief when I interviewed him. "Mr. Hiles knows a lot about logistics, infrastructure and various industries and how they could be properly deployed to help in the development of our community," says Nana Kobina Nketsia.

Like the paramount chief, Martin saw Skyy FM as an effective tool to educate people and help them see how poverty and deprivation was a perfect reflection of poor leadership.

"Africa Has Rulers, not Leaders"

Martin demonstrated his love of Takoradi and the larger Ghanaian community by contributing his expert knowledge in transport and logistics. In all my interactions with him, Martin always elevated the quality of discussions to a new level that forced me to undertake more research on efficient transport and logistics nationwide.

Almost without fail, he would talk about what he believes was an urgent need for the use of Ghana's rivers for efficient inland water transport.

"I always thought there were great opportunities for using the rivers and lakes of Africa for transport," he told me again while researching for this book.

He believes more visionary leaders in Africa would likely implement inland water transport systems, adding, "sadly, Africa has rulers, and not leaders."

After years in Takoradi, Martin Hiles worked as Managing Director of the Volta Lake Transport Company (VLTC) in Ghana, while continuously promoting the use of lakes for transport. He would always argue that water transport represents much better value than road transport.

A soft-spoken man who is careful in his choice of words, Martin Hiles also became a gentle activist in promoting efficiency and transparency in the management of public resources for the wellbeing of citizens.

He was most vocal while working for Carmeuse, a Takoradi-based limestone company which delivered their products all over West Africa by road.

As the regular host of top-rated current affairs discussions on Skyy, I invited Martin as a panel member in 2001. The topic I moderated was *Axle Load Control on Ghanaian Roads*. Within the first ten minutes of the program, Martin revealed what he saw as an extreme waste and mismanagement in the system.

"Every million-dollar spent on road construction in Ghana is lasting one-third of its design life because of axle overload or shortfall in construction techniques."

"Still worse," he continued, "in Ghana, it costs three times the international average to build a road than it would cost anywhere else."

With a remarkably calm demeanour and just a few words, Martin identified what he believed were the major reasons for the poor condition of many Ghanaian roads including their well-known large potholes.

Twenty years after that radio program, I got on the phone to interview him specifically for this book and Martin Hiles' passion to see the development of inland water transport systems in Ghana was still something he talked about with missionary zeal.

A Believer in Inland Water Transport

Martin is about the only person I know who talks so passionately about the benefits of inland water transport, in contrast with road transport.

"Donor monies from Europe and America have been used to build roads in Ghana and Africa for generations," he said.

"One of the biggest realities is that the world can no longer afford to build new roads for the continent and it is time to invest in the more efficient and sustainable inland water transport for a vibrant economy."

He continued: "the rest of the world; India, China, Vietnam and all of Europe from the North Sea to the Black Sea and the Mediterranean are all connected by water bodies that are used for transport and tourism. In America, from the Great Lakes down to the Gulf of Mexico, through the very heart of the north American continent, are all connected by water. The USA considers inland water transport so important that it is run by their army; the United States Army Corps of Engineers."

Drawing on his nearly three decades of experience in Ghana, he said "the population of Ghana and Africa doubled in the last one generation. This growing population needs feeding, moving around, and connectivity. They need access to medicines, hospitals, education - and the numerous rivers can help in all these instances with low cost and immediately available connectivity."

Over a few decades of living in Ghana, Martin developed the heart of a native from Takoradi. Coming from England, where canals were constructed and used for centuries as an efficient transport system, he believes the people of Ghana deserve to enjoy its advantages as well.

Demonstrating his intimate knowledge of Ghana and its geography, Martin said "Ghana has long and gentle rivers like the Volta River, the Black Volta and the White Volta. They flow all year round and can be used easily for inland water transport. I have seen similar rivers everywhere I have been in West Africa, including Senegal, Guinea, Sierra Leone, Niger and Mali."

About 150 kilometres north-west of Takoradi is the Ankobra River which connects areas rich with natural resources to the Atlantic Ocean. Regarding this, Martin says: "Takoradi itself could benefit through the development of the Ankobra River as an inland water transport system to move the bulk of manganese and bauxite most of the way to the coast - specifically avoiding Takoradi itself and its damaged and congested roads."

The "Takoradi boy" now spends most of his time in England. By the end of my interview with him however, Martin said he is preparing to head back to Ghana to carry out more advocacy for inland water transport, with no plans of giving up.

It is hard to find someone with a greater conviction in water transport that has received little attention - or even understanding - over many decades.

One of the outstanding contributions Martin made was his use of Takoradi's first private radio to advocate better development initiatives for the people of Takoradi, Ghana and Africa.

Epilogue

T hank you for reading this far into *Absolute Radio*. I love books, but I hate books that are so huge and voluminous. So, the truth is, I feel a little embarrassed to produce such a big book.

Nevertheless, I feel not even half of the story has been told.

I tried to make it as small as possible but the story kept writing itself through the eyes of the many dozens of men and women I interviewed. Through the 44 chapters in Absolute Radio, these amazing individuals showed us their outstanding qualities.

They were generous with their time, serving up their precious memories of a period like no other in the history of an African twin city called Sekondi-Takoradi.

I expect that the accounts will bring back oceans of memories, including the valuable contributions of many other people in Sekondi-Takoradi and across Ghana.

It is a privilege to be associated with the groundbreaking events and to know so many of the men and women who made it happen.

Ultimately, this is my attempt to express gratitude to a community and a city, along with its people, because they nurtured me.

Acknowledgments

The production of Absolute Radio was a total team effort. My wife, Gabriella and 11-year-old son, Zion, were with me every step of the way, writing, reading and re-reading. Our-seven-year old daughter, Fafali, often fed up with the endless written words, gave the clearest indication of the inconvenience we had to live with in the two years it took to research, interview and write this book.

Absolute Radio is a genuine product of the more than 100 people I interviewed, mostly colleagues who were part of *the inspiring true story of the first private radio in Ghana's Western Region*. We formed an unbreakable professional bond over many years at a place in Ghana that would always remain special.

With the production of this book, I feel I owe a debt of gratitude to each and every one of them, whether their names appeared in this book or not.

Jerome Masamaka, an English and Literature doctoral student at Murdoch University in Perth, Australia, offered many constructive suggestions and reviews over the two years. Dr. Jonas Klutsey, a Political Ethnographer and Dr. Senyo Agbeblewu, both in Perth, were generous in offering their insight as well. Our family friends, Michael and Sarah McLeod were always encouraging and assisted in reading the manuscript along with Corina Sime. Janet Morton, a voracious reader devoured the manuscript and offered valuable perspectives.

Julius Nukpezah, Associate Professor of Public Policy and Administration at Mississippi State University in the United States reviewed and analysed many chapters for quality. I am grateful for his insight and enthusiasm.

Ebenezer Agbaglo of University of Cape Coast proved to be a skilled and insightful proofreader and his feedback was valuable.

Dr. Michael Sewornoo is a communications and journalism lecturer at the University of Cape Coast in Ghana. He was encouraging to me at every turn. Amazingly, Dr. Sewornoo was an employee of Skyy Power FM decades ago in his role as marketing executive. He maintains the same baby face I knew from so many years ago. It is a tribute to his hardwork and talent that he became an expert in international journalism.

Timothy Hudson of Durham in England provided helpful feedback on portions of this work, and I value his friendship. Another friend in England, Akwasi Sarpong of the BBC, was generous in helping me with some research, and so was General Marcus in London.

I want to thank the tireless and exciting octogenarian, Captain Joel Sowu. He was so much a part of Skyy and also a wealth of information, so inspirational and encouraging.

Anny Osabutey, a friend and former colleague at Skyy and Joy FM assisted me with research. Former Chief Executive of Sekondi-Takoradi Metropolitan Assembly, Philip Nkrumah; Western Regional Minister, Kwabena Okyere Darko-Mensah and his assistant, Charles Cobbina, were all helpful during the research stage of the book as they helped me recall many events from the past.

I am grateful to Professor Kenneth Attafuah, a Criminologist. He is a friend from decades ago, and his encouragement spans that period of time right up to now.

In Finland, another old friend from Takoradi, Nana Assyne, was of great value, and so was Samuel Ebo Kwaitoo of the Daily Graphic and Ebo Kooomson, a man who has loved Western Region all his life.

There are many others who were helpful to me through this project, including former colleagues Angela Oppong, Sylvia Odonkor, Lawton and Joycelyn Dadzie, Fati Shaibu Ali, Eddie F, DJ Hallelujah, Eric Kwesi Essel, Kwame Insaidoo, Ralph Menz in Takoradi and Frankie Taylor of Kapital Radio in Kumasi, as well as Fred Chidi, an old guard from Joy FM and Media General.

Special thanks to Kwasi Twum, Chief Executive of the Multimedia Group. His vision established Joy FM, the first manifestation of private and commercial broadcasting in Ghana. Working for him at Joy FM is an experience I cherish.

Also at Joy FM in Accra, Winston Amoah and Joseph Opoku Gakpo were helpful. I owe a lot to former news editors, Kofi Owusu and Matilda Asante. The evergreen Doreen Andoh also of Joy FM was, as always, a breath of fresh air in lending a helping hand for this project.

In Canada, Papa Tony Ashun-Codjiw was a reliable help during the research and writing stage of the book. A fellow Takoradi boy, he was always available to take a hundred phone calls to help refresh my memories on many events.

Also in Canada, Dr. Jonathan Sowah and Eric Sampson, together with my dear friend George Addai were of great assistance. Emmanuel Essien, another Takoradi boy in Italy also assisted me with some background information.

I want to thank Paul Adom-Otchere of Metro TV for helping to clarify some history in the early days of private broadcasting in Accra. My thanks also goes to Ghanaian musician, Afro Moses, who provided some essential background on Western Region and its music.

Another old friend and senior, Ben Dotsei Malor, formerly of the BBC and now with the United Nations, has always been encouraging on this journey.

Also assisting me with some essential background are my friends, Mark Boafo, Edwin Vanotoo and his wife Dr. Linda Vanotoo, three wonderful people with proud links to Sekondi-Takoradi.

I also want to acknowledge William Nyarko, a veteran investigative journalist from the *Ghanaian Chronicle* who has been in the trenches of journalism and even made a bed in the trench for himself and others.

Kojo Ntow, a precocious teenager who made fine contributions to Skyy children's program 20 years ago now works for Ghana's Ministry of Foreign Affairs. From his workplace outside Ghana, he kindly helped me to recall important facts from decades ago.

To Reggie Rockstone, many thanks. Not many people go through life and invent a genre of music. Reggie invented Hiplife in Ghana, and he was gracious to me on the phone in confirming some important events described in this book. I also want to thank one of Ghana's greatest musicians and a fellow Takoradi boy, Kofi Kinaata. As Yuki Ampofo would say, "the vibe in Takoradi was always big" and is still big. Kofi Kinaata is one of the many reasons why.

Susan Elliott and Matthew Scully in Sydney, Australia, showed me the path to broadcast journalism. More than just friends, they are like family and mean so much more to me than I can ever express.

Sincere thanks to some of the friends who have been there for me long before the conception of this book: Benjamin Jacob Nimako, Alexander Akotia, Joseph Kangah, Kwabena Adusei, Evans Nartey, Alexander Yamoah and the late Timothy Howard of Takoradi.

Also, in Takoradi, a truly wonderful man called D. E. Sam and his wife Grace Sam. In Accra, Nicholas and Felicia Akunor have always been there for me and my family.

To Wilson Arthur, Adwoa Amofah and Kennedy Arthur: their creative and entrepreneurial spirit over a quarter of a century created opportunities for so many young men and women across Ghana. It was only a matter of time that a work of this sort would come about to recognise their contribution.

I will always count it a privilege that I lived and worked in Sekondi-Takoradi in Ghana's Western Region. My late Uncle, Sqn. Ldr. Paul Stanley Kpodo-Tay of Ghana Airforce introduced me to Takoradi. I wish he lived long enough to see how his nephew, in a small way, got the chance to help open up Takoradi to the rest of the world.

Like my colleague from Skyy, Kojo Frempong, I say "Takoradi is this place like no other in Ghana." The 14 years I spent there is a period of time I would not trade for anywhere in the world. It is a good feeling to get the chance to pay back for some of the special memories and experiences recollected in this book.

I welcome your feedback on social media which you can find by searching for my name, Phillip Nyakpo, and though my website, **www.nyakpo.com.au**

A**bsolute Radio** is available worldwide in the following formats:

ISBN:

978-0-6454252-1-5 - *Paperback*

978-0-6454252-0-8 - *Audiobook*

978-0-6454252-2-2 - *e-Book*

A catalogue record for this work is available from the National Library of Australia.

Contact Information:

AfricanPod Media

+61493 219 774

Perth, Western Australia

Web: www.nyakpo.com.au

Email: radio@nyakpo.com.au

About the Author

Phillip Nyakpo fell in love with broadcast journalism in 1996, in the newsroom of Channel 7 in Sydney, Australia.

After writing for the *Ghanaian Chronicle*, and later the *Radio and TV Magazine* in Accra, Phillip became one of the first employees of Skyy Power FM, the first private and commercial radio station in Sekondi-Takoradi, the capital of Ghana's Western Region.

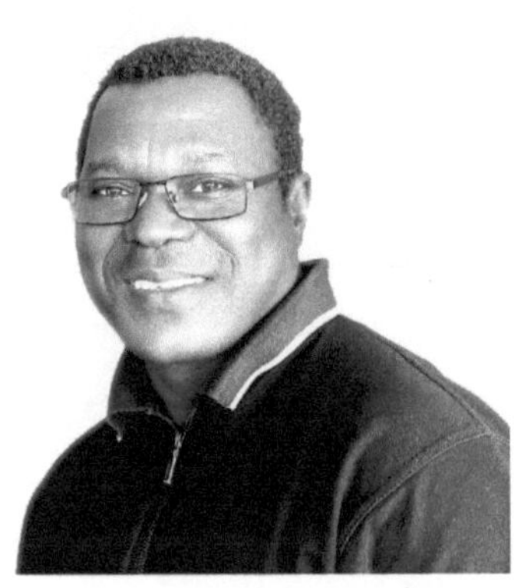

He also worked as the Western Regional correspondent for Joy FM, Ghana's first private radio station.

For nearly ten years in Sekondi-Takoradi, Phillip was editor, reporter, news anchor and the top host for news and current affairs, until 2005, when he left for a stint with the BBC in London, England.

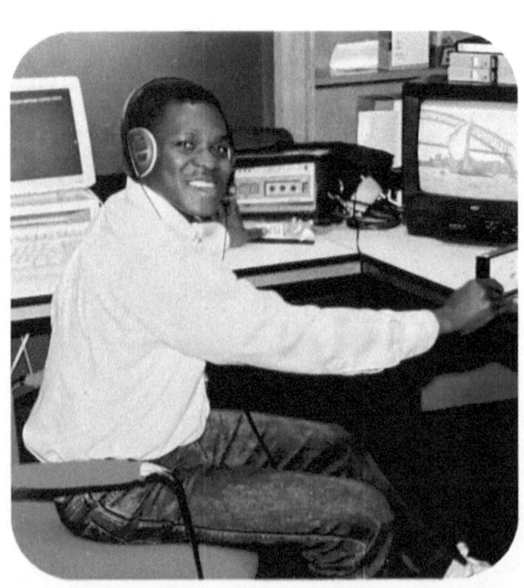

Phillip Nyakpo now lives in Perth, Western Australia with his family, a place he has called home for more than 15 years.

Phillip's work can be seen on www.nyakpo.com.au.

He can be reached on radio@nyakpo.com.au and through *AfricanPod Media* on +61493 219 774.

Phillip at Channel 7 in Sydney, 1996.

www.ingramcontent.com/pod-product-compliance
Lightning Source LLC
Chambersburg PA
CBHW032040050726

47590CB00001B/73